ZEN IN THE ART OF RHETORIC

ZEN IN THE ART OF RHETORIC

AN INQUIRY INTO COHERENCE

Mark Lawrence McPhail

State University of New York Press

Reprinted from J. Habermas, "Towards a Theory of Communicative Competence," *Inquiry* 13 (1970), pp. 360–75, by permission of Scandinavian University Press, Oslo, Norway.

Reprinted from D. Wilkinson, "The American university and the rhetoric of neoconservatism," *Contemporary Sociology* 20 (1991), pp. 550–53, by permission of the American Sociological Association and Doris Wilkinson.

Reprinted from G. Foster, "Cultural Relativism and the Theory of Value," *The American Journal of Economics and Sociology* 50 (1991), pp. 257–67, by permission of the American Journal of Economics and Sociology.

Reprinted from J. Farber, "Learning How to Teach," *College English* 52 (1990), pp. 135–41; C. Paine, "Relativism, Radical Pedagogy, and the Ideology of Paralysis," *College English* 51, no. 6 (1989), pp. 557–70; and J. Smith, "Allan Bloom, Mike Rose and Paul Goodman: In Search of a Lost Pedagogical Synthesis," *College English* 55 (1993), pp. 721–44, by permission of the National Council of Teachers of English.

Reprinted from D. S. Wright, "Rethinking Transcendence: The Role of Language in Zen Experience," *Philosophy East and West* 42 (1992), pp. 113–38, by permission of the University of Hawaii Press and Dale S. Wright.

Published by
State University of New York Press, Albany

© 1996 State University of New York

For information, address State University of New York Press,
State University Plaza, Albany, NY 12246

Production by Christine Lynch
Marketing by Fran Keneston

Library of Congress Cataloging-in-Publication Data

McPhail, Mark Lawrence.
    Zen in the art of rhetoric : an inquiry into coherence / Mark Lawrence McPhail.
        p.   cm. — (SUNY series in speech communication)
    Includes bibliographical references and index.
    ISBN 0-7914-2803-6 (ch : alk. paper). — ISBN 0-7914-2804-4 (pbk. : alk. paper)
        1. Rhetoric. 2. Zen Buddhism—Essence, genius, nature.
    3. Language and languages—Religious aspects—Zen Buddhism.
    4. Language and languages—Philosophy. 5. Truth—Coherence theory.
    I. Title. II. Series.
    P301.M685 1996
    808'.001—dc20   95-15882
                                                                         CIP

10 9 8 7 6 5 4 3 2 1

CONTENTS

Preface: Way of the Warrior   vii

Introduction: Zen and Rhetoric   1

1 To Grasp the Words and Die   19

2 Beginner's Mind   43

3 Otherness   65

4 Emptiness   93

5 One Hand Clapping   113

6 Coherence   131

7 Honoring the Form   149

Notes   169

References   195

Index   215

PREFACE

WAY OF THE WARRIOR

It is the parent who has born me: it is the teacher who
makes me a man.

—Inazo Nitobe, *Bushido: The warrior's code*

One of the reviewers of this manuscript felt that this quotation
seemed "a bit macho." I seriously contemplated removing this
quote, but then thought better of it since part of the project pursued in these pages is a rethinking of the meanings that we attach
to words. We tend to view the word "warrior" as peculiarly masculine and aggressive, but we might also think of it in terms of a
transformative sensibility, one that can help us address the problems of fragmentation and negativity that confront us daily in
our families, our classrooms, and our lives. Another view of the
warrior's way is articulated by Chögyam Trungpa, who sees warriorship as a manifestation of a "basic human wisdom," the same
type of wisdom, I believe, that many have argued cannot be
taught. But, like Trungpa, I believe that this wisdom can be cul-
tivated, for it represents part of what it means to be a human
being. As Trungpa explains: "This wisdom does not belong to
any one culture or religion, nor does it come from the West or the
East. Rather, it is a tradition of human warriorship that has
existed in many cultures at many times throughout history"
(1986, p. 8). Central to this tradition as it emerges in the two
areas of human conduct and inquiry with which I am concerned
here, Zen and rhetoric, is the calling into question of accepted
definitions and divisions.

Thus, in responding to this critic who offered a number of
significant comments and suggestions in response to the first
version of this manuscript, I simply ask that she or he join me in

rethinking the meaning of the term warrior. The comments provided by this reader, which were extremely important in guiding the revision and rethinking of several of the chapters of this book, were offered in what I like to think is the spirit of "rhetorical warriorship." The comments were incisive, engaging, critical: and they were insightful, encouraging, and compassionate. The reader challenged me to rethink, rephrase, and reframe my position, and while I may not have accepted all of the suggestions offered, I am convinced that they were offered in the spirit of helpfulness and the thoughtful recognition of the potential consequences of criticism. "I hope the author will forgive me for focusing on the negative in this review," explains the reader. "There is much in this manuscript I admire. My goal in what follows is to make an acceptable manuscript into a fine manuscript." I thank this reader for providing me with suggestions that I believe have made this a much better book, and I hope the reader will forgive me if I have not honored her or his efforts. I have sincerely tried to absorb what, in my mind, was useful.

I have similarly maintained this attitude in addressing the issues raised by the other individuals who responded to, and commented on, this collection of essays. All of them provided helpful commentaries, balanced between criticism and compassion, and their contributions have made this a much better book. I thank all of these anonymous reviewers, and also thank my good friend and colleague Susan Miller for her careful reading and thoughtful comments, and for being an intellectual inspiration: she is a brilliant scholar and a fine human being. I would also like to acknowledge and thank my colleagues at the University of Utah, especially Sempai Nickieann Fleener, who introduced me to Muso-Kai Karate and Shihan Kiyoshi Arakaki, Leonard Hawes, whose interest in communication, culture, and coherence is guided by a synthesis of discipline and compassion, Chris Oravec, who shares with me a love of Pirsig's Zen and an interest in the classical and romantic dimensions of rhetoric, and Richard Rieke, whose work in race influenced some of my earliest research interests, and whose ongoing commitment to dispute resolution and conflict managment continues to provide me with intellectual and spiritual inspiration.

My colleagues in the Ethnic Studies Program, Ronald Coleman, Karen Dace, and Wilfred Samuels also deserve mention and acknowledgment. They have been like my family here in Salt Lake City, far away from the family into which I was born. And to that family I also give thanks, not only for being a part of my life, but also for being always supportive of my work. I thank my mother and father, the parents who have born me, but most especially my mother Natalie May McPhail, who raised and nurtured me to believe that difference and division did not necessarily define what it means to be human, and that being a man meant a great deal more than being "macho." In this sense, I think, she has been one of my best teachers, for she created the space in my life that allowed me to follow the ways of those teachers of the Way of the word who, I believe, have most helped me become a man.

While there are many individuals that I can call "teacher," the two who most inspired the essays contained herein are Patrick Eaglin and Leland Roloff. Patrick Eaglin introduced me to both the rhetorical and martial arts at a critical time in my life, and although I have not seen him in many years, the spirit he imparted has stayed with me, and emerges again and again in these pages. Lee Roloff introduced me to a part of myself that I only vaguely understood existed, and is perhaps the person most responsible for giving me the faith in my own intellectual abilities that enabled me to write these essays. Both of these men represent the best of what teaching has to offer, the rare and priceless qualities of discipline and compassion. I dedicate this book to them with my deepest love and appreciation.

There are a number of other individuals who I would also like to thank for their guidance and support, especially Jane Blankenship, Edwin Rowley, and Joseph Skerrett, Jr., all of whom have been my teachers, and continue to be my good friends. I am deeply indebted to my all of my students, especially Glenn Kotcher, Felicia Meyer, and Michael Weiss, for kindly allowing me to reproduce their writings in this book, and Uma Swamy, for allowing me to use her name. Thanks to Deborah Borisoff, Keith Erikson, Robert Goepfert, James Robinson, William Starosta, and Bruce Weaver for granting permission to reprint several of the essays contained in this book. And finally I would like to thank Bernard Brock of Wayne State University for his friendship and encouragement, and Dudley Cahn and Priscilla Ross of the State University of New York Press for their editoral expertise, assistance, and support throughout the publication process.

INTRODUCTION

ZEN AND RHETORIC

> The human dilemma of communication is that we can-
> not communicate ordinarily without words and signs,
> but even ordinary experience tends to be falsified by
> our habits of verbalization and rationalization.
>
> —Thomas Merton, *Zen and the birds of appetite*

> The night was dim.
> All you could hear was a swim.
> Of a pollywog:
> Of Tim.
> And then a snake,
> Who was still awake,
> Got Tim.
> And that was the end of him.
>
> —"Tim Pollywog," 1966

I first discovered rhetoric, or perhaps it discovered me, when I was six years old. I wrote the poem "Tim Pollywog" in first grade at the Russell Elementary School, and won an honorable mention for my work in a writing contest. Only in looking back through a critical lens some twenty-nine years later can I describe "Tim Pollywog" as a commentary on the ambiguities of transforma-tion, as a consideration of what in Tibetan Buddhism is called "Bardo," the liminal area between life and death. It is through rhetoric that, in retrospect, I can make such an assessment, claim through the language of critique, the language which in our time determines meaning and value, that one set of symbols provides entry into the understanding of another. Rhetoric gives me the

1

right to contend that what seems to be the simple rhymes of a child are actually a map of the territory of what I have come to call my life, the series of events, structures, and relations that have emerged for me in between the Bardos. Rhetoric reminds me that these states I designate "I" and "me," might well be an illusion, that my attempt to persuade you with these words that there is some coherence in our lives, some shared point of reference, could simply be a lie?

Rhetoric is the two-ness of language that we often do not wish to talk about. Perhaps that is why it has enjoyed, until relatively recently, such a bad reputation in our culture. From the Sophists of the past to the postmodernists of the present, the claim that the world in which we live is a product of the words which we use, and which use us, has always been rather unsettling. The West, in particular, is well known for its "bad conscience"[1] about language, and it is this long-standing view of the word as either divorced from, or a poor reflection of, a reality best apprehended by rational methods of inquiry that has made rhetoric the object of ridicule and scorn. As far back as Plato, reason as the dominant vehicle through which "real" reality is apprehended, has persistently been envisioned as the path to an enlightened consciousness. Yet that enlightenment, that project in which the worth of words was denied by the probabilities of philosophies of matter and mind, has resulted in our own time in a world full of unfulfilled promises of social and spiritual emancipation, in which theories conceived and actions committed in the name of rationality have become all too irrational. In the shadow of such a world, rhetoric, always so at home with uncertainty, has once again become reasonable.

But the West has not been alone in its rejection of the word. In the East, where the realities of rationality and materialism of which the West is so certain are seen as illusions,[2] the word is also seen as at best a poor reflection of reality, and at worst a hindrance to enlightenment. The *Vimalakirti-sutra* offers this description, often quoted by Zen masters, of the word's worth: "In itself, the word is less than the thought, the thought is less than the experience. The word is a filtrate, a residue stripped of its best components."[3] Eugen Herrigel provides a more contemporary account of this assessment when he writes that the "Zen priest cannot evade his duties by mere talk. He cannot preach and demand of others tolerance, patience, mercy and compassion unless he himself religiously fulfills these requirements. Rhetoric does not stand high on the program in Zen" (1974, pp. 86–87). Herrigel rejects rhetoric as "mere words," yet does not recognize its compatibility with the most basic premises of Zen: to see the word and the world as they are, as void; not to be dualistic, which itself implies duality.

Zen originated with the introduction of Indian Buddhism[4] into China in the first century C.E. Etymologically it is rooted in the Sanskrit word *dhyāna*, incorporated into the Chinese language in a somewhat abbreviated form as *ch'an*, and pronounced in Sino-Japanese as *Zen*. The term refers to the Buddhist practice of "laying oneself perceptually open to the essential being of things, intuitive immediacy of perception, awareness of the elemental dynamics of vital relationships generated in peace and silence" (Brinker, p. 2). As D. T. Suzuki (1973) explains, the traditional Buddhist teachings influenced Chinese thinkers, especially the Taoists, who integrated the philosophical aspects of existing doctrines with the practical concerns of everyday life, bringing "about the transformation of Indian Buddhism into Zen Buddhism" (p. 1). As Zen gained adherents and influence in China, it evolved into more than a philosophy or religion, but a way of life governed by the principles and practices embodied in the *sangha*, or community of believers. In addition to attending to the daily affairs of the community, the members of the sangha listened to occasional brief sermons by the master of the monastery and engaged in dialogues that were "bizarre and full of incomprehensibilities, and they were quite frequently accompanied by direct actions" (p. 4). From the twelfth century onward, Zen grew increasingly important in Japanese culture, and found its way to the West at the end of the nineteenth century.[5]

Central to the practice of Zen are the search for enlightenment, or *satori*, and the vehicles for its achievement, *zazen* and the *koan*, a paradoxical question presented to Zen adherents by their masters that cannot be understood or answered logically. *Satori* is often associated with the Zen practice of *zazen* or "just sitting," but it can also be sought through active engagement in a variety of arts ranging from archery, to flower arrangement, to the art of the sword. Zen by its very nature incorporates stillness and motion, action and inaction, contemplation and application. As Helmut Brinker explains in *Zen and the art of painting*: "Between periods of static *zazen*, 'Zen in motion,' *kinhin*, is practiced, as a means of developing the capacity to 'translate' Zen practice into everyday life." Brinker also explains the origin and role of the *koan* in Zen: "The *koan* consist very largely of anecdotes, legendary and biographical details, conversations with, and sayings of the great patriarchs. They were designed to serve the pupil as a tool in his own religious practices, and lead him in the long run to the enlightenment which is his aim" (p. 6). Both *satori* and the *koan* illustrate an emphasis on the direct apprehension of experience unmediated by speech or rational analysis with which Zen is most often associated.

This emphasis on silent contemplation and the rejection of logical methods often gives the impression that Zen is at odds with words, and hence with rhetoric. "It is no wonder that Zen has stressed the all importance of 'No dependence upon letters and words,'" note Lucien Stryk and Takashi Ikemoto. "All masters have discouraged their disciples from pious as well as secular reading, urging them to concentrate upon zazen (sitting in Zen) or koan training to gain satori." This separation of the word and the Way seems somewhat at odds with the spirit of Zen, as Stryk and Takashi point out when they note that "the fact is that numberless Zennists have had an awakening while reading a Buddhist sutra or a Zen writing, or hearing a sutra recited or listening to words uttered in a mondo" (p. xviii). They give the examples of Hakuin, who was enlightened by the phrase "It's for you the leaves stir up a breeze," and Eno, who achieved a satori experience upon hearing a recitation of the *Diamond Sutra*.[6] There is, in Zen, a strong affinity for the word, both in its poetry and in its praxis. As Stryk and Ikemoto remark: "No one can shut his eyes to the conspicuous role letters and words have played in Zen discipline."

Stryk and Ikemoto offer insight into the relationship between Zen and rhetoric which I wish to pursue in this book. They note that "in Zen one must fathom more than the ordinary dualistic meaning of letters and words: this is, one must intuit Nothingness or Buddhahood, identifying oneself with it" (p. xix). Zen provides a way of understanding and enacting words which, I believe, parallels the practice of rhetoric embodied in the doctrines of the Sophists, characterized for example by the *dissoi-logoi*, or Thrasymachus' "theory of the opposite party." The former can be seen in Suzuki's (1964) characterization of Zen as "anti-logical": "Zen is decidedly not a system founded upon logic and analysis. If anything, it is the antipode to logic, by which I mean the dualistic mode of thinking" (p. 38).[7] The latter can be seen in Zen's recognition that seemingly separate positions are always implicated in each other, that "the meaning of the proposition 'A is A' is realized only when 'A is not-A'" (p. 60). If we are to find in rhetoric a Way that is consistent with the principles of Zen, then we might begin by considering approaches to rhetoric that call into question the necessity of duality, and that challenge the hegemony of logic. We find this, I believe, both in the rhetoric of the Greek Sophists and in postmodern rhetoric, in the words of the old and the new, of both the living and the dead.

And here we must take Zen to heart and challenge even this most basic of distinctions between life and death. "The Zen masters have a saying," explains D. T. Suzuki: "'Examine the living words and not the dead ones'" (p. 7). I believe, that in the spirit of Zen, we must examine both. Suzuki makes clear that it is not words themselves *but the ways in which words can be used to fix and categorize the world* which Zen calls into question: "Zen is not necessarily against words, but it is well aware of the fact that they are always liable to detach themselves from realities and turn into conceptions" (p. 5). Because the language of Zen is often depicted as very different from traditional Western conceptions of language,[8] to the extent that we understand rhetoric in terms of such conceptions it will make sense to view the two as incommensurable. If instead, we move beyond traditional notions to a synthesis of the preclassical and the postmodern, we will encounter a rhetoric that points to the radical critique of duality as a starting point for an inquiry into coherence.

That the critique of duality—the negation of negation—might lead us to an understanding of coherence may seem paradoxical. Yet it is this very notion that characterizes the concerns of preclassical and postmodern rhetoricians as well as students and practitioners of Zen. The Sophists, through their various doctrines, challenged the emerging conceptions of knowing, grounded in the necessity of duality, that would later come to dominate Western thinking. Today's postmodernists, responding to the social and spiritual consequences of those ways of knowing, have again called into question the hegemony of philosophical discourse. The paradox, of course, is that the very discursive mechanisms used by Sophists and postmodernists are at the heart of the system of knowledge they call into question: both advance arguments that are, either explicitly or implicitly, *against argument*. Within the context of our own culture, one dominated by ostensibly logical reasoning, such paradoxes are easily dismissed as inconsistent. From another perspective, that of Zen, they are powerfully coherent.

Like the Sophists of old and the postmodernists of the present, Zen calls into question prevailing ways of knowing. This was certainly the case with the Chinese Chan masters, who "challenged the Tang knowledge establishment and its great mass of 'idle knowledge.'" William Powell, in his introduction to *Zen speaks: Shouts of nothingness*, explains how these masters "engaged in a demonstrative form of rhetoric, that, though it reveals a profound grasp of the scriptures, did not make use of specialized knowledge and erudition to make its points." This rhetoric was a form of "intellectual judo, offering no clear target to its opponents. Not only was this approach not openly aggressive, it was executed with a sense of humor that is part of its appeal" (p. 14). Like Sophists and postmodernists, these Zen masters of old articulated a radical critique of duality, one which offered alternative ways of knowing the world and the word, and offered a glimpse of the coherent unity of existence that transcends the negations of rational language and dialectical logic.

In this book I hope to show that Sophistic and postmodern conceptualizations of rhetoric are, like Zen, full of contradiction and paradox, and this is precisely what makes them dangerous: their potential to pull apart all of our preconceptions about the world and invite us to see old things in new ways. They are also dangerous because they possess within them the seeds of a radically emancipatory understanding of language and life. It is not a coincidence that democracy emerged at a time when the views of the Sophists were evolving. They offered unsettling discourses that challenged the common sense of the time: and their counterparts in the East offered something quite similar. As Dale S. Wright (1992) observes in his reconsideration of the traditional view of Zen's rejection of rhetoric, "there is a kind of rhetoric that is incorporated into Zen practice":

> The essential feature of this rhetoric is its strictly emancipatory intention. By means of its "otherness" to ordinary

discourse, and therefore to ordinary "mind," Zen rhetoric sought to free its speakers and hearers, writers and readers, from the constraints of conventional modes of human comportment. The otherness of Zen rhetoric was typically twofold, juxtaposing itself both with the classical language of established Buddhist institutions and with the conventional language of everyday East Asian life. (p. 126)

Wright concludes "that not only is language present in the enactment of the Zen master's enlightened bearing, it also plays a fundamental role in the origins and development of the monastic world that made a uniquely 'Zen' experience of 'awakening' possible" (p. 135). Instead of viewing Zen as separate and distinct from rhetoric, Wright's reading suggests that the Way and the word are very much one and the same, and powerfully implicated in each other.

Like Wright I see rhetoric and Zen not only as a part of each other's programs, but as an inseparable part. I think this is easily missed because, at least in the culture in which we live, we are only beginning to acknowledge how freeing contradiction and paradox can be if we let them. Our cultural habits of naming make those aspects of reality that cannot be conveniently and easily categorized something fearful and unknown: something bad. And so for centuries we have chosen to view in rhetoric's danger not a challenge or an opportunity, but something from which we wish to free ourselves. But we are reminded that we cannot be free from that which is essentially a part of ourselves, and so the struggle of our culture's history has been, at least in my eyes, the attempt to uncover in rhetoric what in one culture is called *Do*, and in another called *Tao*. In short, I have sought to discover in the art of rhetoric a spiritual practice or *Way*. What follows is a brief account of that journey.

Apart from "Tim Pollywog" I had written few poems during my youth, but in high school my interest in poetry resurfaced, perhaps for no other reason than the fact that I needed it to survive. As a child I had done well enough academically to be given the opportunity to attend a private school, but once I arrived there both my grades and self-esteem fell sharply. My only solace was English class, where I continued to do above average work and began developing (although it was not explained to me at the time) rhetorical skills. I had developed an early interest in creative writing and dramatic improvisation, and enjoyed every opportunity I had to experience the written or spoken word. Unfortunately, words were not enough, and my failing grades in other subjects suggested that I needed more direction and discipline in my life. The solution, my mother felt, was a father figure.

My own father had passed when I was only a child, and although I had three older brothers and two older sisters, I lacked a significant role model. When I was thirteen I was sent to live with my oldest sister's boyfriend, and while my grades did not improve I nonetheless received my first lessons in the way of the word. My sister's boyfriend's brother befriended me, and introduced me to two things that have remained with me ever since: the poetic and martial arts. While I struggled with both, I found the compassion of poetry much more to my liking than the discipline of karate, and despite the efforts and concerns of my role models continued to do poorly in school. I eventually dropped out of karate and was kicked out of school, and realized perhaps for the first time the meaning of the first of the four noble truths of Buddhism: that life is suffering.

Fortunately, however, I did not become too attached to that truth. At the next school I attended I continued to develop my creative writing skills, and became a much better student in general. There I encountered teachers who introduced me to the discipline of poetry in its more traditional forms, and I learned how to write using rhyme, meter, and figures of thought and speech. The creative writing that I had been doing, they explained, was not poetry. Free verse, they said, was for experienced writers only, those who had mastered the basics, and I had not even begun to do so. My basic training included not only poetics, but rhetoric as well, for I also received training in expository and argumentative writing and literary analysis. I had developed, largely unconsciously, an appreciation and love of language during that time that has defined the sense of self and selflessness that continues to influence my academic and personal life up to this very day.

When I entered college my emphasis shifted from the written to the spoken word. As a creative writing major I continued to produce poetry, some of which achieved publication, but I decided to become a speech major and studied communication after one of my instructors informed me that my poetry was not "poetry," but "creative writing!" As a creative writing major I wrote few poems, but those that I did write came almost by way of inspiration: effortlessly and quickly. But quantity, not quality determined one's success in the program, so I switched over to speech and learned of a new type of "effortlessness." During my undergraduate years I became a successful practitioner of performance and persuasion in debate, public speaking, and oral interpretation competitions and festivals. It was in one such festival that I first encountered what would become, in my mind, the definitive experience of the way of the word. I was performing a piece by the American poet and critic Robert Penn Warren in which a young boy goes out cross-country skiing with his pet husky, only to watch in horror as the dog escapes from his grip and mortally wounds a fleeing doe. The boy is forced to destroy the doe, and so experiences an epiphanal moment in which he glimpses the interconnectedness of life and death.[9]

As I performed the piece, at one point I looked downward and to my right, and gestured as if petting the animal as I described it. In my mind's eye, I saw the dog there beside me with one blue eye and one brown eye, looking up at me as dogs are wont to do. It was an interesting sensation, one that I had felt only a few times during a performance career that spanned three years in college and one in graduate school. I had mostly experienced performing poetry as a technical affair, and although my performance of "Sila" was not technically "perfect," I felt for the first time the experience of the *poem speaking me.* And I was not alone. At the conclusion of my performance one gentleman told me that I had brought tears to his wife's eyes and, indeed, as she approached I saw that she was weeping. Shortly afterward another gentleman approached me and said *"I saw the dog."* "Me too," I replied.

This was probably the first "spiritual" encounter I had with language. It gave me, albeit briefly, a sense of transcendence, of getting out of myself and into the words of another, of overcoming the obstacle of difference that separated me from the audience. I did not appreciate this experience fully until I entered a master's program in oral interpretation after completing my bachelor's degree. There I learned of the social construction of the self and the sacred condition of selflessness in a program that combined the discipline of a rigidly traditional approach to performance with the compassion of a coherent and transformative vision of the word. It was a place where I initially had nightmares about the high school from which I had been expelled six years earlier, but later learned that I was capable of a level of intellectual analysis and synthesis that I had never before believed possible. My path had led me from poetics to persuasion to philosophy, and throughout my journey I had steadfastly traveled the Way of the word.

That way brought me back to the connection between rhetoric and writing when I began working on a doctorate and applied for a teaching assistantship in a composition program. Although I did not have a formal background in the teaching of writing, I successfully taught composition by teaching principles of classical rhetoric: the five canons and the elements of argument and criticism. Although the director of the program did not agree with my methods, he could not argue with their results: the students were writing clear, well organized, *and creative* essays, and were adept at both argument and narrative. I believe that the forms and models offered by classical rhetoric had given them access to academic voices and also their own voices: they had discovered the connection between discipline and compassion.

I found support for this belief not only in my teaching of both writing and speaking, but also in what would be two of the most important works on rhetoric that I would encounter as a graduate student: Robert Pirsig's book *Zen and the art of motorcycle maintenance*, and Richard Lanham's essay titled "The rhetorical ideal of life." Pirsig's discussion of "classical" and "romantic" modes of thought and Lanham's discussion of "serious" and "rhetorical" premises of style both paralleled my own conceptualization of rhetoric as a vehicle for the teaching of discipline and compassion. Pirsig recalls his own experience as an English teacher whose students made the connection between formalism and creativity. The principles of rhetoric "were no longer rules to rebel against, not ultimates in themselves, but just techniques, gimmicks, for producing what really counted and stood independently of the techniques—Quality" (p. 186). Pirsig's concept of "Quality" closely resembles the stylistic creativity that teachers of rhetoric and composition dream about discovering in the essays, performances, and speeches written and presented by students.

And yet, in search of that style we have all too often attempted to rebel against the rules of rhetoric, seeing them as stifling and burdensome. We have, in short, attempted to free ourselves from rhetoric, and the result has been a debate between form and content, knowledge and expression, that has undermined efforts to legitimate the profoundly transformative and emancipatory possibilities of rhetoric. But this debate, as Lanham suggests, has taught us an important historical lesson: "Perhaps we can see now why the Western paideia has always been a mixed one," he writes in "The rhetorical ideal of life" as part of his commentary on the debate between "serious" and "rhetorical" views of life: "The best education has always put the two views of life into fruitful collision. Divorce and domination present equal dangers. The West has confused itself unnecessarily" (1976, p. 8). That confusion has led to a belief that good writing can somehow be achieved without discipline, and that understanding can be achieved without compassion: in short, that we can be free of rhetoric. On this point I agree with Lanham: "If truly free of rhetoric, we would be pure essence. We would retain no social dimension" (p. 8) Without social dimension it would be impossible for any of us, serious or rhetorical, to achieve a disciplined and compassionate understanding of the processes and products of rhetoric: of Zen in the art of rhetoric.

As a student, teacher, and researcher of rhetoric, this has been my "journey without goal."[10] As a student, the experience of being "written and spoken through" shaped my earliest understanding of rhetoric as a Way. As a teacher I have experienced similar sensations in front of the classroom, and seen them in my students, when words about the word flow effortlessly as if from some unknown source. And as a researcher I have struggled to discover a strategy to challenge accepted divisions and distinctions, to find a way to reconcile unity and diversity that makes room for mind, language, and spirit. Like many of my colleagues in the field I have looked toward the East for answers,[11] yet I have also attempted to look beyond the pragmatics of discourse to its episteme, its way of knowing, to find the connections I seek. I believe that they might be found in the concept of "rhetorical coherence," a concept inherited from the Sophists of old and anticipated in the new rhetorics of our own time, that conceptualizes rhetoric as "the capacity to synthesize diverse conceptions of reality."[12] This capacity is informed by what Pirsig describes as a sensibility "in which the idea of a duality of self and object doesn't dominate one's consciousness" (p. 267), a sensibility which, like Zen, actively seeks the coherence of higher affirmations.

In addition to Pirsig there have been a number of Western writers who have explored how Zen emerges in the arts, some of whom have considered traditional paths and others who have tried to transcend divisions of culture and discipline to illustrate how any human activity can and does reflect the basic sentiments of Zen.[13] Their insights provide a starting point for our consideration of those aspects of Zen that emerge in the essays contained in this book. Part of my project is to offer some new interpretations of the connections between Zen and rhetoric, and to challenge some of the accepted beliefs and assumptions about the relationship between the two. I also wish to provide some directions for an expanded understanding of rhetoric, one which integrates traditional concerns with the contributions of new rhetorics ranging from the social constructivist to the spiritual.[14] I intend to show that a coherent conceptualization of rhetoric offers opportunities to celebrate the unity of diversity, and to see similarity in difference.

The first chapter explores this theme of similarity in difference through a synthesis of narrative and analysis that explores relationships between rhetoric and philosophy, teachers and students, and criticism and compassion. It plays upon the metaphor of death in order to illustrate how the Way emphasizes its inseparability from life, and to suggest that the death of one state of mind can mean the birth of another. It calls on teachers and students to "plunge right into the middle of contradiction and confusion in order to be transformed by what Zen calls the 'Great Death,'" as Thomas Merton describes the experience in *Zen and the birds of appetite* (1968, p. 51). This is the ultimate experience of the warrior of the word who, being born into the house of rhetoric, chooses to grasp the words and die. This grasping of words requires a commitment to the Way that interrogates duality, that calls into question the probabilities of the expert's knowledge and examines the possibilities of "beginner's mind."

The concept of "beginner's mind" guides the discussion of the rhetoric of racism in Alan Bloom's *The closing of the American mind* presented in chapter 2. Bloom's discussion illustrates an interesting tension between his expressed position on race and the epistemological assumptions that undergird his analysis of race relations on American campuses. Bloom asserts throughout the book the efficacy of essential knowledge, but paradoxically fails to apply that standard in his own analysis, which rests upon opinions at odds with several of the prevailing intellectual perspectives on race relations extant in the literature of the field. In cultivating my own position I suggest that invoking such perspectives in critiquing Bloom's position *as* racist merely reifies the essentialism that undergirds his position, and offer instead a coherent conceptualization of rhetoric as a way of moving beyond the oppositions assumed in racial conflict and argument. I assume a position based upon compassion and composure that, according to Gustie Herrigel, "is characteristic of all Eastern art and particularly of the Zen-Buddhist outlook on life." Herrigel's *Zen in the art of flower arrangement* comments on how the beginner's mind offers the possibility of transcending oppositions: "Everything ultimately depends on what is outside and beyond the opposites, on the spirit, and on man's capacity not only to dissolve himself in it through passionate self-immersion, but also to live out of it with equal composure. This is not a negation or a flight from the world" (p. 118). Indeed, the capacity to see through the eyes of the Other, I conclude in this chapter, reflects a powerful commitment to engaging the world and the word on its own terms.

The challenge of engaging the other again emerges in chapter 3, in which the role of argument and criticism in the social construction of difference is examined. My analysis invokes a generally accepted understanding of language attributed to Zen adherents, echoed in David Brandon's (1976) observation in *Zen and the art of helping:* "The symbols we use in language can become a barrier when they are confused with what is out there and inside here. Life is infinitely more complex and beautiful than any of our words and sentences allow" (p. 18). I consider the consequences of conceptualizing and talking about the world in black and white terms, even as it emerges in ostensibly "radical" critical perspectives, those that challenge the hegemonic tendencies of essentialist, patriarchal, and Eurocentric discourses. Like Brandon, I attempt to ask the question that begins to move us beyond argumentative and critical language as our only recourse in discourse: "What words do we use when things are neither true nor untrue, neither black nor white but both?" (p. 19). The answer, I suggest, is a rhetoric grounded in a coherent epistemology, one that acknowledges and recognizes the limitations of dualistic conceptualizations of the word and the world.

Such a rhetoric, paradoxically, is paralleled in what has, until quite recently, been considered one of the most essentialist of our intellectual disciplines: physics. In chapter 4 I turn to physics to suggest that the paradigmatic transformation that has occurred in that discipline holds important implications for our understanding of reality and the way we talk about it. In examining the rhetoric of physics and the physics of rhetoric, I unearth the epistemological assumptions of an actively non-argumentative discourse, one which recognizes the Sophistic insight that opposing positions are always implicated in each other. I offer as an alternative to foundational and externalist essentialisms a coherent essentialism, a vision of essence rooted in the negation of negation characteristic of Zen. "In the Zen view this negation of the separate-distinct I-awareness (separate and distinct from other persons and things) is absolutely essential," observes Winston L. King (1993) in *Zen and the way of the sword.* "Not only does such awareness result in an obstructive undesirable self-centered egoism, but it divides one from that living interactive harmony with the rest of creation that Zen seeks to achieve" (p. 22). Zen's negation of negation provides a transformative vision of essence, one that offers the possibility of integration in a world in which physical and psychological reality have become increasingly fragmented.

It is in an attempt to address such fragmentation that chapter 5 explores the problems and possibilities of a "postmodern" rhetoric, again offering the possibility of actively non-argumenative discourse as a viable vehicle for generating harmony in the face of conflict. In examining some connections that transcend the difference between modernism and postmodernism, the essay offers a possible resolution to the argument between two proponents of these positions, Jean François Lyotard and Jürgen Habermas. The notion of a "postmodern" rhetoric, I argue, is like the Zen koan, "what is the sound of one hand clapping?" In defining a postmodern rhetoric I suggest an alternative to the confrontational negations of contemporary inquiry, and offer a perspective based on the principles of non-confrontation and the redirection of energy devoted to conflict. This, according to Joe Hyams (1979) in *Zen in the martial arts,* is the essence of the martial art known as *aikido.* "The skilled aikidoist is as elusive as the truth of Zen; he makes himself into a koan—a puzzle which slips away the more one tries to solve it" (p. 74). A coherent conception of rhetoric, I suggest, offers the opportunity to understand debates like those between modernists and post-modernists in terms of the common grounds they share instead of the differences that divide them, and represents an approach to inquiry in which rhetoric can be seen as a way and argument understood in light of the "harmony of conflict."[15]

Perhaps the most important implications of such an approach to inquiry can be seen in the opportunities it presents in the institutional arena. Chapter 6 explores those implications in terms of the role that a coherent conceptualization of rhetoric might play in relation to contemporary educational and economic concerns with literacy and diversity. A coherent rhetoric, grounded in the classical concerns of Sophistry and the contemporary emphasis on critical inquiry, calls into question existing material and linguistic arrangements at the epistemological level and challenges the underlying assumptions of essential difference deeply embedded in our social and symbolic institutions. It offers a path similar to that which Horst Hammitzsch (1988) describes in *Zen in the art of the tea ceremony* as "the Tea Way," "a path worth treading, even if a narrow one and difficult to follow. It leads man to the discovery of himself" (p. 9). The Tea Way, like all Zen paths, strives to dissolve division and separation, to achieve a "higher affirmation": "To grasp the idea that 'One is in All and All in One,' that the All cannot be separated from the One—that is the ultimate experience of this Way" (p. 10). I conclude that this idea, which powerfully calls into question our existing educational and economic assumptions, contains within it the seeds of a potentially powerful paradigmatic transformation.

In the final chapter I argue that the sowers of those seeds will be will be those students and teachers willing to follow the Way of the rhetorical warrior. That way is envisioned not so much in new rhetorics, but in new ways of thinking about and understanding rhetoric, its relationship to the One, and the potential it holds for the many. The Way of the rhetorical warrior is as ancient as the Parmenidean assertion of Being that "the one way, that it is and cannot not be, is the path of Persuasion, for it attends upon Truth."[16] This is also the Way of the Zen Master, who is according to Eugen Herrigel "like a flash of lightning from the cloud of all-encompassing Truth." Herrigel concludes in *Zen and the art of archery*, that the follower of Zen must dare to leap into the Origin, so as to live by the Truth and in the Truth, like one who has become one with it. He must become a pupil again, a beginner; conquer the last and steepest stretch of the way, undergo new transformations. If he survives its perils, then is his destiny fulfilled: face to face he beholds the unbroken Truth, the Truth beyond all truths, the formless Origin of origins, the Void which is the All; is absorbed into it and from it emerges reborn. (pp. 89–90)

In returning to the origins of rhetoric we might gain insight into understanding it as Richard Lanham does, as "a way of life as well as a view of life, a coherent counterstatement to serious reality" (p. 6). What "truth" this Way might offer us today remains to be seen. I attempt to uncover some semblance of it in its argumentative and narrative manifestations in the works of two student writers. I hope here to suggest the possibility of a pedagogical praxis that illustrates the word as Way, the realization of the rhetorical ideal.

Initially I will consider how a coherent view of rhetoric can make room for preclassical, traditional, postmodern, and non-Western views of language, can synthesize persuasion and narrative, dialectic and dialogue. As a way of making this move, I offer the metaphor of rhetoric as a martial art, as a disciplined practice that leads to an enlightened compassion, as a synthesis of technique and art that interrogates duality and strives for coherence. In support of this notion I will offer my own voice as well as the writings of two students who I believe achieved empowerment through language. The essays illustrate in very different ways how the issues raised by Pirsig's *Zen* helped lead these students to an understanding of how social and psychological divisions might be transcended and transformed.

The first essay illustrates Pirsig's "knife of reason," and reflects Ray Bradbury's (1990) consideration of the relationship between quantity and quality in *Zen in the art of writing*: "Quantity gives experience. From experience alone quality can come" (p. 123). The student, through an insightful analysis, is not only able to synthesize seemingly separate conceptions of quality, but to also understand the implications of such a synthesis for both social and central conceptions of the self. His careful management of the technical and creative aspects of rhetoric offers, in Bradbury's words, "a new definition for Work. And the word is LOVE" (p. 131). Bradbury's observations are also applicable to the second essay, which illustrates one student's struggle with, and subsequent analysis of, the relationship between failure, success, and one's sense of self. His discussion of failure mirrors the student's own experience:

> To fail is to give up. But you are in the midst of a moving process. Nothing fails then. All goes on. Work is done. If good, you learn from it. If bad, you learn even more. Work done and behind you is a lesson to be studied. There is no failure unless one stops. Not to work is to cease, tighten up, become nervous, and therefore destructive of the creative process. (p. 124)

As one reads the student's account of the encounter with Pirsig's *Zen*, one experiences an almost eerie parallel between the student's essay and Bradbury's, a mysterious connection between the thoughts of an experienced writer and a beginning student of composition, between the expert's and the beginner's minds.

I will conclude with an amplification of what teaching rhetoric as a martial art can mean for contemporary rhetorical theory and practice. As an alternative metaphor for rhetoric, the martial arts move us away from the notion that our language is somehow "amoral," that if our students use it to harm others we are simply, like the Aristotelian teacher of wrestling, not responsible. It forces us to confront Adrienne Rich's important admonition, that as teachers of rhetoric "we need to be acutely conscious of the kind of tool we want our students to have available, to understand how it has been used against them, and to do all we can to insure that language will not someday be used by them to keep others silent and powerless" (1979, p. 68). The martial arts metaphor, which synthesizes discipline and compassion, nonviolence and self-defense, dialectic and dialogue, offers a glimpse of what a coherent rhetoric might look like, and what it could mean for a world in which the disciplines of language have increasingly lost their ability to create and communicate the social reality of compassion.

Zen in the art of rhetoric: An inquiry into coherence is about the importance of reclaiming that ability in our works and our words. It is about discovering the available means of living and speaking in the world that can help us become, in Pirsig's words, "a part of the world and not an enemy of it."[17] In looking to Pirsig and those other writers who have found Zen in a diversity of arts and appetites, I hope to have contributed coherently to the conversation in which they have engaged in order to inform, delight, and enlighten those who celebrate the rhetorical ideal of life. What they have taught us about Zen is first, that it is not easy despite its simplicity, and second that it offers a profound connection with all things despite its emphasis on detachment. We can see the importance of this connection for each of us, and its relationship to the word and the Way, in the comments of D. T. Suzuki: "Love to be articulate requires a means of communication, which is language. Inasmuch as Zen is one of the most significant human experiences, one must resort to language to express it to others as well as oneself" (1973, p. 6).

This is the sentiment that undergirds these essays. They are not easy essays, and like Zen they will require some work on the part of the reader just as they have required some work on the part of the writer. But despite the density of vocabulary, the theoretical complexities (if any, in fact, do exist), and the philosophical nuances, they are quite simply about love: the need for it in our lives, and especially the need for it in our language. And so I ask the reader to stay with them through their more convoluted and difficult passages, and seek within them the simplicity of their message: that there is a reality beyond the illusory differences that separate us in our lives, languages, and methods, and that reality is as much a part of rhetoric as it is of Zen. Buried in these pages I believe, there is something for almost everyone: as you read them absorb what is useful, and be compassionate in your judgment of that which is not, for ultimately they are nothing more than the amplified poems of a child who first found the simplicity of rhetoric at the age of six, and has continued to follow the Way of the word ever since.

1

To Grasp the Words and Die

> Zen has always emphasized the essential identity or,
> perhaps, intimate linkage of appearance-disappearance,
> life-death in an unbroken chain. Death comes out of
> life, and life appears out of death or non-existence.
> Which is the true reality?
>
> —Winston L. King, *Zen and the way of the sword*

Uma Swamy entered my office for her half-hour writing conference and placed her essay in front of me.[1] Uma believed that she
was not a good writer: her attitude manifested itself in her writing in the form of careless errors, inferential leaps, and "awkward" sentences. When she reviewed her writing during confer-
ences she often was able to correct and revise her work
satisfactorily, so I surmised that her problems with writing were
due primarily to her negative feelings about the activity. Because
when reading her work I could see her struggling, not so much
with the language as with herself, I tried to be as tactfully positive, and at the same time helpful, as possible.

Uma and I over the past several months had spent a great
deal of time working on her writing, and I had consistently
stressed the importance of paying attention to detail, yet as I
read through the essay I noticed a number of what I perceived to
be careless errors as well as an overall lack of focus. "Oh oh,"
Uma remarked "your forehead's wrinkling. I guess it's not too
good, huh?" Without looking up from the page that I was reading
I handed her the first page of the essay. She began making cor-
rections and audible comments like "oops," "hmm," and "what
did I mean by *that*?" With that statement, we both looked up
and laughed.

"How's the semester going?" I asked.

"The usual," she replied. "You know, I stayed up until three o'clock writing this."

"And you can see where it needs improvement, right?"

"Yeah, I guess. I don't know why I don't see these things while I'm writing. I see them now."

"Attention to detail, Uma," I said, watching her frown and roll her eyes as if this were the thousandth time she'd heard me make the same remark.

"Yeah I know, but it's hard. And I'm trying. But you know I'm not a good writer." This time *I* frowned, and gave her my most tactful "I don't want to hear that" look. "So, what have you been up to lately," she asked, trying to match my tact by changing the subject.

"I'm working on an essay about the importance of teaching rhetoric and criticism called "To grasp the words and die."

"Why are you calling it *that*?"

"Initially I got the idea from the words of Kato Kiyomasa, a samurai warrior who wrote that when one is 'born into the house of the warrior, one's intentions should be to grasp the long and short swords and to die.'[2] When one is born into the house of rhetoric," I explained, "one's intentions should be to grasp the words and die. Rhetoric is how we grasp the words. Criticism is how we die. In order to be a good writer you've got to give something up, like the belief that you are not a good writer. You do that by reflecting on the process that you're involved in and the way you feel about it. You can't let the rules of writing scare you; you have to master them, control them, so that they don't control you. Language is like a double-edged sword. It's how power is created and maintained, and yet it is also how power is called into question. Historically, rhetoric has been the best way of calling power into question because it is first and foremost a critical activity. That's why I teach rhetoric and criticism, because they deal with both power and empowerment."

I mentioned how Georges Poulet's essay, "Criticism and the experience of interiority," related the process of reading to "dying," and explained Paulo Friere's belief that the teacher must experience a 'death of consciousness,' must "make his Easter" in order to provide students with a truly liberating and liberalizing education. Finally, I admitted: "I like the way it sounds," and continued to read Uma's essay, making sure not to wrinkle my forehead.

"Uma," I said after reading through the essay, "you know how to deal with the mechanical problems and spelling errors, so we're not going to spend too much time on that. But you still need to be more focused and organized: remember, almost every essay you write will be critical, and you can use the three points of criticism as an organizing scheme. Start out by telling the reader what you are going to do through *description*, then present your analysis through *interpretation*, and finally tell the reader why what you've presented is important through *evaluation*."[3] I wrote the words one on top of the other in the margins of her essay, underlined the first letter of each, then circled all three in order to indicate that they all worked together to form a single process.

"*Die*," she said.

I couldn't believe it. There it was, the answer to her question concerning the title of my paper: the justification for which I had been searching. And it made perfect sense. But I never saw it. I had struggled with the problem of connecting criticism to dying, had arrived at some marginal justifications, had rationalized some seemingly reasonable connections, but had missed the most obvious explanation, perhaps because I had looked too hard. *Description. Interpretation. Evaluation. Die!* I was reminded of Shunryu Suzuki's comment in *Zen mind, beginner's mind*: "In the beginner's mind there are many possibilities, but in the expert's there are few."

RHETORIC AND MOTORCYCLE MAINTENANCE

I was in the last year of my doctoral program in rhetoric at the University of Massachusetts when I discovered Robert Pirsig's *Zen and the art of motorcycle maintenance*. I had written an essay on the shift between pre-Socratic and Platonic thought in ancient Greece and how it accounted for a problematic view of language in Western culture. During my three years of course work I had come to believe that there was something very wrong with the understanding of rhetoric that we had inherited from the Greeks as it was articulated in the Platonic dialogues. I believed that an understanding of rhetoric's bad reputation could be found in Plato's preoccupation with *essential* reality. My professors explained to me that I should "just read the dialogues and know what they say. You can re-write the history of rhetoric *after* you get your degree."

When I had completed the paper, I asked my roommate to read it to see if it made sense. About an hour later she returned and exclaimed, "you have to read this book I just finished. It deals with a lot of the same things your paper talks about." She handed me a copy of *Zen* and pointed out the section on rhetoric and the ancient Greeks. As I read through it I felt a strange mixture of excitement and disappointment: Pirsig had indeed dealt with the same issues, but far more clearly and articulately. I had thought that I had discovered something original only to find that it had been done before, and had been done more effectively at that. Nonetheless, Pirsig's treatment of rhetoric's connection to "Quality" made me realize that I *had* discovered something, that what I had to say was important, useful, and perhaps even true.

To paraphrase Pirsig, I had been doing it right all along. I began reading more about the Sophists and pre-Socratics, and making connections between their views of language and many of the contemporary conflicts in social, political, and literary theory. I also made another important discovery: that the view of language in Western culture paralleled the views which Europeans had of Africans and African culture. Henry Louis Gates provided support for this view with his observation that "[e]thnocentricism and 'logocentricism' are profoundly interrelated in Western discourse as old as the *Phaedrus* of Plato, in which one finds one of the earliest figures of blackness as an absence, a figure of negation."[4] And I found many more connections which suggested what contemporary black thinkers call the "Afrocentric" view of communication paralleled perspectives articulated by many of the early Sophists.

My dissertation became an exploration of the problem of racism using contemporary theories of language and communication. I began to believe that racism might be best understood as a participatory activity negotiated through symbolic interaction, based upon an agreement to disagree which I described as "complicitous." This conclusion was in many ways at odds with some contemporary theories of race relations, which view racism as a "white problem" (Bowser and Hunt, 1981), but consistent with views of theorists like David Wellman, who sees racism as a manifestation of the same competitive behavior that whites engage in with each other (1980), and Albert Memmi, who asks in *The colonizer and the colonized* "Who can completely rid himself of bigotry in a country where everyone is tainted by it?" (1967, p. 23).

It was the work of Vincent Crapanzano, who follows Memmi's line of argument,[5] that provided me with the concepts and vocabulary necessary to articulate the relationship between rhetoric and racism that I had been trying to explain. Crapanzano's discussion of "essentialism" and its connection to racism had at one and the same time both clarified and complicated the connections I had drawn between rhetoric and race. Rhetoric, when seen from an essentialist perspective is problematical precisely because it calls into question a singular reality, what Richard Lanham calls "serious reality" (1976). Race confronts that same reality by posing differences which call into question the assumptions which "serious reality" engenders, differences that can only be explained within the contexts of relative and contingent "rhetorical" realities.

Essentialism attempts to "free us from rhetoric," but as Richard Lanham explains "we cannot be freed from it" since freedom from rhetoric would force us to "divest ourselves of what alone makes social life tolerable, of the very mechanism of forgiveness." Lanham's explanation suggested that rhetoric offered a vehicle for transcending the black and white judgments of essentialist thought through its recognition that, ultimately, to be true to ourselves, we have to judge others as we would have them judge us. Lanham's "rhetorical ideal of life" provided a "Golden Rule" of judgment that, I believed, could humanize the problematic discourse of negative difference.

I began to believe that the problem of race, like the problem of rhetoric, was basically a problem of judgment based on *essentially* negative differences, differences that were at the very core of Western thought. The assumption of ontological difference, of a world composed of separate and distinct beings has, since the ancient Greeks, been axiomatic in Western thought, and it has shaped and defined both descriptive and prescriptive assertions about the nature of reality. Both physical and human nature have been viewed from the standpoint of a logic of identity that strives for certainty, that attempts to determine reality in the last instance, to discover final truths. Both philosophical idealism

and realism, and the foundationist and externalist epistemological strategies they often emphasize, assume the existence of a
justificatory ground separate and distinct from human beings and
situated in the formal or substantive properties of reality.[6] And
yet, this seemingly self-evident assumption has not brought us
much closer to understanding our selves or the world in which
we live in any enduring sense, for we continue to judge and act
against the Other, whether we define that Other in terms of class,
gender, language or race, in ways that we would never apply to
ourselves.

This became most apparent to me when, in writing my
dissertation I asked the following questions based upon the conclusions at which I had tentatively arrived: if racism is based on
the problem of negative difference, then am I not perpetuating
that problem when I argue for positions that assume that whites
are *essentially* different than blacks? How can I know that, as
Robert Terry[7] suggests, "*to be white in America is not to have
to think about it*," without accepting the assumption that
whites and blacks are *in fact essentially different*? If I assume
that I possess some knowledge or faculty that a white person
does not, have I not committed the same fallacy that whites
have been accused of committing against blacks, the fallacy of
special pleading, which occurs when "one disputant tries to
reap the benefit of an argument which he later pleads has a special reference to his own case but which somehow does not
apply to others"?[8]

In short, I began to reflect upon the implications of judging a
white person, or any other person for that matter, on the basis of
standards and assumptions which I could not likewise apply to
myself. Such a judgment would violate what Chaim Perelman
and L. Olbrechts Tyteca call "the rule of justice," which "requires
giving identical treatment to beings or situations of the same
kind."[9] If black people and white people are "of the same kind,"
then to make a judgment about whites that I could not apply to
myself would be to make a consciously bad judgment. And yet, as
I reviewed the literature on race, and examined blacks and whites
discoursing on racial issues, it was clear that the rule of justice
was consistently being violated by all of the participants in the
discourse. The problem of race, I concluded, needed to be
addressed not only as a problem of language, but as a problem of
epistemology if its solution was ever to be isolated.

This conclusion led me to a line of thinking in contemporary physics which suggests that the problem of negative difference has had a profound influence on human symbolic action and material interaction. David Bohm proposes that the belief that the physical and social worlds are composed of separate and distinct entities, or "fragments" as he calls them, "is evidently an illusion, and this illusion cannot do other than lead to endless conflict and confusion." Bohm relates his discussion to the relationship between essence and race when he asserts that

> the widespread and pervasive distinctions between people (race, nation, family, profession, etc., etc.) which are now preventing mankind from working together for the common good, and indeed, even for survival, have one of the key factors of their origin in a kind of thought that treats *things* as inherently divided, disconnected, and "broken up" into yet smaller constituent parts. Each part is considered to be essentially independent and self-existent.[10]

I would discover later that Bohm's research in physics pointed to the importance of coherent dialogue as a vehicle for transcending the limitations of epistemological strategies that emphasize reductionistic and fragmentary notions of essence.[11]

My initial confrontation with Bohm's work, however, provided a physical parallel to the symbolic manifestations of negative difference, and further implicated essentialist thinking in the problem of racism. I began to wonder whether or not the material divisions perpetuated by racism were the result of a way of thinking, and this insight returned me to the book that had first inspired me to explore the relationship between rhetoric and race, Pirsig's *Zen*. In his discussion of the birth of rational philosophy in the time of the Sophists of ancient Greece, Pirsig eloquently explains the problem of negative difference when he argues that the divisions of "mind and matter, subject and object, form and substance" are "dialectical inventions": perhaps the "illusions" of which Bohm speaks? The legacy of these divisions and illusions continues to haunt us today in the realm of race relations in particular, but also in the realms of human relations in general. As a student of rhetoric I had discovered that the same language that had created these divisions could potentially remedy them, and as a teacher of rhetoric I believed that I could offer students a chance to enter the discourse well armed, able to protect themselves, and with an understanding of the incredible responsibility the power of the word entailed.

RHETORICS OF POWER AND EMPOWERMENT

In empowering students it became clear that the complicity of reason and the university needed to be exposed. Robert Pirsig's previous personality, a character he calls "Phaedrus," refers to the university in a series of lectures to his students as a "Church of Reason," the primary goal of which is "Socrates' old goal of truth, in its ever changing forms, as it's revealed by the process of rationality. Everything else," he writes, "is subordinate to that" (p. 133). The metaphor which Pirsig uses to characterize reason is a knife, an instrument that dissects and categorizes the world, defines it in terms of its essential elements. Pirsig's Phaedrus becomes obsessed with only one side of the blade of this knife, however, the side that discriminates and subordinates parts to the whole. Although he seeks a critical sensibility which emancipates, his search for essential reality leads only to a critical sensibility by which he is himself enslaved, a critical sensibility defined by an almost fanatical faith in the power of reason.

It was this same faith in reason that I saw as central to the discourse of negative difference and its impact on our understanding of rhetoric and race. It was also central to the relationship between students and their teachers, and like Pirsig, I began to see it as a vehicle for creating followers instead of leaders, consumers instead of critics. "The student's biggest problem was a slave mentality which had been built into him by years of carrot-and-whip grading, a mule mentality which said, 'If you don't whip me, I won't work'" (p. 175). Like Pirsig, I began to believe that this mentality arose out of a certain way of looking at rhetoric, and consequently, of looking at the world.

And I found support for this belief in *The trial of Socrates*, in which I. F. Stone argues that Socrates "and his disciples saw the human community as a herd that had to be ruled by a king or kings, as a sheep by a shepherd" (p. 38). The ancient "philosopher king" of both Socrates and Plato, the only person wise enough to know that he knows nothing, is replaced by the

teacher in modern essentialist education. The result is an educational praxis that is both elitist and oppressive. As Stone
explains:

> It followed—at least for Socrates and his disciples—that
> since virtue was knowledge and knowledge was unattain-
> able, ordinary men, the many, had neither the virtue nor
> the knowledge required for self government. By this
> labyrinthine metaphysical route Socrates was back to his
> fundamental proposition that the human community was a
> herd, and could not be trusted to govern itself (p. 40).

Stone concludes his chapter on "Socrates and Rhetoric" by suggesting the logical end of the Socratic rejection of rhetoric: "The
negative dialectic of Socrates—if the city had taken it seriously—
would have made equity and democracy impossible. His identification of virtue with an unattainable knowledge stripped common men of hope and denied their capacity to govern themselves"
(Stone, p. 97). This negative dialectic, which for centuries mas-
queraded as dialogue, reduces rhetoric to a slave of philosophy,
and creates in the minds of the many a "slave mentality."

Pirsig recognizes that this "slave mentality" arises in the
student's mind precisely when rhetoric is reduced, as both
Socrates and Plato had done, to a simple set of techniques used by
those who have discovered the "Truth," for persuading those
who cannot learn it own their own. Unlike Plato and Socrates,
Aristotle saw in the human condition a capacity for self-govern-
ment, and viewed rhetoric as a critical activity, defining it as
"the faculty [power] of discovering in the particular case what
are the available means of persuasion."[12] The question then
becomes one of ends: *why* do we discover these available means
of persuasion? To persuade others? *Or to understand how others
are attempting to persuade us?* The answer, of course, is both; but
for centuries emphasis has mostly been placed on the former,
and the latter has suffered so greatly that it has only been recognized in the privileged discourses of contemporary critics that
rarely reach students, most of whom in any case have been per-
suaded that they "do not yet know enough" to understand what
these critics are saying anyway.

Pirsig's character Phaedrus decided to emphasize the latter,
and began by asking himself and his students the question which

circumscribes all means and ends: "And what is good Phaedrus, and what is not good—Need we ask anyone to tell us these things?" In a society which asserts that we do indeed need someone to tell us these things, to explain what is good and what is not good, such words are subversive. They call into question the need for teachers and critics and other sources of externalized authority which negate the individual's sense of self and ability to make decisions on her own.[13] In a society in which schools are a place where "you let the dying society put its trip on you," where they "teach you by pushing you around, by stealing your will and your sense of power, by making timid square apathetic slaves out of you—authority addicts,"[14] the calling into question of externalized authority is dangerous.

And because one of the purposes of rhetoric is this calling into question of authority, it becomes a dangerous subject to teach, unless of course one can disguise it as something less dangerous, as a simple system of "forms and mannerisms," as a way of talking about the world, but never as a way of creating it. So schools don't teach rhetoric, at least not until it is much too late in a student's career to enable them the openly question and criticize the teacher in a legitimate search for "truth."[15] Pirsig's Phaedrus attempted to subvert this system by teaching students that they *did* know what is good and what is not, that they *did* have something important to say, that rhetoric was more than forms and mannerisms. Rhetoric, for Phaedrus, was *the Good*, the edifice of Quality that held society together. The price of this insight for Phaedrus was, for all intents and purposes, mental death—madness.

But Phaedrus survived his ordeal, and became the personality we know as Pirsig, and explained it all in *Zen*.[16] Using his experiences as a teacher of composition he argued passionately that schools don't teach students to seek the truth, but merely to believe what they are told. And what they are told is that they do not know enough to know what the truth is, but that one day, if they work hard and listen to their teachers, they will be able to know: they will have access to the privileged discourse that, as David Bartholomae explains, allows them to "invent the university": the discourse of essential knowledge. They will then become writers "who can successfully manipulate an audience," who can "both imagine and write from a position of privilege," and who can "see themselves within a privileged discourse, one that already includes and excludes groups of readers." They will become players in a system of power relations in which self and Other are at odds and in conflict, and thus they "must be either equal to or more powerful than those they address" (1986. p. 9). They must not only learn to exercise power, but also to maintain its well-defined parameters.

What Pirsig and Bartholomae do not explain, however, is how this problem of privileged discourse relates to the problem of race. For that we need to consider Jerry Farber's essay *The student as nigger.* School for Farber is a place where students are forced to submit to the system and its disempowering methods of instruction, where the goal is to achieve good grades and "please the teacher." In a discussion of rhetoric as it is traditionally taught in the writing class he argues that the "very essence of Freshman English is that term paper they force out of you," a paper defined by grammatical rules and divorced from rhetorical implications: "In perfect order, impeccably footnoted, unreal and totally useless—that term paper, that empty form, is pretty much the content of the course: submission—alienation—learning to live a pretend intellectual life, pretend caring about pretend things" (p. 23). This is precisely how Lanham describes rhetoric when viewed from a "serious" or essentialist perspective: "Hold always before the student rhetoric's practical purpose: to win, to persuade. But train for this purpose with continual verbal play, rehearsal for the sake of rehearsal" (p. 2). This is the "empty rhetoric" both condemned and at the same time constrained by philosophy, the good slave that loves and mimics its master to survive, and accepts a subservient position never to be called into question.

But this acceptance, Lanham explains, runs counter to rhetoric's critical impulse, and rhetoric when defined within the context of its own coordinates, offers a type of emptiness more consistent with the philosophy of the East than the West. Such rhetoric offers

> a training in tolerance, if by that we mean getting inside another's skull and looking out. It offered the friendliest of advices on how to tap into any and all sources of pleasure. It habituated its students to a world of contingent purpose, of perpetual cognitive dissonance, plural orchestration. It specialized less in knowledge than in the way knowledge is held, which is how Whitehead defines wisdom" (p. 7).

This is a rhetoric not only of persuasion, but also of inquiry; not merely a counterpart of dialectic, but also a vehicle of dialogue. It is a rhetoric based upon a reality of diversity and contingency, that recognizes a variety of complementary truths, no one inherently better than the others, and all implicated in each other. This is a rhetoric capable of interrogating the essentializing consequences of physical and psychological division, one that is equally able to consider the evidence of personal experience as that of authority, a knife capable of cutting through the illusions and delusions of rational and material reality to a coherent theory of knowledge situated somewhere between "a positivist reality and a Platonic, between realism and idealism."[17] Equipped with this double-edged sword of the word, I left graduate school, took my first teaching position, and found myself following the way of the warrior.

THE WAY OF THE WARRIOR

Through the train's/ unwashed window,/ snaking slow over/ Longfellow,/ I spy the river/ wrinkling;/ an unfinished/ portrait/ sketched by some/ psychotic artist/ living on the Hill/ amidst the swell/ of tenements up/ into skyscrapers—/ scratching/ the muffled blue,/ and drinking/ the symmetry of sky./ Home is a place/ where you may find/ a reason/ to love life,/ or find the/ difference/ between dreams/ and what dreams/ seem to be, or/ find the hurt/ of knowing,/ too, that else-/ where so much/ more of life/ is longing/ to be loved;/ and that may be,/ of all things/ found, the/ hardest hurt to/ have to learn./ Yet even now,/ as this same/ train accepts/ the subtle/ promise of a tunnel's/ northward/ darkness,/ I hope that home,/ my tendril heart,/ forgives me/ for my dreams./ But dreams/ are not an/ easy thing/ to be/ forgiven for.

I had written the poem "Between two cities" in my junior year in college, and analyzed it for the first time when working on my master's degree. As a writer I had intended to honor the form of my favorite poet, Robert Penn Warren, whose poem "Pondy Woods" had inspired me to begin writing poetry at age thirteen. As a critic, armed with the knife of analysis, I discovered that, beneath its surface, "Between two cities" spoke to the tension and tensiveness of being between two states of thinking and being. As a teacher, returning to the school from which I had received my undergraduate degree, I hoped to offer my students some sense of the stylistic and substantive experience of a reader and writer caught in between two cities of the mind.

I began in an introductory literature course by explaining Pirsig's notion of the dialectical knife, and what he calls the "classic-romantic dichotomy," the split between science and art. At the top of the board I wrote "classic" and "romantic", and began listing dichotomous terms below them: philosophy and rhetoric, yes and no, right and wrong, black and white, good and bad, true and false, male and female. With this last set I heard a loud gasp, and turned to see a young man staring at the board. "That's it," he said, "Oh my *God*, that's *it*." Most of the other students, those who were paying attention, looked at him quizzically, but he just stared at the board in rapt contemplation, discovering something that he had already known. I continued my list, and concluded it with the final definitive pair: teacher and student. The young man who had gasped left the class quickly with a disturbed look on his face.

The next several classes involved an amplification of the dichotomies, their connection to literature and criticism, and the relationship between language and power with an emphasis on its role in the classroom. At the conclusion of one class I indicated the assigned readings, and explained that each student would focus on one text and report on it to the rest of the class. Instead of everyone reading all of the poems, short stories and plays in the anthology, I explained, I thought it would be more useful to have each student focus on specific texts and play the role of "teacher" for her peers by presenting her own critical insights to the rest of the class. As I looked around the room, I noticed that several students looked uncomfortable with the assignment, especially one young woman sitting in the last seat to the right in the front row.

"Is something wrong," I asked?

I heard her say, very quietly and without looking up, "*You are an asshole.*"

"O.K.," I said, pausing and taking a slow breath. "I just thought that this would be the most productive way of using our class time, and that it would allow us to deal with some of the issues concerning rhetoric and criticism that we've been discussing. The only other alternative that I can see is having everyone read everything, and I just felt that we should focus on quality instead of quantity. In any case, if you have another alternative I'd be more than happy to hear it, and if the class would rather do that, then it's fine by me." The student seemed a little less exasperated, and eventually said, "I guess that's a good way of doing it."

"So, do you still think I'm an asshole?"

The young man who earlier in the semester had experienced his epiphanal moment, gasped again.

"What's wrong," I asked.

"I've never heard a teacher say asshole before!" he said.

"What do you mean," I said. "She called me an asshole."

The young woman looked me, shocked and horrified. "I said you are *impossible*."

"Oh," I said, "I thought you said I was an asshole."

The young man looked at me, incredulous. "But would you have *really* reacted that way if she had called you an asshole?"

"I reacted the way I reacted," I said, trying to sound like a Zen master. "Whether she believes I am impossible or an asshole, she is entitled to say how she feels. If I had reacted in any other way; if for example I had berated her, or thrown her out of class, and lectured you all about respect when addressing the teacher, and found out in the course of the discussion from one of you that she said that I was impossible, then what could I do? Accuse you all of lying to protect her? Then, I really would be an asshole, wouldn't I?" It was, I felt, a lesson in the rhetorical ideal of life, of power, empowerment and tolerance.

Unlike a Zen master, however, I wasn't able to maintain the same mindset in all situations. I was crossing Longfellow Bridge on the train that runs between Cambridge and Boston reading Allan Bloom's *The closing of the American mind*. As I read Bloom's discussion of race relations in the university I became very angry. "This man," I thought, "is a racist. This is textbook racism: blaming the victim, claiming that white students have done all they can to remedy the problems of racism, arguing that affirmative action leads to mediocrity! I've been to the University of Massachusetts, where black students were attacked by a mob of white students following the 1986 World Series, and the University of Michigan where a series of racist incidents occurred during the same year. *This man does not know what he is talking about.*" I began thinking of the essay that I would write in response to this obviously bigoted book, when I realized that I had suddenly fallen into the abyss of my own analyses. I was guilty of special pleading, had fallen prey to the rhetoric of racism. The problem of negative difference had again reared its ugly head, and it was looking right at me! I had tossed tolerance out the window because I didn't agree with what Bloom had to say. So much for practicing what I preached!

"You are an asshole."

As the train approached "the subtle promise of a tunnel's northward darkness," I realized that I had been duped, drawn into an argument that I myself had claimed was problematical. Once again, I had to reflect on what it meant to live between two cities, to live with myself and what I claimed to believe in. Two years later I found myself between two cities once again as an instructor in a basic writing course at a large midwestern university. I was the second reader for a group of student portfolios, and the assessment director had asked us to record our responses. I had received the portfolio of a student who described himself as "vice president of college Republicans," and who had written essays on the university's proposed mandatory racism class and on a request by students of color for "minority lounges." He opposed both, and I had to make an "objective" assessment of his writing, regardless of how I felt about his politics. The following excerpts from the response I gave to his portfolio give some sense of what I experienced as a critical reader and teacher in a position of power.

"This cover sheet is very interesting. The student begins, 'Like a highly-guilded sword, the written word is both art and weapon.' I like this. I find it both creative and insightful, but I know that this is a part of my own bias about words and swords. As I read through the cover sheet I find the writing clear, organized and interesting, even though I've been told that the writer is the 'vice president of college Republicans,' and that his essays deal with racism. At this point, I think I know what I am in for, but read on, through two revised essays and the impromptu. All the way through I am sure that this student is a 'very good' writer, although I know that many of his arguments are fallacious at best, and having done a great deal of research into the relationship between language and race, racist by any reasonable standard.

"Nonetheless, when I finish my first reading of this portfolio I give [the student] a score of '1' because, regardless of how much I disagree with his position, and regardless of how well I can argue against it using both formal and substantive 'critical' analyses, his writing in my mind, based on the assignment, and our collective 'general characteristics of effective writing' standards, is quite good, and in fact, superior. At this point I go back to the two revised essays and give them a second read, trying to make sure that I have not overlooked any complex structures, insightful arguments, or stylistic uses of language. Here I see some holes in the argument, some leaps in logic, and an interesting mixture of fact and fallacy.

"[He] writes in 'Look Who's for Segregation Now': 'When a handful of [student assembly] representatives had the courage to cite that this violated [the Student Assembly's] constitution because it discriminated on the basis of race, [one student organization] sent in a small army of thugs to [the Student Assembly] the following week, savaging the offending representatives with unfounded charges of racism, and in general intimidating the hell out of [them.]' *Thugs. Savaging.* This is, in my mind and based on my knowledge of the subject, textbook racism, but the argument that he is making prior to this is textbook argumentation—one of the Aristotelian special *topoi*, using an opponent's argument against him or her—and in fact, it's not a bad argument in terms of form and substance. So [his] first score remains a '1', and at this time I am sure of this score. I do not need to reflect on what kind of '1' this is, high, medium or low, or whether or not a workshop is in order. It is a strong '1'. The kid is a good writer.

"This is the most interesting part of this process of reading a portfolio. I saw lots of strengths, few weaknesses, and three pieces of writing that were written by a very capable writer who had understood the assignments given to him and composed to the best of his ability. I also saw a student who knows how to traffic in argumentative racist discourse in a way that, in its own right, exemplifies this thing we call 'critical thinking.' I think anyone who 'objectively' reads this portfolio would feel the same way. Perhaps [the student] puts it best. 'One essay deals with the mandatory racism class, the other with minority lounges. I argue against each for reasons I hope you will agree with. If not, I'm sure you will at the very least enjoy how they are written. . . . So as to you dear reader, I offer up these guilded swords. If you be not a warrior, then by all means simply revel in their beauty.'"

Reading this student's portfolio was like reading Allan Bloom's *The closing of the American mind:* both challenged me to reflect *critically* on my own beliefs concerning what it meant to be "open minded." Both confronted me with the experience of being "aware of a rational being, of a consciousness; the consciousness of another, *no different from the one I automatically assume in every human being* I encounter."[18] I could easily judge either of these two individuals in terms of *their* ignorance, of *their* not knowing what *they* were talking about: but I knew that, by doing so, I would be subscribing to the myth of difference, *of negative difference*, that is at the root of those discourses that we choose to term "racist." I knew that to do so would be to knowingly and willingly violate the rule of justice, to reaffirm my own smug sense of superiority; I knew that to do so would make me, *essentially*, no different than those I would condemn.

And I knew that I derived that knowledge from a critical faculty, one which discovers "in the particular case what are the available means of persuasion," one which enabled me to understand race as a *rhetorical* phenomenon. Thus, I had to see Allan Bloom and the student as individuals who, like me, make judgments based upon their experiences and understanding of a world in which we all live. To see my own opinions and judgments as somehow superior would be to impose my own agenda on them, and to limit the possibilities of discourse to the mutual exclusivity of truth and falsity that is at the heart of essentialism, of a serious reality that would do away with the rhetorical capacities of tolerance and forgiveness. Allan Bloom induced me to recognize my epistemic complicity; the student influenced me to "make my Easter," to look into own beliefs about what it means to be a human being who treats others as they would treat me. They helped me to look into myself and *Die*.

This is the type of death that results, I believe, from what Habermas calls the "emancipatory cognitive interest,"[19] the human capacity for critical self-reflection, a process which enables us to move beyond argumentative essentialism to some common ground of understanding. I experienced how wonderfully radical this notion was when working with a student who had been assigned to write on Friere's "Banking Concept of Education."[20] At one point during our discussion she asked: "isn't he just changing the currency?" From her own perspective she believed that Friere's "radical" approach to education substituted one agenda, "the liberation of the oppressed," for another, "the oppression of the liberated." Who was I to tell her different?

She saw through the discourse of negative difference to an underlying agreement to disagree, and recognized the same inconsistency that Charles Paine has commented on in his essay, "Relativism, radical pedagogy, and the ideology of paralysis." Paine suggests that many 'radical' critics "do themselves a disservice by conceptualizing ultimate goals and rigid political positions; and at times they seem surprisingly naive in thinking that sound method or correct content by themselves will lead to the creation of desirable political values and to successful radical teaching" (p. 558). In short, they participate in the same essentialist discourse that they attempt to overthrow, without recognizing—or acknowledging that they, in fact, are simply "changing the currency."

Paine's essay does much to highlight the paradoxical position of radical pedagogy in terms of its relationship to criticism. "That is, critical thinking—the ability to transcend limited or oppressive consciousness, becoming critically aware of the status quo, one's society, and one's own consciousness as historically contingent—is fundamental" to the agenda of 'radical pedagogy' (pp. 558–59). Certainly the self-reflexive function of criticism is central to the radical pedagogical agenda, but a recognition of its self-legitimizing function must also be addressed to offer students the full range of "alternative possibilities"[21] presupposed by critical thinking. Paine concurs: "We perhaps should make it clear that we are teaching one type of critical thinking among potentially numerous types, one that allows us to recognize the oppression of the dominant order" (p. 564). He warns against the dangerous possibility of shifting from one form of essentialism to another, and demands that we interrogate, and take responsibility for, the justificatory strategies upon which we base our arguments for emancipation and empowerment:

> Since we acknowledge that there are no transcendent anchors to consult, no transcendent goals to justify the way things are or the actions we take, and no transcendent goods to teach our students, we must cultivate the courage to assume full responsibility for our actions, influence, and belief, which we try to pass on to our students. (p. 569)

Paine offers a powerful challenge to those who wish to engage in radical and emancipatory pedagogy. He invites us to tread the path of the warrior by asking the question with which Pirsig prefaces his "inquiry into values:" "*And what is good, Phaedrus, and what is not good—Need we ask anyone to tell us these things?*"

FACING THE GODS?

Need we ask anyone to tell us these things? Traditionally, the philosophical answer to the question has been, "Yes, we do. We need the dialecticians, *those who know the truth,* to tell us what is good and what it not good." This is the answer which we have inherited through essentialist educational philosophies, that has been justified by the Socratic injunction that the one who knows— the teacher—should rule, should decide what is good and what is not. The rhetorical answer has, however, been far less clear-cut and—at least for most philosophers—far less satisfactory. It defies the logic of essentialism, of "true and false discourse," by offering what Jean-Pierre Vernant identifies as the "logic of polarity," that is exemplified in the rhetoric and the "anti-logic" of the Sophists, the *dissoi-logoi.*[22] One sees a similar "logic of polarity" in the Zen notion of the "center of being." As Herrigel (1974) explains in *The method of Zen:* "The center of being is *beyond* all opposites just because it dwells within them, and *within* all opposites just because it 'is' beyond them. It is without contradictions and yet full of contradictions" (p. 80). One also sees it in the realms of "plural orchestration," and "perpetual cognitive dissonance" that are the essence of the "rhetorical ideal of life."

And just as the "logic of polarity" can lead to "the center of being," the "rhetorical ideal of life," which necessitates surrendering the central self, can lead to the "egolessness" that the student of Zen seeks. "The essential thing is," writes Herrigel, "to become egoless in a radical sense, so that 'egoself' does not exist any more, either as a word or as a feeling, and turns into an unknown quantity" (p. 93). In Zen, this "unknown quantity" that goes beyond words and feelings is situated in the lived experience of the here and now, and is, at least for Herrigel, foreign to rhetoric. Herrigel's understanding of rhetoric is, however, a rhetoric defined in "serious" terms, a rhetoric that has haunted us since the "triumph of philosophy and the end of tragedy."[23] And this, suggests Lanham, is the tragedy of rhetorical education in the West. "The recurring attempts to make rhetorical training respectable in serious terms all go astray. The contribution rhetorical reality makes to Western reality as a whole is greatest when it is most uncompromisingly itself, insists most strenuously on its own coordinates" (p. 6). Rhetoric and language have been neglected and negated, precisely because their paradoxical natures could not be adequately explained in "serious" terms. The result has been the creation and perpetuation of oppressive social and pedagogical situations which use the power of words to disempower, and undermine the transformative capacities of language.

This potential for transformation is explained by James Hillman: "The relation between word and force is also reflected in society, suggesting to me that the rule of coercive violence increases when our art of convincing words declines. *Peitho* takes on an overwhelming importance both in the healing of the soul and the healing of society" (p. 20). *Peitho*, the ancient art of rhetoric, empowers precisely because it offers the possibility of change, and the possibility to negotiate the contexts and constraints of communication between persons, of reality, and of *power*: "Through words we can alter reality; we can bring into being and remove from being; we can shape and change the very structure and essence of what is real. The art of speech becomes the primary mode of moving reality" (p. 21). Only recently have we begun to transcend an understanding of rhetoric as "mere words," and moved to the painful recognition of the words at the center of our social and psychological worlds.

Indeed, even contemporary critical theory, perhaps the most powerful manifestation of the "serious" premises of reality, has returned to the centrality of language and its emancipatory possibilities: Habermas, echoing the ancient Greek rhetorician Isocrates, contends in *Knowledge and human interests:* "What raises us out of nature is the only thing whose nature we can know: language. Through its structure, autonomy and responsibility are posited for us. Our first sentence expresses unequivocally the intention of universal and unconstrained consensus." This "unconstrained consensus" is manifest in what Habermas calls "the ideal speech situation," an environment which is free of constraint and domination in which true and productive dialogue can occur.[24] Habermas connects this ideal speech situation to the emancipatory function of critique: "In self-reflection knowledge for the sake of knowledge attains congruence with the interest in autonomy and responsibility. The emancipatory cognitive interest aims at the pursuit of reflection as such" (p. 314). While Habermas envisions this liberatory move as an ideal, its realization becomes possible when that ideal is understood and enacted rhetorically.

If this is the ideal that we are trying to realize in our class-rooms and in our society, it is imperative that we consider fully how the double-edged sword of criticism both nurtures and negates the freedom that we desire for ourselves and our students. Critical inquiry is a privileged discourse, and as such, can alienate and exclude just as it can affirm and include.[25] The challenge that confronts theorists and practitioners of education, especially those committed to issues of diversity and liberal humanism, is to create an environment that offers students more than just another oppressive discourse substituted for one that precedes it. The challenge to radical pedagogy is nothing less than the democratization of academic discourse, and that means that we, as the holders of power in the classroom, must be ready and willing to take responsibility for the things we say we believe in, and "make our Easter." We must, in short, grasp the words and die.

To Grasp the Words and Die

I have attempted in this opening chapter to offer some concrete examples of what it means "to grasp the words and die" by exploring classical and contemporary considerations of criticism and its social, political, and pedagogical problems and possibilities. As a critic of race relations and rhetoric, I have tried to illustrate the difficulties involved in coming to grips with the realities of humanism and pluralism in what I believe to be an epistemologically oppressive environment. As a teacher of rhetoric and criticism, I have tried to share with students an understanding of the power of words and the double-edged agenda of critical inquiry, that they might protect themselves in that environment.[26] As a theorist of education and language I have tried to think through the implications of invoking the full emancipatory potential of criticism to make real the "ideal speech situation."

To do this, I believe, we must in some sense "die." As critics we "die" whenever we engage a text. Jane P. Tompkins writes of Georges Poulet, that when he "examines the internal processes through which literature realizes itself in the individual reader, he is struck by the essentially passive nature of the reader's role. The reader gains his experience by forgetting, foregoing himself; dying, so to speak, in order that the text may live" (p. xiv). I believe that we can extend Poulet's analysis to the death of a "state of mind," a death that we encounter as critics involved in either written or oral interpretation. Whether we analyze the forms or structures of a text, or engage it at a level which forces us to give up some part of ourselves and at the same time "face the Gods," we invoke the double-edged sword of critique that allows the word to live.

As teachers of criticism we must be willing to transform the nature of the student-teacher relationship in such a way as to bring about the sense of community and respect that all of us, regardless of orientation, seek to achieve. We must "die as elitists so as to be resurrected on the side of the oppressed, that they be born again with the beings who were not allowed to be" (Freire, 1973). And yet, we must not make the mistake of replacing one oppressive discourse—one agenda—for another, regardless of whether we choose to define it as "radical," "conservative," or "liberal." We might follow the advice of the Zen master Daiyu: "If you really want to attain the Way, you must die completely once: only then can you realize it."[27] Unlike the classic tradition of Zen, however, the teacher's agenda must be open to question and consideration in order for an environment free from constraint and domination to develop.

As critics of education, we must be willing to call the positions that we hold dear into question, to suspend judgment in order to discourse on the process of judging. This is how Wayne Booth (1986) approaches pluralism in his classroom. Booth notes that he has "elected one pluralism among many—what could be called either 'pragmatic pluralism' or 'rhetorical pluralism.' The ultimate truth of any one pluralistic scheme has been ignored, or at least bracketed, while we have thought about how to open up life to life's pluralities" (p. 479). "Rhetorical pluralism," as I understand it, might well mean the death of the one—the teacher—for the liberation of the many.

In short, as teachers we must become warriors, and in the tradition of the Samurai, we must not be afraid to "die." Here I am of course referring to the death of a state of mind, which could allow for a democratization of pedagogical discourse. We can begin by providing students with the critical tools necessary to extend analysis beyond isolated texts and contexts, and bring the discussion of power and language into the classroom, where both linguistic and social reality are born. As warriors, we must deal with the consequences of essential knowledge and its influence on the pedagogical philosophies to which we subscribe. In a war against ignorance and closemindedness, we must think carefully about the implications of privileging any one position at the expense of others. Such an approach to education is, in my view, truly radical.

This approach to education is central to the rhetorical enterprise. I concur with Thomas O. Sloan that the most noble legacy of rhetoric is "an abhorrence of coercion through a liberalizing of the mind."[28] As we look toward the future of educational theory and *praxis* we need only recognize that we cannot be free of rhetoric and that, being born into its house, it should be our intention to grasp the words and die. As teachers this will mean reflecting on our own pedagogical practices and how they may contribute to the closing of our student's minds in ways that we may not wish to acknowledge. As critics, it will mean examining our own justificatory strategies to consider how they might be implicated in those whom we criticize.

This is the purpose of the next chapter, which will further explicate my earlier discussion of Alan Bloom's *The closing of the American mind* in order to illustrate the pitfalls and possibilities of critical analysis. Focusing on Bloom's discussion of race relations, I will consider how the justificatory strategies underlying Bloom's position lead to a conception of knowledge grounded in foundationist assumptions, assumptions he seems unwilling to apply to his own position on race and racism in American education. A critique of Bloom's position, however, runs the risk of reifying an essentialized conception of knowledge that perpetuates a dualistic understanding of race and rhetoric. By approaching Bloom's discussion from the perspective of what Zen masters call a "beginner's mind," I hope to suggest that an analysis grounded in rhetorical coherence might offer an opportunity for reopening the American mind.

2

BEGINNER'S MIND

However long or short life may be, no matter under what conditions we have to live it, we all want to make the best of it—the best not only in the technique of living, but also in understanding its meaning. But that implies apprehending a glimmer of its mystery.

—Gustie Herrigel,
Zen in the art of flower arrangement

In *Zen mind, beginner's mind*, Shunryu Suzuki writes: "The beginner's mind is the mind of compassion" (1988, p. 21), a mind that approaches established ideas openly and without preconceptions.[1] It is with this type of compassion in mind that I wish to consider Allan Bloom's (1987) discussion of race relations in *The closing of the American mind*. Bloom's book offers an excellent opportunity to explore the complexities which undergird the argumentative dichotomies created by essentialist epistemology in education and society. My analysis emphasizes Bloom's opinions concerning race relations in the university community, and relates this discussion to his positions on gender and contemporary criticism to argue for the consideration of rhetoric as a corrective to the philosophical and social problems created by essentialist discourse. I suggest that Bloom's arguments are undermined by the very assumptions of knowledge he implicitly and explicitly defends, and that his book offers an excellent opportunity to consider the crisis of epistemology which now confronts many academic disciplines. This approach to the *American mind*, I believe, provides new insights into the relationship between race and epistemology by interrogating the

43

notion that there is a significant difference between the assumptive grounds of the arguments articulated by Bloom and those who might disagree with him.

RHETORIC AND THE PHILOSOPHY OF *THE AMERICAN MIND*

Bloom's book is a serious critique of American higher education, which contends in its subtitle that our system "has failed democracy and impoverished the souls of today's students." This critique requires rhetorical consideration because it exemplifies quite clearly the assumptive grounds of the debate between rhetoric and philosophy. "In liberal education," writes Bloom, "the worst and the best fight it out, fakers vs. authentics, sophists vs. philosophers, for the favor of public opinion and for control over the study of man in our times" (p. 342). Bloom's commentary might be read as a rehearsal of the *physis-nomos* antithesis, a contemporary manifestation of the continuing debate between foundationist and conventionalist conceptions of truth, between idealism—the position which assumes a single transcendent reality, and historicism—the position which assumes that truths are determined by social and historical conventions. While, ostensibly, Bloom's book is about the quality of education in America, many of his critics argue that, essentially, *The closing of the American mind* is about power relations in the academy, about who should rule and who should be ruled, and the principles and practices upon which such rulership should be based.

Bloom's attack in many ways echoes the Socratic indictment of the rhetorical dilemmas inherent in social democracy, and ultimately points to the same Socratic conclusion. Like Socrates before him, Bloom assumes that "the one who knows" should rule, and that knowledge should be reserved for a philosophical elite, well versed in the art of learned disputation and possessed of the love of wisdom. This is the basic assumption that guides much of Bloom's reasoning and argumentation, and his becomes yet another voice in the controversy that has been an important part of the evolution of education in Western culture since the times of the ancients that he so admires: the battle between knowledge and opinion, and its implications for discovering that which is true and good for woman and man. On the one hand, Bloom articulates the importance of essential knowledge for the proper nourishment of students' souls, so that they might realize 'real' truth and goodness.[2] On the other, he defends the privileges afforded by the belief in essential reality, and chooses not to acknowledge the inconsistencies of his own position when considered in terms of the assumptions upon which his argument is based. This becomes clear when we focus on Bloom's discussion of race, and also applies when we consider his arguments against feminism and deconstructionist literary criticism.

Bloom believes that the university has an essentially unchanging role in terms of its relationship with the larger society, and that it should be insulated from social problems and influences that undermine the products and processes of the educational experience. This belief is undergirded by essentialist assumptions[3] that carry with them a whole set of assertions and prescriptions concerning the nature of knowledge and existence, assertions and prescriptions that have been called into question by many of the same scholars "preoccupied with questions of Health, Sex, Race, War," who Bloom feels have contributed to the closing of the American mind. These questions, which derive answers based on externally verifiable historical realities, challenge the assumption that social problems can be remedied by transcendent truths or idealistic solutions, an assumption which lies at the root of foundationism. They thus represent a shift from foundationism to conventionalism as a justificatory strategy, and while this shift ostensibly offers an alternative to the essentializing consequences of perennialism, it has the potential of replacing one form of essentialism with another.[4] Before considering this possibility in terms of critiquing Bloom's view of race relations, the connection between racism and essentialism will be considered.

ESSENCE AND EPISTEMOLOGY:
THE RHETORIC OF NEGATIVE DIFFERENCE

Writing on the problem of race, Vincent Crapanzano explains that from an essentialist point of view, "once an object or being is classified, it is forever that object or being. It has an identity. It partakes of a particular essence" (p. 20). Crapanzano argues that Apartheid, South Africa's former separatist system of government, "is an extreme case of the Western disposition to classify and categorize just about everything in essentialist terms," and he points to a clear epistemic connection between problems of race and systems of knowledge in that society and in general in his explication of "essentialist classification."

> Essentialist classification is static. Any change in identity, in essence, in regularity, or in place poses a problem; indeed it threatens the classificatory system itself. Such change must be accounted for in terms of "transformations," "evolution," "growth," or "conversion," which are somehow compatible with the classificatory system itself. Or, as in the case of human society, we try to interdict changes that risk toppling the classificatory system. We legalize them out of existence. We deny them. When applied to human beings, essentialist thought precludes that small space of freedom that is at the heart of our humanity and enables us to engage in a vital manner with those about us. (p. 20)

Crapanzano's description of essential thought is reminiscent of the Platonic conception of justice articulated in *The republic,* a justice of each thing being in its proper place in accordance with its nature. While ideally, such a conception can be defined and defended on intellectual and theoretical grounds, in practice it has resulted in many of the very social "problems" that Bloom believes have harmed the university and the educational experience it offers.

This, I believe, is why Bloom's brief discussion of race relations in the university is so very important. Bloom seems to suggest that the de facto socioeconomic segregation that has marked American education for centuries has all but disappeared, and he completely ignores that fact that such segregation has had a significant impact on race relations in American society as a whole. Such a view is wholly inconsistent with much of our contemporary knowledge of race relations,[5] but Bloom chooses his "facts" carefully in order to prove his case, a case clearly presupposed by essentialist assumptions. This is the major argumentative inconsistency of Bloom's position: while he advocates an educational system which protects and preserves essential truth, he ignores those truths—based on essential knowledge—that are inconsistent with his own position. His beliefs, based on opinion and personal experience, are somehow elevated to the status of truths, while essential knowledge about those beliefs is ignored, and relegated to the status of opinion. Thus, his argument presupposes a standard which he cannot apply to all cases, but only to his own. Within the context of essentialist epistemology, such an argument would be defined as relativistic.

Yet Bloom adamantly opposes relativism, and on this ground rejects the intellectual legitimacy of feminism and deconstructionism, both of which indict essentialist thought by asserting that all truths must be placed within an historical context. These two areas of inquiry, along with contemporary race relations theory, have played an important part in exploring how the principle of negative difference functions linguistically to create and legitimate inequitable power relations in society and discourse. The concept of negative difference is a basic aspect of rational analysis, the Aristotelian principle of non-contradiction (A cannot be not A) being its most obvious manifestation, and thus is a central element of essentialist logic and language. Yet contemporary theorists in literary criticism, race and gender, arguing that language constructs as well as reflects reality, have illustrated quite convincingly that essentialist language defines social realities in negative and often inequitable terms. The discussions of many of these theorists converge on the common ground of rhetorical inquiry, an area of inquiry historically antithetical to the philosophical assumptions adhered to and defended by Allan Bloom. In order to explicate the connections between Bloom's views on race, gender and deconstruction, a rhetorical consideration of the polemics elicited by the book, a close analysis of Bloom's position on race, and a discussion of the arguments presented in terms of the historical epistemological conflict between rhetoric and philosophy might offer some useful insights into the theoretical controversies and practical dilemmas reopened by *The American mind.*

Bloom's arguments have elicited responses from individuals both inside and outside of the academy, some in agreement, some in opposition, some which straddle the fine line between the two. Michael W. Hirschorn writes that "Mr. Bloom's book is sharply critical of what he argues is the failure of higher education to instill in students a love of learning. He offers a withering attack on professors for preaching the doctrine of 'relativism.'"[6] This relativism, Bloom suggests, leads to a lack of "intellectual achievement" and "wisdom," and undermines the role of the university in society. Bloom suggests that a return to the "Great Books" and the enthronement of philosophy at the center of the academy will cure, or at least reform, our ailing educational institutions.

Hirschorn continues: "Secretary of Education William J. Bennett recalled that after a recent speech to a group of Republican grocers in the midwest, the first question was: 'Allan Bloom says that relativism is a terrible thing. Are you for it or against it?' He was against it." Hirschorn also quotes Bennett as saying "I feel very much gratified in my views by this book" (p. A22). Opponents of Bloom, such as Howard R. Swearer, president of Brown University, disagree with Bloom's 'Great Books' solution, and even Mortimer J. Adler, a long-time defender of perennialism who is "sympathetic to Mr. Bloom's point of view, but not Mr. Bloom," argues that Bloom "has historical myopia, " and "can't see beyond his nose" (pp. A1, A22).

Reviewer Martha Nussbaum suggests that Bloom has philosophical myopia as well, and while she agrees with his opposition to relativism and historicism, takes him to task on his knowledge of Greek philosophy in general, and the positions of the ancients on the role of women in particular. Nussbaum argues that Bloom "simply ignores all texts that contradict his thesis," and applies this argument to Bloom's assertions "that feminism is 'not founded on nature,' and that it ends 'in forgetting nature and using force to refashion human beings to secure that justice.'" She also takes issue with Bloom's lack of definition for what he generally calls 'relativism,' arguing that his position "is long on rhetoric, painfully short on argument. Central terms such as 'relativism' go undefined and unanalyzed, in a way that would have caused Socrates to ask many irritating questions" (1987, p. 24). Nussbaum implies that Bloom's attack on feminism is grounded less in knowledge than opinion, questions Bloom's philosophical abilities, and offers some insights into the argumentative inconsistencies that undermine Bloom's position.

Nussbaum depicts Bloom as the defender of "a philosophy that is not practical, alive, and broadly distributed, but contemplative and quasi-religious, removed from ethical and social concerns, and the preserve of a narrow elite" (p. 24).[7] Bloom's position echoes the Socratic essentialism articulated in Plato's *Cratylus*, provides the assumptive grounds of a philosophy that seeks transcendent and immutable truths and assumes that all things exist in and of themselves and have an unchanging nature, and claims for the dialectician, the one who engages in the art of learned discourse— the one who knows—the privilege of "true" knowledge. This is an understanding of philosophy that has attempted to reduce rhetoric to "mere words," and that has denied rhetoric the status of an art of social definition vital to the health of the polity, as well as its rightful place in the academy.

The historical relationship between rhetoric and philosophy is one in which, at least until recently, philosophy has assumed a privileged position in relation to rhetoric.[8] Traditionally it has been claimed that philosophy through dialectic has access to true knowledge, while rhetoric is concerned only with opinion. Philosophically, dialectic has been described as an art of rational disputation that uses a question and answer method of arriving at essential definitions of reality in order to achieve the truth. Rhetoric, on the other hand, has been seen as an art of persuasion, concerned with opinions and probabilities as opposed to truths. In recent years, however, this situation has been transformed in such a way as to place rhetoric in a more favorable light. In its theoretical, practical, and productive manifestations rhetoric has become a focal point of philosophical examinations of logic, society, and literature, and at each level the old divisions constructed by the idealist and realist presuppositions of Western philosophy have become more tenuous. Rhetoric can no longer reasonably be reduced to relativism, nor separated from argument, but must be seen as a vehicle for understanding and interrogating "the problematic and the questionable."[9]

Rhetoric has thus provided an important commentary on the philosophical defense of essential knowledge, one which many philosophers—certainly Platonic philosophers—would rather reject than deal with on its own terms. "Rhetoric's real crime, one is often led to suspect, is its candid acknowledgment of the rhetorical aspects of 'serious' life," explains Lanham. "The concept of a central self, true or not, flatters man immensely. It gives him an identity outside time and change that he sees nowhere else in the sublunary universe. So, too, the theory of knowledge upon which seriousness rests" (p. 7). This theory of knowledge upon which seriousness rests, whether Platonic or positivist, reflects the essentializing consequences of argumentative strategies that emphasize negative differences and assume that there is one *true* reality that can be understood dialectically, through the art of learned disputation, that is separate and distinct from the relative truths of opinion. It assumes that knowledge is generated through rational, critical discourse, and is verified by those who have thoroughly contemplated and understood the subjects of that discourse. The epistemological necessity of negative difference, upon which essentialist justificatory strategies are grounded, is implicated in problems of race, gender, class, classification, and those very systems of language which legitimate the theory of a singular reality grounded in knowledge as opposed to opinion.

BLOOM ON RACE RELATIONS: THE PHILOSOPHY OF KNOWLEDGE AND A RHETORIC OF OPINION

Based upon this theory of knowledge Bloom's discussion of race is clearly opinionated and ill-informed. Bloom asserts that the "discriminatory laws are ancient history," that "there are large numbers of blacks in the universities," and that "there is nothing more that white students can do to make great changes in their relations to black students" (p. 92). But these views are not supported by much of the qualitative and quantitative contemporary knowledge concerning race relations in this country.[10] Bloom not only asserts that the days of discrimination are over, but also contends that the differential treatment that black students are subjected to is something that these students have brought upon themselves. Black students, Bloom contends, do not share "a special positive intellectual or moral experience; they partake fully in the common culture, with the same goals and tastes as everyone else, but they are doing it by themselves. They continue to have the inward sentiments of separateness caused by exclusion when it no longer effectively exists" (p. 93).

When considered in contrast to the observations of contemporary educators and race relations scholars, Bloom's views are at best ignorant, and at worst racist. The problematic nature of Bloom's discussion of race is immediately evident in some of the responses that it has elicited. Scott Heller in *The Chronicle of Higher Education* writes: "A national best seller that has castigated America's colleges and Universities is racist, elitist, and 'profoundly wrong' in its view of students, especially members of minority groups." Heller attributes this opinion to Clifton R. Wharton, Jr., former chancellor of the State University of New York, who argues that Bloom presents "a perspective so detached for the actual complexities of the situation, so supercilious in its pseudo-Olympian 'objectivity,' as to make ordinary garden variety racism look almost benign" (1988, p. A1).

Wharton continues: "Students have become 'the problem' for Mr. Bloom in the same way that black folk were 'the problem' for a racist society, as viewed by W. E. B. DuBois. . . . Today we call this maneuver, Blaming the victim" (p. A12). For Wharton, Bloom's position is not based on any *essential* understanding of the true nature of race relations in the university, either as experienced by those in the academy or as detailed by the learned disputations of contemporary race-relations scholars. Indeed, Bloom's views are directly refuted by the works of scholars such as William Ryan, whose "seminal study of the impact of racism and elitism" titled *Blaming the victim* (1971) provides theoretical support for Wharton's arguments. Bloom's beliefs are also contradicted by the theoretical analyses of researchers like Benjamin Bowser and Raymond G. Hunt who define racism as "a white problem" (1983), and David Wellman, who in *Portraits of white racism* argues that racism is basically "a defense of privilege" (1976).

Many of Bloom's assertions are based more on his own beliefs about black students than the students' actual experiences or extant empirical research that addressed the situation of black students on college campuses at the time of his writing. Bloom argues, for example, that blacks are well represented in the university community, but the evidence available suggested otherwise.[11] Various reports indicated that blacks were not only underrepresented, but their numbers were declining. In the same issue of the *Chronicle of Higher Education* that listed *The closing of the American mind* as number one on college campus reading lists, Michelle Collison reported the American Council on Minority Concerns' observation that between 1980 and 1984, the number of black men on college campuses declined by 25,300, and the number of black women by 9,761 (1987, p. A 26).

Despite the reality of declining enrollments, however, Bloom's arguments suggest that any segregation which still exists is the fault of black students rather than the institutions they attend. "The universities are formally integrated, and blacks and whites are used to seeing each other," he writes. "But the substantial human contact, indifferent to race, soul to soul, that prevails in all other aspects of student life simply does not usually exist between the two races. There are exceptions, perfectly integrated black students, but they are rare and in a difficult position" (pp. 91–92). Bloom's assertions are called into question by contemporary studies of race relations in the academy. Talmadge Anderson explains: "It is fallacious to assume that the opportunity and situation for Blacks are improving and that progress is being made toward real equal opportunity and access. Conversely, the number of Black faculty, administrators, and students at white colleges and universities is declining, and, on some campuses, are nonexistent" (1988, p. 271). Whether Bloom does so intentionally or unintentionally, it is clear that he chooses to ignore relevant information concerning the present and past realities of the experiences of blacks in predominantly white educational environments.

Bloom's suggestion that black students segregate themselves takes race relations in the university out of its historical context, and is based on another fallacious assumption: that relationships between blacks and whites can be "indifferent to race." Such a suggestion is best understood when considered in light of contemporary race relations theory, specifically the work of Robert W. Terry. Terry contends that many whites deal with the social reality of race by asserting that race does or should not matter, and also offers an explanation that describes how many whites are able to dissociate themselves from the realities of race.[12] Bloom's assertions are based neither on experience nor evidence, and consequently he seeks to substitute opinion for knowledge.

This is most evident when he suggests that white students play little or no part in the perpetuation of racism in the university. "These students have made the adjustment, without missing a beat, to a variety of religions and nationalities, the integration of Orientals and the change in women's aspirations and roles. It would require a great deal of proof to persuade me that they remain subtly racist" (p. 92). While Bloom asks for proof of subtle racism, he is as unwilling to acknowledge the existence of such proof as he is the existence of racism. Bloom's position is clearly at odds with established knowledge in the field of race relations that suggests that such subtle racism does indeed exist. As Benjamin Bowser and Raymond G. Hunt have convincingly shown, "racism in America is a white problem. It is a white problem not merely because of hostile reactions to minorities to overt expressions of white racism, but because racist attitudes, behavior, and social structures have direct and indirect impacts on whites" (p. 13).

Bloom's arguments seem to suggest that black students are responsible for the self-imposed segregation that undermines their academic experiences, and that white students are not to blame for this situation. But it is precisely this attitude that, according the race relations scholars, creates the environment which Bloom ostensibly wishes to see remedied. Bowser and Hunt continue: "Constructive change in the field of race relations has been impeded, on the one hand by a persistent failure to deal directly with the structural aspects of racism in American society, and, on the other, by a persistently wrongheaded conceptualization of racism as a 'minority problem'" (p. 19). This essential truth about race relations is rather far removed from the 'facts' presented by Bloom in *The American mind.*

Yet Bloom would just as soon blame the problem not only on the victims of racism, but on those institutional structures developed to help them. His attack on affirmative action exemplifies a number of the discursive strategies characteristic of symbolic racism, reflecting "what a psychoanalytic approach would probably call projection: White doubt about qualifications are projected as alleged self doubts upon blacks."[13] Bloom fails to take into account the historical realities of American racism, ignores the reality of racial advantage that results in separatism and unequal achievement, and dismisses the resistance to racial integration, reflected in both attitudes and actions, that consistently surfaced at the time of his writing.[14] Such an argument, as David Wellman explains, could easily be labeled racist: "A position is racist when it defends, protects, or enhances social organization based on racial advantage. . . . Sometimes it is expressed in crude terms but . . . often it is not. White racism is what white people do to protect the special benefit they gain by virtue of their skin color" (p. 236). Bloom substitutes the subtle machinations of intellectual argument for the "crude terms" of traditional racism, and yet his position reflects the same reliance on special pleading characteristic of the rhetoric of racism.

In justifying his position, Allan Bloom ignores the material manifestations and consequences of racial inequality, blames the victims of this inequality, and suggests that the experience of blacks in the university community is somehow essentially different than that of whites. "For the majority of black students, going to the university is therefore a different experience from that of the other students, and the product of the education is also different." I wonder how many black students Allan Bloom knows, and with how many he has had more than surface relationships or conversations?[15] I also wonder on what basis he justifies the assertion that "[t]he black student who wishes to be just a student and to avoid allegiance to the black group has to pay a terrific price, because he is judged negatively by his black peers and because his behavior is atypical in the eyes of whites" (p. 95). Even I cannot be sure whether this statement accurately describes the experiences of a majority of black students in the university, though I write from experience.

Having spent most of my life in predominantly white educational institutions, some of them considered "good universities," I have not paid a much greater price than most of my peers, nor have I been any more alienated by blacks than by whites; and I do not consider myself to have been one of Allan Bloom's "perfectly integrated black students." While I have always been conscious of the reality of racism in the university, I have also come to believe that racism is one manifestation of a way of viewing the world in terms of *essential* differences. This belief has led me to agree with Wellman's claim that racism "need not be distinct, in its content or emotional loading, from the more routine forms of competitive behavior white people engage in with other whites" (p. 236). Racism is one of many ways that we differentiate ourselves from others and justify our differences on the basis of principles or practices that assume some privileged point of reference, either foundational or external, that grants our beliefs the status of knowledge.

When we see racism as a defense of privilege, its epistemological implications become clear, and this is why it is useful to consider *The closing of the American mind* in terms of Allan Bloom's position on race. Allan Bloom is defending a privileged belief system that engenders intellectual elitism and which, like racism, is presupposed and legitimized by an essentialist understanding of what is "true" and "real." Bloom's discussion of race in *The American mind* is clearly an extension of his personal "subjective" beliefs, and while it cannot be justified in terms of its consistency with a system of either "principled" or "objective" beliefs, Bloom's position might best be viewed and understood in terms of its *coherence* within that system. Because many of Bloom's arguments cannot stand when the principles of knowledge which he explicitly and implicitly defends are applied to his own positions, at least in terms of his discussion of race, Bloom is guilty of the fallacy of special pleading. The argumentative inconsistencies in his position, which also emerge in his discussions of feminism and some deconstructionist literary theory, not only illustrate the weaknesses of Bloom's critique of those positions he opposes, but offer an important commentary on the paradoxical role of essentialism in the legitimation of argumentative discourse.

Bloom assumes that certain beliefs determine what is essentially true and real, and that the *foundations* of knowledge (i.e., transcendent principles and eternal verities) are grounded in those privileged beliefs, and his attacks are basically aimed at opponents who espouse positions that call into question his underlying foundationalism. Many of his critics, in response, justify their positions on the basis of beliefs that reflect *externally verifiable* grounds of justification (i.e., social inequality and material inequities).[16] While the positions can be understood as mutually exclusive and independent of each other, we might also attempt to find some common ground between them in order to avoid the "warfare of fixed opinions" that results only in winners and losers. As Gladys Parker Foster (1991) suggests, the losers in such warfare might well be those whose minds are the battleground for the war: our students. Foster argues that "most of the attacks on Bloom have been academically bankrupt", although one of Bloom's sharpest critics, Sydney Hook,[17] while disagreeing with Bloom on many points, "agrees that many young people really are missing something," and "contends that Bloom has opened what should be a serious debate," a debate that, unfortunately, "has not been forthcoming" (p. 258). Foster illustrates the failure of the debate around Bloom's book to generate productive alternatives:

> Bloom himself, seems to offer no clear alternative to cultural relativism other than some reprehensible position such as cultural absolutism, intolerance, ethnocentrism, and/or

bigotry. And the academic community, in failing to address the question of cultural relativism, is vulnerable to the charge of believing in nothing, of nihilism, and of providing no way to distinguish between good and bad or between right and wrong. The general public is seemingly left with some not very attractive choices: right wing elitism, ethical relativism, or nihilism. (p. 258)

Foster offers a careful analysis of the debate that indicates some points of agreement between Bloom and his opponents, but more importantly suggests that the issue raised by Bloom is one that is extremely old: the issue of "the relationship between value and science." This is an issue which raises questions often unanswered, suggests Foster, precisely because such answers pursue an either/or approach to judgment that assumes value and science as mutually exclusive. Both Bloom and his critics would take issue with this assumption, albeit for different reasons, but an interrogation of this assumption might provide some directions for reopening the American mind. As Foster notes: "The lack of an answer to the question explains why Bloom made his arguments and why he has received so much attention. Instead of name-calling, we in academia should note his message and, as he suggested, begin a dialogue" (p. 259). Foster turns to "Dewey's approach to the theory of inquiry" as an approach that synthesizes Bloom's high regard for reason with an "instrumentalist theory of value" that provides "an alternative to both cultural relativism and cultural absolutism, or, in a broader context, ethical relativism and ethical absolutism."[18] The move toward Dewey's "inquiry into inquiry" exemplifies an attempt to explore the debate in terms of epistemic justification, and to find coherence between values and science, subjectivity and objectivity, principles and practices.

FROM DIALECTIC TO DIALOGUE:
FINDING COHERENCE IN THE AMERICAN MIND

Because of its attacks on blacks, women, and literary critics, *The closing of the American mind* has been labeled racist, sexist, and elitist. This, however, is not where the analysis ends, but where it must begin, since these responses to Bloom raise an important meta-ethical consideration. To the extent that these critics reject Bloom argumentatively, they affirm his position at its most basic, *essential* level. Bloom's rejection of race, gender, and contemporary criticism is grounded in a reaction to the rhetorical imperative which all of these disciplines have in common: the critique of privileged discourse, the calling into question of the assumptive grounds of foundationism by recourse to conventionalist justificatory strategies. Because this shift is justified argumentatively, by means of a dialectical affirmation of truth, to argue against Bloom based upon dialectically derived truths is to affirm the very system of knowledge which he defends. To argue that Allan Bloom is wrong because he does not *know* what he is talking about, is to implicitly defend and legitimate essential knowledge, which is what Bloom is explicitly doing. This element of complicity in argumentative discourse is a product of essentialist thought and language, and while it has been ignored by rational philosophers for centuries, it has always been a central concern for rhetoricians, for it points to the paradoxical and creative aspects of language that cannot be defined in essential terms.

Perhaps this element of complicity illustrates the most valuable lesson that Allan Bloom's book can teach us: that those who profess to being dedicated to discourses of tolerance and affirmation are as willing to indict as intolerant and reject those positions with which we do not agree. To argue against Bloom's positions by simply shifting to equally essentialist justificatory strategies is to support those positions at their most basic level, the adherence to dialectically derived truths to form judgments based on essential knowledge. Bloom's attack is, indeed, against race, gender, deconstruction, and education: yet it is also an attack against the dilemmas and inconsistencies inherent in democracy. Like Socrates, he is pointing out that those who claim to be tolerant, who believe that all voices deserve to be heard, will silence in their intolerance the voices of those with whom they disagree. Allan Bloom presents an important critique of the assumptive inconsistencies of those positions that profess to transcend privileged discourses through adherence to principles of tolerance and pluralism by pointing out that, *essentially, we are tolerant of all positions except those that are in opposition to our own,* and in order to disprove those positions we resort to essential knowledge.

I am not here suggesting that all critics who disagree with Allan Bloom fall prey to this argumentative inconsistency, but many critics who question the legitimacy of essentialist thought are often, like Allan Bloom, willing to draw the dialectical line precisely at the point where our own privileged discourses can escape the indictments inherent in our own arguments. Like Allan Bloom, we violate the rule of justice in order to legitimate the rightness and righteousness of our own positions. This is an accepted element of argumentation based upon both foundationist and externalist justificatory strategies, one which dates back to the beginnings of philosophy in Western culture and is sustained in the metanarratives of modernism, and one which critics in the areas of race, gender, and language are now beginning to seriously examine.

Certainly in terms of race, the adherence to essentialist justificatory strategies is in many ways antithetical to social and educational systems which attempt to foster equality and just judgment. In ancient Athens, such a view promoted, in I. F. Stone's view, an intolerable elitism. In contemporary South Africa, essentialism created a republic founded on principles of elitism and racism not much different than those that legitimize rule by "the one who knows." Crapanzano concurs when he notes that racism's epistemological roots lie deep within the grounds of essential knowledge, the type of knowledge which offers access to true reality. Crapanzano's analysis suggests that racism is, at least at some level, intimately related to essentialist intellectual inquiry and critical discourse.[19] Because both Bloom and his critics are privileged by such discourse, it seems unlikely that either opponents or proponents of *The American mind* will willingly explore the theory of the opposite party inherent in the position of the other side.

Thus, in order to fully explore the argumentative paradoxes and dilemmas of judgment posed by Bloom's discussions of race, gender, and critical theory in *The closing of the American mind*, we must consider the role essentialist conceptions of knowledge play in the construction of social reality. The underlying problematic which informs critical analysis in the areas of contemporary race, gender, and literary theory, is a basic aspect of essentialist epistemology, the principle of negative difference. Racism, sexism, and the linguistic elitism that has privileged philosophy at the expense of literature all arise out of an affirmation of this principle, a principle ultimately perpetuated by dialectical argumentation, and potentially, *by the act of criticism itself*, even as it is practiced by scholars in these disciplines. Because the language of critical analysis is often circumscribed by essentializing justificatory strategies, critical inquiry that partakes of essentialist assumptions often fails to achieve a self-reflexive understanding of the complementary nature of argumentative positions and the dialogic potential of discourse.

Thus, the most important contribution which Bloom's book can make to the practice of critical inquiry is the extent to which it will cause Afrocentricists, feminists, and deconstructionists to reflect upon the complicitousness with which we have defended our own privileged critical positions through dialectical and argumentative discourse. To argue with Allan Bloom in a manner that depicts him as Other is to lose, *precisely because it means engaging in a game in which there must be winners and losers, in which someone must be right and someone wrong.* This is the underlying logic of essentialism, that there is one true reality that can be discovered and defined through dialectical argumentation. It is this approach to linguistic interaction that critics concerned with privileged discourses attempt to transcend, yet we sometimes fail to reflect on the implications of the dialectical presuppositions which undergird the arguments presented in defense of our own positions. Limited by what Paul de Man (1983) describes as a "rhetoric of blindness," we fail to see the assumptions of the opposition inherent in our own positions.

De Man observes that critics often fail to take note "with regard to their own insights, of the discrepancy, hidden to them, between their stated method and their perception" (p. 111), and this blindness results in a complicitous acceptance of the underlying assumptions of the positions they critique. De Man's deconstructive vision parallels the rhetorical imperatives of the Greek Sophists, and echoes Thrasymachus' "theory of the opposite party." Thrasymachus' conceptualization of argument acknowledges the fact that all polemic is presupposed by an agreement to disagree, to take positions that are assumed to be mutually exclusive and *essentially* at odds with one another. Such a conceptualization, despite the fact that it was articulated over twenty-five hundred years ago, has only relatively recently become a part of a tradition of critical intellectual inquiry that has for centuries been constrained and circumscribed by philosophical realism and idealism.

To a large extent critical discourse is legitimated through an essentialist logic which results in judgments based on negative differences. Ultimately, to the degree that we engage in essentialist discourse, this includes the criticism practiced by feminists, deconstructionists, and contemporary Afrocentric thinkers, who sometimes fail to see the alternatives to such a black and white universe of discourse, and ignore the generative possibilities inherent in rhetoric that are so important a part of our own theories of language. Yet these theories have deep roots in Western thought, and can be traced back to the generative, non-dialectical systems of language articulated in the rhetorics of the ancient Greek Sophists. The *dissoi-logoi* were part of an ancient art of rhetoric that taught that, because we cannot escape from the problems which accompany being human, we must live with difference and the sometimes tragic polarity it implies. This is a lesson, however, that essential philosophy, with its emphasis on bivalence—the law of the excluded middle—has found so difficult to impart. Perhaps it is time for a return to Sophistry.

As Vernant suggested, with the death of tragedy came the demise of rhetoric, and with the rise of philosophy began the ascent of the privileged discourse of rational essentialism, a mode of discourse that undermines the possibility of achieving a truly liberal and democratic system of education, precisely because it creates a climate of negativity and intolerance. *The closing of the American mind* can teach us a great deal about how that climate was created and how it can be changed. I must agree with philosophy professor Sharon Schwarze when she suggests that "we should thank Bloom for bringing out the illiberal nature of all these liberally educated people. And his book should be read and digested—then argued with" (1987, p. B4). Although I may not agree with Bloom, and although I may be able to point out and expose the weakness and inconsistencies in his argument, I cannot deny him the right to argue, to offer the truths that are for him foundational, essential, and very real. Perhaps by approaching Allan Bloom's *American mind* in this manner, more scholars will be able to engage in a "rhetoric of inquiry," to get beyond "the warfare of fixed opinions" and "try out our reasons on each other, to see where we might come out" (Booth, 1981, p. 31). More importantly, such an approach might lead to attempts to find common grounds between Bloom and those whose educational theories appear at odds with his, might provide a way of moving beyond dialectic and toward dialogue.[20]

Following this way might help us transcend the illusion of mutual exclusivity created by essentialist epistemology and perpetuated by the type of argument that those who defend Bloom as well as oppose him seem to advocate. Schwarze offers a pertinent example when she argues that it "is not 'women, blacks, Hispanics, and people from different cultures' who are the marginal voices in our current democratic conversations. It is the classics that are the marginal voices because we refuse to take seriously their claim that there are standards of good and bad, better or worse" (1987, p. B4). Although Schwarze casts the debate in dialectical terms, she offers an insight important to the creation of dialogue: that when we recognize that marginality is not the privilege of any particular group's discourse, but may impact upon the voices of women, blacks, Hispanics, people from other cultures, *and* classicists, *at one and the same time,* we will be able to see beyond the black and white judgments of essentialist language, and recognize the discursive imperative articulated by Aristotle, that applies to classical as well as contemporary thought, the imperative of "alternative possibilities" that emerges perhaps most clearly and coherently in the realm of rhetoric.

REOPENING THE AMERICAN MIND: A RHETORIC OF COHERENCE

The closing of the American mind is an important contribution to the debates between rhetoric and philosophy, the social and central selves, and between those who would uphold the eternal verities of *physis* and those who would argue in favor of the conventionality of *nomos.* To suggest that one of these positions is true at the expense of the other is to engage in a discourse of negative difference, a discourse that I believe has helped to contribute to the social and material realities of racism, sexism, elitism, and—although Allan Bloom might not agree—a discourse that has largely been responsible for the closing of the American mind. It is a discourse that would do away with rhetoric, and Allan Bloom, like Plato and Socrates before him, might wish to free us from rhetoric. But as Lanham so eloquently observes,

If truly free of rhetoric we would be pure essence. We would retain no social dimension. We would divest ourselves of what alone makes social life tolerable, of the very mechanism of forgiveness. For what is forgiveness but the acknowledgment that the sinner sinning is not truly himself, plays but a misguided role. If always truly ourselves, which of us shall scape hanging? (p. 8)

In searching for a new beginning, a reopening of the American mind, I'd like to return to where this essay began, to the notion of "beginner's mind." As Suzuki explains, "for Zen students the most important thing is not to be dualistic" (p. 21). Although this notion arises out of an Eastern tradition, one somewhat foreign to Western essentialist thought, an important parallel can be found in Pirsig's discussion of the preclassical *mythos* of ancient Greece: "What is essential to understand at this point is that until now there was no such thing as mind and matter, subject and object, form and substance. Those divisions are just dialectical inventions that came later" (p. 337). Both the Zen notion of beginner's mind and Pirsig's conception of a non-dialectical state of mind converge in the realm of dialogic coherence.

Dialogic coherence sees difference as both foundational and external, and as something more than each of these can *in and of themselves* explain. Like the Sophistic *dissoi-logoi* it assumes that while we can choose to believe that we can have one or the other, *essentially* we cannot have one without the other, for the two are at some level always implicated in each other. It recognizes that both permanence and change come into play in human inquiry, and that difference exists as much within our minds as in an external world. If we can incorporate a similar understanding of the divisions of difference created by dialectical argumentation into our own systems of knowing, into our own mythos, we might be able to find it easier to reconcile the products of these divisions, the negative differences which now exist in the realms of race, gender, and language. Perhaps then those of us who disagree with the Allan Blooms of the world will be willing to find some common ground with our opponents and judge them by the rule of justice, not necessarily as they judge us, but *as we would be judged,* and in accordance with the rhetorical ideal of life, judge them with the compassion of a beginner's mind, that we might all "scape hanging."

Yet to judge Bloom compassionately, as we ourselves would wish to be judged, necessitates recognizing the epistemological implications at work in our own justificatory strategies, as well as reconceptualizing the very notions that differentiate and separate us from one another: the notions of self and Other. Here again we might consider what the philosophies of the East have to offer, since "Buddhist teachings are concerned with either or both of the two fundamental facets of Buddhism, self-help and helping others, wisdom and compassion."[21] Reflecting on the ways in which we conceptualize self and Other and justify those conceptualizations in terms of foundational or external beliefs can facilitate a move from a dialectical either/or understanding of the world, and toward a dialogical both/and understanding. In the next chapter I will explore how the problems and possibilities presented by such a move is reflected in the realms of oppositional criticism and practice, and how the emergence of dialogic coherence in those realms offers the possibility of social and psychological transformation.

3

OTHERNESS

> This awakening is seeing people as they really are. It
> means seeing them with the eyes of love and without
> the continuous carping and criticism which is so much
> a part of my experiencing others. Often I can hardly
> hear what another says because of the internal noise
> that goes on in the judging of them.
>
> —David Brandon, *Zen and the art of helping*

The problem of judgment considered at the end of the last chapter
in the realm of race relations has important epistemological implications that extend beyond a reopening of the American mind to a
reopening of the Western mind.[1] The contemporary critical consideration of otherness manifest in the writings of Afrocentric,
feminist, and rhetorical scholars exemplifies most clearly these
implications, in that these writings signal an epistemic shift away
from materialist and idealist philosophies and the evaluative
strategies they engender, toward a symbolic—or as I will suggest,
coherentist—approach to knowing and being. This approach parallels Stephen C. Rowe's "rediscovery of the West," which posits
that an "encounter with the otherness of the East provides the
ground upon which it becomes possible to reclaim our own
Western integrity, while at the same time we are enabled to open
to the realities of such otherness as Zen" (1994, p. 2). Reclaiming
our integrity may necessitate pursuing the paradoxical "inquiry
into nothingness and relatedness" that Rowe suggests undergirds
our ability to confront, within ourselves, the Other.

In confronting the Other we encounter something that is
unrelated, and in that lack of relation construct our symbolic realities. As James Baldwin explains in *If Beale street could talk*: "It's

astounding the first time you realize a stranger has a body—the realization that he has a body makes him a stranger. It means that you have a body too. You will live with this forever, and it will spell out the language of your life."[2] Baldwin describes the material manifestations and linguistic implications of the Other, a figure which has become a central concern in contemporary oppositional criticism.[3] The heroine of his novel is a young woman named Tish, and in a short section in which Baldwin describes the recognition of the Other as stranger, Tish confronts the social and physical realities of negative difference, the complicity it engenders, and its impact on human communicative interaction. Although Tish lives in a "fictive" world, her insights have important implications for critical discourse in the "real" world.

The Other illustrates the problem of language in Western culture in its most extreme form, as a figure made flesh which reifies the existence of an essential reality, a reality "out there," separate and distinct from the human agents that interact within it. This belief in separateness has, indeed, made us strangers, and has created a language of negative difference which manifests itself in the social and symbolic spaces of race, gender, and rhetoric. These spaces have, for centuries, been circumscribed by philosophical perspectives that privilege specific conceptions of reality, that emphasize idealist or realist alternatives without recognizing their interrelatedness, that posit an essentialist conception of the "truly" real that limits knowing and being to the terms of a language of negative difference. The calling into question of this language of negative difference has become a key strategy in many feminist, Afrocentric, and rhetorical theories of discourse. Scholars in these areas have explicated various indictments of the phallocentric, Eurocentric, and essentialist linguistic strategies defined and perpetuated by dominant population groups, and have begun the difficult task of addressing the complicitous nature of critical discourse.

It is important to consider this strategy in terms of the underlying epistemological transformations which it represents, transformations that signal a move away from foundationist and externalist and toward coherentist justificatory strategies. This chapter will explore this move from complicity to coherence as it is manifest in critical discourses that converge at the juncture of gender, race and rhetoric. By focusing on this juncture I shall continue my explication, begun in the last chapter, of how racism and sexism are products of a conceptualization of language peculiar to essentialist epistemology, and prefigured by the historical conflict between rhetoric and philosophy. I shall also suggest that contemporary race, gender and rhetorical studies provide the foundation for an epistemic stance that situates critical self-reflection within a context which makes possible a more positive approach to linguistic definition.

COMPLICITY AND NEGATIVE DIFFERENCE

My explication of complicity as a theory of negative difference is rooted in the linguistic theories articulated by the ancient Greek Sophists, particularly Thrasymachus of Chalcedon whose "theory of the opposite party" clearly illustrates the problem of complicity as it functions in argumentative discourse. Thrasymachus observes that individuals "who are at variance are mutually experiencing something that is bound to befall those who engage in senseless rivalry: believing they are expressing opposite views, they fail to perceive that their actions are the same, and that the theory of the opposite part is inherent in their own theory."[4] This "theory of the opposite party" calls into question the principle of negative difference which is the basis of essentialist justificatory strategies. Essentialism is a consequence of epistemological foundationism, and posits a reality in which material and symbolic processes exist in and of themselves, in which they are justified either on the basis of some privileged foundational belief or on the basis of belief in some externally validated, reliably referenced "reality." It assumes an essential reality on the basis of which judgments can be verified or legitimated, and contributes to a linguistic praxis which emphasizes argumentation and critical discourse, precisely because such discourse is aimed at the discovery of *essential* truths.

It also results in social praxes which perpetuate the principle of negative difference in human interaction. As suggested above, the isolation of racism as an object of critical analysis obscures the underlying epistemological essentialism which also undergirds problems of gender, class, and classification. In his discussion of the "rhetoric of domination and subordination," Crapanzano connects essentialism with the problem of complicity. Following Memmi and Mannoni, he argues that the belief that individuals can respond to oppression without recognizing their complicity in its perpetuation fails to consider the political and linguistic complexities which circumscribe systems of domination.[5] Crapanzano's analysis provides a starting point for a discussion of complicity precisely because it isolates and interrogates the essentialist presuppositions of language that undergird the theory of negative difference.

Those presuppositions are deeply rooted in Western conceptualizations of language, and provide a common point of reference for our understanding of the relationship between race, gender, and rhetoric. Henry Louis Gates suggests this connection between race and the theory of negative difference when he contends that Blackness as a figure of negation points to an *essential* difference, one intimately connected to the assumptions of knowledge in Western discourse as evidenced by Plato's *Phaedrus*.[6] Steve Whitson also explicates how negative difference functions in relation to both rhetoric and gender in the *Phaedrus*, where Plato has "relegated rhetoric to the negative pole of binary oppositions that privilege a particular truth claim: presence/absence, light/dark, man/woman, truth/appearance, and philosophy/rhetoric."[7] Both Gates' and Witson's analyses suggest that the epistemological assumptions of both racist and sexist language can also be traced to the essentialist presuppositions of language clearly evident in the debate between rhetoric and philosophy.

These presuppositions are explored by Lanham in his examination of the "serious premises" of epistemology which underlie Western discussions of style as it relates to rhetoric. The significance of Lanham's essay is its explication of the essentialist presuppositions of "serious" reality and the resulting historical disenfranchisement of rhetoric by philosophy. The relationship between rhetorical and philosophical reality is grounded in, and perpetuated by, the same assumptions concerning language and reality that create the social divisions of race and gender. Lanham contends that rhetoric constantly calls into question the assumptive grounds of "serious" reality, in much the same way that race and gender studies have challenged the legitimacy of Eurocentric and phallocentric discourses. Contemporary rhetorical theory, like oppositional critical theory, has witnessed a re-emergence of the primacy of language that necessitates a consideration of how the principle of negative difference functions in argumentative and critical discourse.

One manner in which in which this principle functions is manifest in the critique of foundationism engaged in by oppositional critics who justify their positions on conventionalist grounds, and thus substitute one hegemonic discourse for another. Oppositional criticism that emphasizes the "social realities" of oppression that define race, class, and gender relations only partially addresses the implicatory nature of phenomena anticipated by the rhetorical turn in contemporary critical theory. That turn, which signals a turn away from foundationism and externalism and toward coherentism as a justificatory strategy, emphasizes the socially constructed nature of subjective and objective "realities," and raises the important—and paradoxical—question: *What kind of 'reality' does an oppositional and dialectical language create?*

When viewed in light of this question, the rhetorical turn in contemporary critical studies confronts critics of race, gender, and language with the problematical possibility that we have, through argumentative discourse, participated in the creation of the realities of racism, sexism, and logocentricism. This is the phenomenon of complicity, and it is rooted in the tendency of critical discourse to privilege itself even as it calls privilege into question. Jean Baudrillard explains complicity in terms of *seduction*: "This is what happens initially when a discourse *seduces itself*; the original way in which it absorbs meaning and empties itself of meaning in order to better fascinate others: the primitive seduction of language" (p. 150). In attempting to privilege itself, oppositional criticism can be seduced by the very "abduction of meaning" that it attempts to oppose. Baudrillard continues: "Every discourse is complicit in this abduction of meaning, in this seductive maneuver of interpretation; if one discourse did not do this, then others would take its place" (p. 150). Confronting oppositional criticism, then, is the distinct possibility that it represents a mere replacement of one oppressive discourse for another and a reproduction of the very principles and practices that it ostensibly rejects.

ARTICULATING IDENTITY: ESSENCE IN OPPOSITIONAL DISCOURSE

Ernesto Laclau and Chantal Mouffe indicate how complicity functions in oppositional critical theory and practice in their explication of the concept of *articulation*.[8] According to Laclau and Mouffe, the problem of radical antagonism emerges within discursive structures in such a way as to undermine the practical possibilities inherent in discourse. Within this context, hegemony can be seen as an agreement to disagree, which rearticulates itself in the collaborative nature of hegemonic praxis. To the extent that critics of race, gender, and language oppose hegemonic discourses based upon positions which subscribe to this rhetoric of negative difference, they become complicitous with those discourses, and in effect, reify them. Laclau and Mouffe explicate the concept of articulation as it applies to the complicitousness of feminist and antiracist struggles:

> The political space of the feminist struggle is constituted within the ensemble of practices and discourses which create the different forms of subordination of women; the space of the anti-racist struggle, within the overdetermined ensemble of practices constituting racial discrimination. But the antagonisms within each of these relatively autonomized spaces divide them into two camps. This explains the fact that, when social struggles are directed not against objects constituted within their own space but against simple empirical referents—for example, men or white people as biological referents—they find themselves in difficulties. For, such struggles ignore the specificity of the political spaces in which the other democratic antagonisms emerge. (p. 132, 1989)

Both feminist and antiracist theoretical struggles find themselves in difficulty when they critique the essentialist tendencies of foundationism through recourse to an equally essentialist conventionalism. Such critiques ignore the assumptive grounds of the linguistic spaces in which epistemic antagonisms occur, and thus, complicitously rearticulate the problem of negative difference in their own critical discourses.[9]

Complicity thus manifests itself in terms of an adherence to the problematical assumptions of epistemic position and privilege that characterize ideological as well as formalistic critical discourse. R. Radhakrishnan makes the point powerfully clear in "Ethnic identity and poststructuralist difference": "The assumption that there exists an essence (African, Indian, feminine, nature, etc.) ironically perpetuates the same ahistoricism that was identified as the enemy during the negative/critical or 'deconstructive' phase of the ethnic revolution" (1987, p. 208). Radhakrishnan then asks the question most central to the problem of complicity at the linguistic level: "Doesn't this all sound somehow familiar: the defeat and overthrow of one sovereignty, the emergence and consolidation of an antithetical sovereignty, and the creation of a different, yet the same, repression?" (p. 208). His analysis of feminist historiography suggests some strategies for critics of language sincerely committed to transforming, and not simply reconstructing, the problem of negative difference.

Indeed, it is within the arena of feminist literary and political theory that the problem of complicity has become increasingly evident and problematical, perhaps because it is within this space that issues of gender, race, and classification most clearly converge. Catherine Dobris and Cindy White suggest that this complicity is most evident in terms of the inconsistencies of feminist discourse in regard to women of non-dominant populations: "Exclusivity, ignorance and blaming the victim all contribute to a feminist discourse that is devoid of the experiences of non-dominant women," they argue, contending that "while the dominant discourse of feminism presents itself as all-inclusive, it is clear that members of non-dominant groups construct images of feminism that project a white, Christian, heterosexual, middle-class identity, leaving most other women excluded from its purview" (p. 17).[10] Their insights provide an important point of departure for the consideration of how complicity is problematized within contemporary feminist theory.

bell hooks explicitly recognizes the problem of complicity and its articulation in feminist theory and practice in *Feminist theory: From margin to center*: "Women must begin the work of feminist reorganization with the understanding that we have all (irrespective of race, sex, or class) acted in complicity with the existing oppressive system. We all need to make a conscious break with the system." hooks comments on the consequences of replacing one essentialist discourse with another when she suggests that feminists "cannot motivate [other women] to join a feminist struggle by asserting a political superiority that makes the movement just another oppressive hierarchy" (1984, pp. 161–62). hooks suggests that contemporary feminist *praxis* contains within it the possibility of perpetuating the same type of privileges legitimated by the "oppressive" system from which it must break, and argues for a recognition of complicity as a first step in transcending that possibility.

Barbara Christian, in her critique of French feminism illustrates how critical discourse, ostensibly aimed at transcending the hegemonic dialectic, reifies it. She registers her concern that this particular school of feminist scholarship "has become authoritative discourse, monologic, which occurs precisely because it does have access to the means of promulgating its ideas" (p. 60). Christian confronts the same problematic in black feminist literary criticism. "Since I can count on one hand the number of black feminist literary critics in the world today, I consider it presumptuous of me to invent a theory of how we *ought* to read" (p. 53). Like hooks, Christian's analysis of the complicitous privileging of discourse enables her to transcend the problematical dualities of race, gender, and identity and confront the underlying epistemological concerns which problematize feminist theory and practice.

Christian generalizes her analysis of these concerns when she contends that many "critics do not investigate the reasons why that statement—literature is political—is now acceptable when before it was not; nor do we look to our own antecedents for the sophisticated arguments upon which we can build in order to change the tendency of any established Western idea to become hegemonic" (1987, p. 55). One way to facilitate the type of change that Christian and many other critics of race and gender are attempting is to recognize that our complicity with hegemonic discourse begins with the very language we use to call that discourse into question: critical, argumentative language. Christian's observations that "the new emphasis on literary critical theory is as hegemonic as the world which it attacks" and that "the language it creates as one which mystifies rather than clarifies our condition, making it possible for a few people who know that particular language to control the critical scene" (p. 55), might be extended to a general discussion of the epistemological presuppositions of argumentative language. In contemporary oppositional criticism the problem of negative difference is manifest in an adherence to principles of essentialist epistemology and the problematical divisions it constructs in terms of symbolic and social action.

Michael Awkward concurs, and returns us to the junction of race, gender, and language in his discussion of the essentialist presuppositions of justificatory positions taken by contemporary black and feminist literary critics concerning cross-gender/racial critical abilities. Using principles of psychoanalytic criticism, he responds to the assertion that men are incapable of doing "feminist" criticism, and compares the assertion to the arguments presented by black critics during the 1960 regarding the abilities of whites to analyze Afro-American literature. Awkward suggests that psychoanalytic theory deconstructs traditional feminist criticism by exposing its essentialist presuppositions in terms of its "problematic appeals to an authority of female experience," and calls into question "the neither biologically or culturally justified nature of feminist criticism's practice of a wholesale reverse discrimination." He concludes: "To simply reverse the binary opposition man/woman, when we are painfully aware of its phallocentric origins, is to suggest complicity with the male-authored fiction of history. No feminist should be comfortable with such a suggestion, despite the potential institutional gains" (1987, p. 23). One can easily extend Awkward's analysis to the practice of criticism itself, which is a privileged discourse in the mouths of its practitioners that is rarely, if ever, turned back upon itself.

Indeed, no critic, I would argue, should be comfortable with such a simple reversal of any of the binary oppositions which criticism so eloquently calls into question. And yet, when grounded in essentialist justificatory strategies, critical discourse is often limited to perpetuating just this type of dialectical binary opposition. Criticism, whether or not it calls into question privileged discourse, *is itself a privileged discourse, and consequently too often strives to perpetuate one position at the expense of another.* This is the rhetoric of "serious" reality, the rhetoric of dialectical critical discourse that becomes little more than an ideological discourse of self-legitimating privilege. This is the discourse which oppositional criticism calls into question, but which at the same time legitimates the theories and practices of critics who would oppose Eurocentric, phallocentric, or other discourses of negative difference. The problem of complicity demands a self-reflexive reassessment of the underlying assumptions of critical inquiry and their reification of "serious" reality, and calls forth the notion of a rhetoric of coherent judgment.

This, I believe, is precisely what Paolo Valesio attempts in *Novantiqua: Rhetorics as a contemporary theory.* Valesio argues that

> the real "enemy" of rhetoric is: not logic but ideology. If the struggle has been between rhetoric and logic, it would not have raged with such a continuity and force; but it did, and still continues to do so, because rhetoric is more or less clearly perceived as a threat to the assurance that any ideological system requires and confirms—and this perception is quite correct. (p. 61)

Valesio reconstructs the debate between rhetoric and philosophy by arguing that rhetoric is not a counterpart of dialectic, but *is* dialectic, when he asserts that dialectic is *"the dominant form in which rhetorical structure manifests itself"* (p. 113). This reconstruction of the relationship between rhetoric, dialectic, and ideology transcends the problematic of negative difference which has historically circumscribed symbolic and social interaction.

Valesio suggests that rhetoric, in its capacity to call into question privileged discourses, transcends the principle of negative difference by its insistence that all discourses are "at every point shaped and slanted according to specific argumentative structures" (p. 62). The implication of this insistence cannot simply be dismissed, for it suggests that when critics of race, gender, and language engage in argumentation we risk rearticulating—being seduced by—the very ideological structures that we are attempting to transcend. Radhakrishnan, in his analysis of feminist historiography, concurs: "Could it not be the case that we are either flogging a dead horse or that our interest is not in achieving a 'break,' but in the eternal and timeless maintenance of a 'tradition of opposition' that has perforce to keep alive the very tradition it questions?" (1988, p. 201). The challenge for feminist criticism, Radhakrishnan suggests, is to transcend the problem of negative difference embedded in the language of gender, and this challenge, I believe, is applicable to all practitioners of criticism concerned with issues of gender, race, class, and classification.

While complicity manifests itself as problematic in contemporary feminist theory and practice, to isolate this one arena of discourse would be to ignore the extent to which the same issues exist in terms of race, class, and classification. Complicity arises out of a failure to acknowledge and call into question the essentialist presuppositions of critical discourse grounded in either foundationist or conventionalist justificatory strategies. The underlying principle of essentialism at work in both idealism and realism is the principle of negative difference, which is central to argumentative and critical discourse and, thus, a basic element of our linguistic and symbolic interaction. This raises an important theoretical question which confronts scholars in women's studies, communication, and contemporary black thought: to what extent are oppositional critics, through our participation in the prevailing essentialist linguistic systems, complicitous in constructing "oppressive" social realities? As critics we are confronted by an important epistemological dilemma, in the sense that breaking with the system is reifying the system in its most basic form: negation. This paradox points to the underlying problematic of complicity.

To the extent that we all participate in discourse, practical and theoretical, presupposed by essentialist assumptions, might it not be possible that we participate in the construction of oppressive social realities? As scholars and social critics we are privileged by principles of negative difference that we readily use to participate in the argumentative and agonistic symbolic systems that sustain and perpetuate epistemological privileges. If criticism is to be radical in terms of its own presuppositions, it must look to its own assumptive ground for an epistemic stance that transcends the tradition of opposition of which Radhakrishnan speaks: "The task for radical ethnicity is to thematize and subsequently problematize its entrapment within these binary elaborations with the intention of 'stepping beyond' to find its own adequate language" (1987, p. 216). In order to step beyond the binarity of essentialism, I believe it is necessary to step into it: that is, to confront it on its own terms, in its own language, to call into question the necessity of negation by legitimating it through affirmation.

COMPLEMENTARY DIFFERENCES:
THE COHERENCE OF COMPLICITY

Finding an "adequate language" for oppositional criticism entails reflecting on those tendencies that problematize both foundationist and conventionalist justificatory strategies, not simply to reject them, but to recognize their interdependence and tactical value. Such a view goes beyond essentialist conceptualizations of reality by positing the possibility of articulating a social reality in which differences might be complementary, and not merely antagonistic. The possibility of such an affirmative transformation is clearly articulated within the context of the narrative paradigm, in the rhetorical realm of literature where, as Baldwin suggests at the beginning of this chapter, how we experience otherness powerfully influences the problems and possibilities of our language. Similarly, Virginia Woolf indicates the impact of subscribing to the discourse of negative difference on human consciousness in the final chapter of *A room of one's own:* "Perhaps to think, as I had been thinking these two days, of one sex as distinct from the other is an effort. It interferes with the unity of mind" (1978, p. 145). The challenge for contemporary critics is to remove this interference, to begin to give voice to that element of the Other that is within each of us, and find within discourse the possibility of achieving a unity of mind and method that transcends and transforms negative difference.

Certainly, this is what James Baldwin does with the character of Tish; he transcends the reality of gender in order to live within the space of the Other, and this is a rhetorical move. If we can make this rhetorical move in the realm of fiction, perhaps we can learn to make it in the realm of critical theory and eventually in the realm of social *praxis* as well. This will, of course, demand an understanding of rhetoric which, at first, seems peculiarly different than the traditional view of rhetoric which we have inherited, defined by philosophy and limited to the "forms and mannerisms"[11] of persuasive discourse. This traditional view, Lanham suggests, is in opposition to the actual practice of rhetoric, and this opposition "goes far to explain the two persistently puzzling facts about the history of rhetoric: why it has been so deplored and why it has so endured" (p. 5). Philosophy for centuries has denigrated rhetoric, I would argue, in a fashion similar to how Europeans have denigrated Africans and how men have denigrated women, through critical discourses that have focused on, and reified, *essential* differences. "Such criticism," writes Lanham, "points to differences so fundamental they indicate a wholly different way of looking at the world" (p. 5).

As oppositional critics we can be seduced into believing that these differences not only indicate different ways of knowing and being, but that they are based on essential distinctions between self and Other: such distinctions are not only questionable, but dangerously incoherent. Yet, despite the complicitousness with which some oppositional critics have accepted essentialized conceptions of language and identity, theorists concerned with problems of race, gender, and language have provided important directions for conceiving of a rhetoric that facilitates coherent approaches to knowing and being. Arthur Smith's suggestion that "*Rhetoric as concept is foreign to the traditional African ethos,*" primarily because of its emphasis on persuasion, exemplifies a complicitous acceptance of the essentializing tendencies he eschews. Although Smith rejects traditional notions of rhetoric in his later work,[12] some of his early writings suggest that an African-centered conception of rhetoric is grounded in a coherent conceptualization of reality, and emphasizes dialogic and inclusive linguistic practices.[13]

The rejection of persuasion by Smith is paralleled in Sally Miller Gearhart's (1979) equating of rhetoric as persuasion with violence. Gearhart, however, offers as an alternative to a rhetoric grounded in persuasion a rhetoric based on dialogue, the ethical implications of which have been explored by several scholars in the field of communication, and which point to a coherent approach to knowing and being.[14] Gearhart's "womanized" rhetoric challenges the basic epistemological assumptions of traditional rhetorical theory and practice, and suggests that rhetoric as persuasion uses a conquest conversion mentality that precludes true dialogue: "In the conquest model we invade or violate. In the conversion model we work very hard not simply to conquer but to get every assurance that our conquest of the victim is really giving her what she wants" (p. 196). Her analysis emphasizes the importance of rhetorical theory and practice as a means of transcending discourses of negative difference. Gearhart does not simply reject rhetoric, but emphasizes instead its reconceptualization. Her indictment of the field "is not an attack on the tools of rhetoric; nor does it suggest that we, its practitioners, serve the world best by forsaking education or committing suicide. With our expertise in persuasion, rhetoricians and rhetorical theorists are in the best position to change our own use of our tools" (p. 196). Gearhart suggests that dialogue represents a "womanized" rhetoric which is different than persuasion in that each party seeks to contribute to an atmosphere in which change for all parties can take place. Dialogue offers a coherent approach to discourse in that it recognizes the interrelatedness of seemingly distinct positions, and assumes common epistemological and ontological foundations "Our physical being, our movement, our thought, our metaphors: all are forms of energy in constant and infinitely varied exchange" (p. 196).

Physicists David Bohm and F. David Peat (1987) offer a similar conceptualization of dialogue that, like Gearhart's, is actively non-argumentative. They contend that communicative dialogue could be used to facilitate scientific discovery and social development, and differentiate dialogue from "ordinary" argumentative and persuasive uses of language: "A key difference between a dialogue and an ordinary discussion is that, within the latter, people usually hold relatively fixed positions and argue in favor of their views as they try to convince others to change" (p. 241). Argument and persuasion, Bohm and Peat suggest, may lead to agreement or compromise, but rarely recognize or integrate the generative possibilities of discourse. Additionally, discourse that focuses on issues of ethical and moral judgment, "degenerates either into a confrontation in which there is no solution, or into a polite avoidance of the issues. Both these outcomes are extremely harmful, for they prevent the free play of thought in communication and therefore impede creativity" (p. 241).

Creativity, according to Bohm and Peat, is generative, and is grounded in possibility and potential. Dialogue, they suggest, "is not compatible with a spirit that is competitive, contentious, or aggressive" (p. 241). The process of dialogue is grounded in principles of rhetorical discourse which place a premium on positive and affirmative communication as well as the opportunities and possibilities for growth created by such communication for participants: "If they are able to engage in such a dialogue without evasion or anger, they will find that no fixed position is so important that it is worth holding at the expense of destroying the dialogue" (p. 242). In a more recent work Bohm suggests that through a recognition and understanding of the interrelatedness of the diverse positions which make up the system of beliefs "we can talk together coherently and think together."

Bohm suggests that dialogue might facilitate "a coherent movement of communication, coherence not only at the level we recognize but at the *tacit level*—at the level for which we have only a vague feeling."[15] It is at the tacit level that philosophers and rhetoricians accept the mutual exclusivities and binary oppositions of argument as necessary and essential. The significance of coherence for philosophical and rhetorical discourse is that it brings these tacit assumptions to the surface and allows for a consideration of their collective dimensions through dialogue. And it is through dialogue, notes Bohm, that we are able to achieve in both consciousness and communication "some sort of coherence and order."[16] Bohm's concept of dialogue exemplifies the power of finding similarity in difference, and the possibilities it presents for rhetorical theory and *praxis*.

Dialogue signals a move beyond argumentative essentialism and toward an epistemology that recognizes the inseparability of difference and sameness, and the importance of this inseparability for intellectual and social understanding. Bohm's conceptualization of dialogue exemplifies the praxis of a coherent theory of rhetoric: it offers a practical strategy of discourse—a way of thinking about and using language—that addresses the critical, political, and epistemological consequences of social and psychological fragmentation. Bohm's explication of dialogue, like Gearhart's, emphasizes the importance of moving beyond argumentative and persuasive language in order to facilitate positive exchange and understanding. It also illustrates a coherent conceptualization of knowing and being that "tends to give rise to a unity in plurality," and which recognizes the interrelatedness of both positions and people. It places a premium on empathy in order to transcend discourses of struggle and domination.

The same notion emerges in contemporary composition studies' recognition of the limitations of traditional argument: "In confrontations between young and old, East and West, white and black—in short," write Young, Becker, and Pike, "whenever commitments to values are powerful and emotions run high— logical demonstration may seem irrelevant and conventional argumentative strategies suspect" (1970, p. 274). As an alternative to traditional rhetorical strategies, they offer "Rogerian" argument, which "places a premium on empathy between writer and reader and on the peculiarities of the topic." Rogerian rhetoric emphasizes understanding between writers and readers, recognizing areas of positional agreement, and acknowledging shared ethical grounds and aspirations. Young, Becker, and Pike note

that "users of the strategy deliberately avoid conventional persuasive structures and techniques because these devices tend to
produce a sense of threat, precisely what the writer seeks to overcome" (p. 275). Rogerian rhetoric emphasizes the dialogic capacities of language, and exemplifies a movement beyond essentialist assumptions toward a coherent conceptualization of human
symbolic and social action.[17]

Mikhail Bakhtin (1990, p. 269) suggests that this dialogic
conceptualization of language is *essentially* rhetorical, and has
powerful implications in terms of our recognition of the ideological dimensions of all forms of discourse. "It is precisely those
aspects of any discourse (the internally dialogic quality of discourse and the phenomena related to it), not yet sufficiently
taken into account and fathomed in all the enormous weight
they carry in the life of language, that are revealed with great
external precision in rhetorical forms," he explains in "Discourse
and the novel." Bakhtin expands the conceptualization of rhetoric
beyond its traditional boundaries in order to illustrate its ideological implications as well as its potential for affirmation and
coherence. "We are taking language not as a system of abstract
grammatical categories, but rather language conceived as ideo-
logically saturated, language as a world view, even as a concrete
opinion, insuring a *maximum* of mutual understanding in all
spheres of ideological life" (p. 271). Dialogue allows for the recognition of the interrelatedness of positions and propositions that
transcends the dualistic essentialism of persuasive discourse, and
provides for an understanding of rhetoric as coherence.

Rhetoric as coherence considers how beliefs are contextual-
ized in discourse, and how the system of beliefs is understood
in terms of both its dialectical and dialogic manifestations. As
such, the privileging of positions necessitated by argumentative
and critical discourse gives way to an interpretive frame that
explores underlying commonalties that circumscribe any shared
system of beliefs. A coherent rhetoric might best be envisioned as
the *t'ai chi* symbol of the Taoists, the Yin and Yang, which recognizes the interpenetration of opposites as the basis of material
and social existence, echoing Thrasymachus' "theory of the opposite party." Like the Yin and Yang, a rhetorical conceptualization of coherence provides an understanding of how each position
is implicated in the other through an acceptance of this underlying assumption, and points to the possibility of a dialogic con-

ceptualization of rhetoric that can move us beyond argumentative essentialism.

The epistemological and ideological consequences of argumentative essentialism can be traced as far back as the Platonic dialogue *Gorgias*. In this dialogue, Socrates questions Gorgias and his two students Callicles and Polus, and induces them to admit that rhetoric has to do with persuasion. Using dialectic, the question and answer method of philosophy which emphasizes definition and through which an understanding of "true" reality can be achieved, Socrates questions Gorgias until he admits that rhetoric is "a creator of persuasion." At this point Socrates goes on to argue that rhetoric is in fact not an art, but a mere set of techniques used to pander to an audience. This argument has shaped definitions of rhetoric ever since. However, it seems unlikely that Gorgias would have defined rhetoric as persuasion when he states in his *Encomium on Helen* that "persuasion by speech is equivalent to abduction by force."[18] Gorgias, who readily admitted to being a teacher of rhetoric, called into question the Platonic assertion of the primacy of dialectic, and this is the basis of Socrates' attack on rhetoric. When viewed as persuasion, rhetoric is used to impart the knowledge of a pre-existent reality, one arrived at through dialectical attenuation and understanding and grounded in either foundationist or externalist justificatory strategies. This is the conceptualization of rhetoric which we have inherited from Plato and Socrates via Aristotle. It is also the definition of rhetoric articulated in the Platonic dialogue *Phaedrus*.

The *Phaedrus* seems initially to be a reversal of Socrates' earlier condemnation of rhetoric, but actually it is an explanation of the hierarchical relationship between rhetoric, dialectic, and knowledge. In the *Phaedrus*, Socrates suggests that rhetoric can be an art of persuasion, but only when used by the dialecticians, who alone have an understanding of "true" reality. Socrates equates dialectic with love, and argues that the dialectician understands the true nature of human souls and uses rhetoric accordingly to lead each soul toward the light of truth. The philosopher, who is the consummate dialectician, is the guardian of the knowledge of "true" reality, that is arrived at through the process of definition and which distinguishes things in terms of their "natures." This is the underlying logic of essentialist epistemology, or "serious" reality, and it attempts to free us from rhetoric in the same way that the Socratic charioteer attempts to free us from the "dark horse" of the soul which would lead us from the singularity of "true" reality.

This "dark horse" is the same figure of negation that Gates and Whitson explicate, and it is at this juncture that the relationship between rhetoric, race, and gender becomes quite clear. The language of contemporary race, gender, and literature attempts to create a discursive space that goes beyond a rhetoric of persuasion—one which reflects a pre-existent reality—and offers the possibility of *a rhetoric of coherence*, one that defines and constructs reality in such a way as to interrogate the privileging of one position at the expense of another. Coherence allows us to consider seemingly competitive positions as complementary, offers a powerful representative anecdote[19] for a reconceptualization of essence, and emerges in rhetoric in two ways: metaphysically and epistemologically.

Metaphysically, coherence represents the tendency of rhetoric, as Lanham observes, to offer "a coherent counterstatement to 'serious' reality,"[20] and epistemologically coherence theory provides the foundations of knowing within which rhetoric can assert itself as a legitimate science of symbolism. Coherence theory synthesizes alternative possibilities by focusing on their shared and mutually dependent foundations, and views all propositions as contingent upon, and thus inseparable from, one another. Coherence theory is characterized by an epistemic stance that, as Roderick Chisholm (1965) observes, posits "a being for whom all truths are evident, but also, that each of us is identical with that being, and therefore with each other," and transcends essentialist conceptualizations of knowing and being by positing that the truth of a given proposition must be measured in terms of its context, that is, in relation to its assumptive presuppositions and to all of the other propositions with which it is consistent *and* inconsistent.

Chisholm rejects coherence as a viable epistemological ground, but tempers his own rejection of the concept by recognizing that "if we reject the theory, we must find some other way of dealing with the problems it was designed to solve," problems that are basically metaphysical in origin.[21] Two writers whose discussions of coherence are useful in terms of its metaphysical implications are H. H. Joachim and Brand Blanshard. Joachim (1906) suggests that coherence points to the existence of a "significant whole" as the essential ground of truth: "A 'significant whole' is such that all its constituent elements reciprocally involve one another, or reciprocally determine features in a single concrete meaning" (p. 66). He views essence as a holistic synthesis that transcends analytical divisions, and views thought as an organic and transformative process.[22] Coherence, he suggests, is a *quality* which "penetrates its materials; and they—if we call them 'materials'—are materials which retain no inner privacy for themselves in independence of the form. They hold their distinctive being in and through, and not in sheer defiance of, their identical form; and its identity is the concrete sameness of different materials" (p. 77). Coherence reconciles the distinctions of essentialist conceptions of knowing and being by recognizing their interrelatedness and their contingent nature, and conceptualizing judgment in light of this recognition.

Brand Blanshard (1940) suggests that coherence provides a vehicle for recognizing the interrelatedness of propositions and also indicates its importance for judgment: "The degree of truth of a particular proposition is to be judged in the first instance by its coherence with experience as a whole" (p. 264). Blanshard sees coherence as exemplary of a complementary view of reality and concerns itself with the human capacity to *"hold beliefs about the technique of acquiring beliefs"* (p. 285). Truth is assumed by coherence theorists to be systemic, as much generated by human beings as a reflection of an external reality. Its metaphysical assumptions indicate an almost spiritual conceptualization of truth as a holistic singularity, and this is echoed in Chisholm's assessment of coherence as a conceptualization of self-evidence that transcends distinctions between beings. This holistic emphasis of coherence offers important directions for critical theory in its movement away from the competition of beliefs that characterizes both criticism grounded in foundationist or conventionalist justificatory strategies, to a consideration of the cooperative construction and conceptualization of truth.

Coherence theory reconstructs the traditional relationship between rhetoric and philosophy precisely because it points to the underlying complementarity of any ontological or epistemological stance. Philosophy can no longer distinguish or separate itself from rhetoric without reference to the extent to which they are interrelated and contingent upon one another. This reconstruction transforms the debate between rhetoric and philoso-

phy, and through implication, our conceptualization of the negative differences of race and gender as well. The debate between
philosophy and rhetoric has two purposes closely aligned with
those that circumscribe antagonisms of race and gender: first, to
privilege one position at the expense of the other by constructing
an arbitrary distinction between the two; second, to reify the
first position by using the second to legitimize the first as essentially real. Real reality must invent the inferior other in order to
remain real, in order to survive. This is best achieved by harnessing the power of the word to disempower the word and by
articulating in language an argumentative discourse that fails to
apply its own principles to itself.

Criticism, when it fails to acknowledge its underlying principles of justification, tends toward this type of discourse. And to
the extent that oppositional critics, in replacing foundationist
with conventionalist justificatory strategies, also engage in critique and assert the existence of essential differences through
that engagement, we too participate in the discourse of negative
difference. Therein lies our complicity. Oppositional criticism
cannot escape this complicity as long as it attempts to "ignore
the simple fact that no case can be argued, no proposition
stated—however radical in its intent—without falling back on
the conceptual resources vested in natural language. And that
language is in turn shot through with all the anthropocentric
'metaphysical' meanings which determine its very logic and
intelligibility."[23] When critics participate in essentialist argumentative critical discourse we subscribe to the very epistemological sensibility which we hope to transcend, and are privileged
by the theory of knowledge that, ostensibly, we are calling into
question.

Oppositional criticism, seduced by the very epistemic stance
that it has called into question, is merely another manifestation
of essentialism's articulatory power. This seduction—this rearti-
culation of the discourse of negative difference—poses an important challenge in terms of oppositional criticism's ability to articulate a method that transcends the simplistic negativity of
merely rejecting the language out of which it arises. Oppositional
criticism, in short, must acknowledge its complicity before it
can transcend the discourse of negative difference in which it is
grounded and recognize that the sociological realities of race,
gender, and language are deeply rooted in the common ground of

human consciousness, its classificatory and symbolic systems, and their material manifestations. This is precisely the move that Laclau and Mouffe call for when they argue for a strategic shift from opposition to construction.

Laclau and Mouffe's observations are particularly salient in an intellectual and political climate undermined by the consequences of social and psychological fragmentation characteristic of what Cornel West calls "postmodern culture," a culture in which the "hidden injuries of class, intra-racial hostilities, the machismo identity taken out on women, and the intolerance of gay and lesbian orientations generate deep anxieties and frustrations that often take violent forms" (p. 43). These are the negations and divisions that oppositional discourses that recognize "language as a system of differences" are meant to address and resolve, but to no avail. "If language is a system of differences" note Laclau and Mouffe, "antagonism is the failure of difference; in that sense, it situates itself within the limits of language and can only exist as a disruption of it—that is, as metaphor" (p. 125). The limits of argumentative language emerge in the tendency of oppositional critiques to suffer the same essentializing consequences of those discourses to which they stand in opposition. As Laclau and Mouffe explain:

> If the demands of a subordinated group are presented purely as negative demands subversive of a certain order, without being linked to any viable project for the reconstruction of specific areas of society, their capacity to act hegemonically will be excluded from the outset. This is the difference between what might be called a "strategy of opposition" and a "strategy of construction of a new order." (p. 189)

"Acting hegemonically," according to Laclau and Mouffe, means constructing "a new 'common sense' which changes the identity of the different groups in such a way that the demands of each group are articulated equivalentially with those of the other" (p. 183). This entails not simply a shift away from foundationism to conventionalism, from the ideal to the real, but a reconstruction of essence that integrates the real and the ideal in a non-oppositional manner. Such a reconstruction can be seen in the words and works of two of our most radical contemporary critics, Martin Luther King, Jr., and Mohandas Karamchand

Gandhi, both of whom translated the theoretical principles of dialogue and coherence into the practical realities of social action and transformation.

DIALOGIC COHERENCE IN THE RHETORIC OF NONVIOLENCE

The rhetoric of nonviolence advocated by King and Gandhi exemplifies a form of oppositional criticism that provides a coherent integration of foundationist and conventionalist justificatory strategies and acknowledges the interdependence and interrelatedness of both beliefs and beings. Both men exemplified in their thinking beliefs grounded in the basic assumptions of coherence: a unified ground of being, the interpenetration of opposite positions, and recognition of the potential for symbolic action to shape and transform social action. The rhetorics of King and Gandhi exemplify a coherent synthesis of foundationist and conventionalist justificatory strategies that transcends the limitations of oppositional discourse through recourse to a constructive and inclusive vision of human symbolic and social action.

Martin Luther King's use of nonviolence as a form of moral action clearly illustrates a coherent metaphysical and epistemological grounding. According to Dorothy Pennington, King viewed nonviolence as "the ultimate form of persuasion," quoting King's own claim that the "ultimate aim" of nonviolent action was "to persuade" (p. 120). Although grounded in traditional rhetorical principles and strategies, King's agenda was radical in the sense that it called into question the social inequities of American society by an affirmation of the underlying principles of democracy. King called for a realization in praxis of the foundational ideals that defined American ideological traditions, and did so not only in word but also in deed. In doing so he not only addressed the theory of negative difference that circumscribed the paradoxical denial of equality to America's poor and disenfranchised, but also addressed some of the underlying assumptions that led to this denial. According to Payne (1989), King's rhetorical strategy transcended both physical and psychological distinction by synthesizing the material with the spiritual, and establishing an "interconnection between material conditions and spiritual ideals" with which to transform social reality: "Although his rhetoric was steadily and traditionally spiritual, King always understood that solutions to his people's troubles lay in material and economic equality" (p. 52) King's insight into the need for a synthesizing vision reflected his adherence to a coherent conceptualization of human thought and action.

This coherence also emerged in his rhetoric, as evidenced by his "Declaration of Independence from the war in Vietnam" as well as his "Letter from Birmingham jail." In his declaration, King recognized that the resolution of conflict demanded a coherent conceptualization of human being. He explains that nonviolence "helps us to see the enemy's point of view, to hear his questions, to know his assessment of ourselves." King notes that this capacity to see through the enemy's eyes helps us to recognize the extent to which the existence of the other is dependent upon, and intimately related to our own existence: "For from his view we may indeed see the basic weaknesses or our own condition, and if we are mature, we may learn and grow and profit from the wisdom of the brothers who are called the opposition" (p. 43). His "Letter from Birmingham jail" further suggests a coherent conceptualization of human existence. In it he writes: "We are caught in an inescapable network of mutuality, tied to a single garment of destiny. Whatever affects one directly affects all indirectly" (1964, p. 77). King's emphasis on the interrelatedness of human existence illustrates his reliance on coherent ontological and epistemological assumptions, assumptions which emphasized similarity over difference as a method for transcending the social and psychological divisions that undermine human unity and cooperation.

Although he was at first skeptical of nonviolence as a viable strategy for African-American liberation, King eventually saw Gandhi's use of nonviolence as influencing his own choice of it as a strategy for social transformation. According to Flip Schulke and Penelope McPhee, he "began to be convinced that Gandhi was indeed a great man, who had liberated India from British rule without firing a single shot and had caused political and social change by harnessing the power of love" (1986, p. 20). Studying under L. Harold DeWolf and Edgar Sheffield Brightman at Boston University, King encountered "the philosophy of personalism," a philosophy that clearly reflected coherent assumptions.[24] King translated his personal idealism into moral action, and grounded his understanding in a diversity of competing views which he was able to recognize as complementary. Like Gandhi, he recognized that human division was as much grounded in the epistemological as the material, in the symbolic as well as the social. Nonviolence provided a concrete strategy of social action that transcended distinctions between the symbolic and the social, and synthesized the ideals of human cooperation and equity with the pragmatics of judgment guided by both the Golden Rule and the rule of justice.

Like King, Gandhi saw nonviolence as the foundation of human unity and a vehicle for the transcendence of conflict and division: "Interdependence is and ought to be as much the ideal of man as self-sufficiency. Man is a social being. Without inter-relation with society he cannot realize his oneness with the universe or suppress his egotism" (1982, p. 87). Gandhi's recognition of interdependence as necessary to the resolution of human conflict informed his use of nonviolence as a strategy for social transformation, and reflected a coherent conceptualization of human belief and being. His social and symbolic strategies were undergirded by a recognition of the interrelatedness of two aspects of human consciousness that have been at odds to one extent or another throughout the long history of rhetoric: faith and reason. He saw the two intimately related to one another: "Faith is a function of the heart. It must be enforced by reason. The two are not antagonistic as some think" (p. 83). According to Robert Bode (1987), Gandhi's synthesis of faith and reason provides the foundation for a rhetorical theory that weds the foundational with the external, and that "articulated concerns for the well-being of people of all nations, the whole of the human family" (p. 68).

Bode's explication of Gandhi's rhetorical theory focuses on its emphasis on nonviolent action, maintenance of human relationships, openness, and flexibility. Taken together these qualities indicate a coherent approach to human symbolic action, and a recognition that human beings are ultimately social actors capable of making choices that may lead to transformation. Bode suggests that Gandhi extended the principles of nonviolence to language, and "believed that violence was found in forms of speech. He therefore repeatedly admonished that *Satyagrahis* should have neither a trace of bitterness in them nor violence in their language" (p. 49).[25] Bode suggests that Gandhi recognized the difficulty of transcending existing assumptions concerning language which would allow for the development of nonviolent forms of speech, and "implied that there were difficulties to be overcome as people tried to create new patterns of speech that were nonviolent" (p. 51). Gandhi believed that the strategy of nonviolence could be applied to a number of situations, both physical and symbolic, and Bode suggests that "creative thinkers" might find ways of implementing such applications in areas ranging from interpersonal to international communication (p. 55).

Bode's analysis of Gandhi's rhetorical theory is important for two reasons: first, it brings together the writings of other rhetorical scholars who have viewed nonviolence as a useful vehicle for considering alternative theoretical conceptualizations of rhetoric; second, it offers an explication of the ethical implications of nonviolence for a praxis grounded in strategies of judgment. Quoting Oliver, Bode points to the coherent assumptions which characterize Indian rhetorical practices: "Everything, no matter how special or particular or unique it may appear, is actually akin to everything else. Even contradictory elements or incidents or behaviors are really reflections of precisely the same reality." Bode also cites Bondurant's suggestion that nonviolence emphasizes "the synthesis of opposite claims," Frank's suggestion that critics and theorists of rhetoric can function as social actors "in the development of the art and science of peacemaking," and Carlson's claim that Gandhi's rhetorical strategy needs to be considered from a dramatistic perspective. (pp. 13–14). I would extend the observations of these scholars even further to suggest that Gandhi's rhetorical theory also offers important implications for an actively non-argumentative conceptualization of rhetoric.

The ethical implications of Gandhi's strategy provide support for just such a move. Bode suggests that Gandhi's rhetorical theory offers "a unique ethical perspective" (p. 110), and differentiates the ethics of Gandhi's rhetorical theory from existing approaches in a manner that indicates its importance for actively non-argumentative rhetoric. "Gandhi's rhetorical theory assumes that maintaining relationships is paramount. Communicators should recognize the primacy of persons and relationships." Bode continues: "Gandhi sought to maintain relationships even with his opponents. He believed also that conflicts could draw persons nearer. Such a communication orientation places the survival of relationship above and beyond winning an argument or accomplishing a selfish end" (p. 115). The assumptions of Gandhi's theory reflect a coherent conceptualization of rhetoric that echoes the concept of dialogue articulated earlier by Gearhart; Young, Becker, and Pike; and Bohm and Peat. Dialogue, as defined by these writers, is explicitly nonargumentative, and while scholars have thus far suggested that it is distinct from traditional theories of rhetoric, I wish to suggest that it is more accurately described as an amplification of the traditional paradigm that recognizes the coherence of discourse and emphasizes its potential for social and symbolic transformation.

FROM COMPLICITY TO COHERENCE: TOWARD A RECONSTRUCTIVE RHETORIC

The notion of a non-argumentative rhetoric has important implications for oppositional and radical critics, for it consciously recognizes the potentially essentializing consequences of argumentative discourse, and interrogates the underlying justificatory claims that connect theory to practice. Such a rhetoric recognizes the link between realism and idealism, and recognizes their implication in each other in order to draw upon the strengths of foundational justification, for example, its commitment to principle, as well as those of externalist justification, that is, its application to empirical phenomena. Rhetoric as coherence is less concerned with rejecting the essentializing consequences of classification than with reconstructing the system of classification. An amplification of the insights of Kress and Hodge (1979) suggests directions for further theory and practice.

> The basic system of classification is itself abstract, and isn't manifest until it is made actual by human agents engaged in social interaction. This abstract character is its source of strength, in that the system itself is never scrutinized, so it is not usually open to criticism's weakness, because it is constantly being subtly renegotiated by individuals who are responding to forces outside the language system. Classification only exists in discourse, and discourse is always at risk. (p. 64)

Rhetoric allows us to call discourse into question, and a rhetoric of coherence will allow us to renegotiate the risks of interaction and perhaps transform our classificatory systems so that we might emphasize similarity and affirmation.

In constructing a coherent theory of rhetoric, we need to recognize the complicity that is created by negation, both in symbolic and social interaction. As Kress and Hodge observe, "Negatives can create a universe of alternative meanings, which the speaker formally renounces but which exist as a result of his renunciation. His relationship to his meaning is peculiarly ambivalent" (p. 145). As we begin to scrutinize, reconceptualize, and reconstruct our classificatory systems, we will find forces within the language that might formulate a discourse devoid of domination that, in its affirmative approach to language, thought, and action, will be both radical and revolutionary. Such an approach to language will enable critics to engage in a rhetoric which actively recognizes, and seeks to transform, the illusory black and white divisions of race, gender, and the language of negative difference.

While oppositional critical discourse has been at the forefront of this transformative move, the resources available for articulating a coherent conception of rhetoric can be found in a discipline that for centuries had been defined in the essentialized terms of foundationism and externalism: physics. Indeed, the movement from the metaphysics of the ancients, to the macrophysics of the moderns, to the microphysics of contemporary quantum theory, have radically altered our understanding and articulation of that which we refer to as "reality." As B. Alan Wallace reminds us, contemporary physics provides a coherent conception of reality that parallels the basic assumptions of Buddhism: "The Buddhist centrist view regards both materialism and idealism as extremes. The objective physical world is empirically knowable in relation to our modes of experience, as is the subjective cognitive world." The Buddhist view, which eschews an essentialized understanding of existence, situates terms in the realm of the contingent, the realm of rhetoric: "The terms *subject* and *object* are used, but they denote a mere conventional duality, rather than the absolute duality that we encounter in Cartesian-based Western thinking."[26] As we shall see in the next chapter, just as oppositional critical theorists have interrogated the duality of subjectivity and objectivity, so too have philosophers and rhetoricians of science, whose insights set the stage for a rhetoric of physics that calls into question our most basic beliefs about the essential separateness of self and Other, and bring us closer to an actively non-argumentative conception of discourse.

4

EMPTINESS

The circle as "perfect manifestation," as a form without beginning and without end, represents the annul-
ment of all contradictions to absolute unity and,
accordingly, to "true emptiness."

—Thomas Merton, *Zen and the birds of appetite*

In *The transformative vision: Reflections on the nature and history of human expression*, Jose Argüelles explicates a vision of
reality that transcends objective idealism and material realism,
the emergence of which is resulting in contemporary transformations of knowledge.[1] These transformations reflect an increasingly widespread intellectual preoccupation with the fragmented
and divisive vision of existence manifest most clearly in the
objectivist and materialist conceptions of reality posited by modernist theory and praxis. Argüelles argues that contemporary
approaches to ontology and epistemology are challenging the
assumptions of modernism by positing a conceptualization of
reality that transcends materialism and objectivism. He integrates "the psychophysical aesthetic and the perennial philosophy" to offer an historical analysis of human artistic expression
from the Renaissance to the modern period, illustrating the emergence of the transformative vision.

This chapter amplifies Argüelles' vision by offering a coherent integration of two areas of inquiry considered disparate, if
not mutually exclusive, since their inceptions: science and language. In science, the discoveries of relativity and the quantum
nature of matter have challenged traditional ways of thinking
about physical reality, and in language studies the explication of
constructivist epistemologies have transformed our understand-

ing of social reality. Efforts to bring the two realms together, however, have not yet fully considered the symbolic and psychological implications of what these discoveries suggest about the nature of reality: "Only in a few fringe areas of atomic physics and avante-garde art have there been genuine breakthroughs to an immaterialist or supermaterialist understanding of the universe" (Argüelles, p. 158). I would like to suggest that another area of human inquiry, rhetoric, also offers a transformative vision of reality, one that becomes particularly powerful when viewed in light of the breakthroughs of contemporary physics.

The relationship between rhetoric and physics offers a common ground between symbolic and physical theory and practice pointing to just such an immaterialist or supermaterialist conceptualization of reality. I will explicate the rhetoric of physics first by exploring how rhetoricians approach and explore the language of science in general and physics in particular, then by examining how views of quantum physicists about language have been radically transformed during the past century, and finally by considering how the epistemological common grounds of quantum theory and rhetoric offer a synthesis of material and social reality. I will consider how rhetoric functions as both method, as a way of arguing about the relationship between language and science, and as a figure, a metaphor, for the reality that these arguments presuppose. The rhetoric of physics illustrates how the discoveries of quantum physics complement contemporary conceptions of rhetoric as epistemic, and offers powerful implications for the theoretical and practical possibilities inherent in how we choose to understand our language and our world.

Rhetoricians on Scientific Inquiry

Since the publication of Thomas Kuhn's seminal work, *The structure of scientific revolutions,* the symbolic foundation of scientific knowledge has been an epistemological preoccupation that has cut across disciplines, and those areas of inquiry dealing with language have been no exception. In the realm of rhetoric this preoccupation has manifest itself on many levels: in literary criticism, composition, and perhaps most powerfully in speech communication and argumentation. During the past ten years, numerous scholars have explored the relationship between science and rhetoric and the epistemological implications of that relationship. In literary criticism, N. Katherine Hayles has provided an excellent study of parallels between literary structures and field theories in physics,[2] in composition studies several writers have explored relationships between science, writing, and the social construction of knowledge,[3] and in speech communication studies the exploration of philosophical relationships between rhetoric and science has been extensive as exemplified by the rhetoric of inquiry and the conceptualization of rhetoric as epistemic.[4]

The connections drawn between rhetoric and science have, however, not been drawn without resistance. Douglas Ehninger agrees when he points out that "historically rhetoric and science have been regarded as mutually exclusive, if not antithetical, modes of human activity. Science, we have been taught, deals with 'facts'; rhetoric with 'informed opinions.' The aim of science is to describe the world; the aim of rhetoric is to reform or regenerate it" (1984, p. 455). Indeed, questions concerning the status of rhetoric began at its birth, for it was conceived at a point in time when the human mind had begun to discover through philosophical inquiry a world made up of many parts that emerged out of a single "factual" reality. The birth was made difficult by the fact that rhetoric was relegated to the realm of opinions and appearances, and was thus made out to be at worst an enemy of "true" reality, and at best a poor representation of it. This is most clearly seen in the *physis-nomos* antithesis of the ancient Greeks, in which rhetoric was associated with *nomos*, or conventional law, and "real" reality—reality discovered through philosophical inquiry— with *physis*, or physical law.[5] *Physis* designated objective reality, and rhetoric was confined to *nomos*, where it could, if governed by reason, help point to truth, but never discover or create it.

Contemporary rhetorical studies suggest, however, that rhetoric *does*, in fact, both discover and create reality. The conceptualization of rhetoric as epistemic, and its "descendants"— the theory of argument and the rhetoric of inquiry—attempt to place rhetoric on an equal footing with philosophy itself by illustrating the rhetorical nature of the various human sciences. Epistemic rhetoricians have argued that all considerations of what we call "reality" are fundamentally rhetorical, and that symbolic interaction forms the foundation of both social and material constructions of the world. Arguments for the epistemic nature of rhetoric were offered over two decades ago by Robert Scott in his essay "On viewing rhetoric as epistemic" (1967), and in a recent essay Scott allies the "rhetoric of inquiry" and contemporary studies of argumentation with the rhetoric as epistemic camp (1990).

Richard Gregg's *Symbolic inducement and knowing* sets forth a consideration of the epistemic nature of rhetoric that begins with the Greek Sophist Gorgias of Leontini and synthesizes his views on the symbolic nature of knowing with contemporary rhetorical, philosophical, and scientific theories (1984). The conceptualization of rhetoric as epistemic has done much to redefine the divisions and boundaries between rhetoric and science and rhetoric and philosophy. Barry Brummett's exploration of "postmodern rhetoric" considers how the notion of social constructivism calls into question objective realities that exist apart from human beings, and he argues for a holistic approach synthesizing theory and method in experience (1976). In that essay Brummett argues that the "need for an organizing perspective is as important in the study of rhetoric as it is in the 'hard' sciences" (p. 42), but in more recent works he argues against the efficacy of the epistemic position.

Brummett in his "Eulogy for epistemic rhetoric" suggests that epistemic rhetoric is on its last legs (1990), yet in their response to Brummett's article, Richard Cherwitz and James Hikins argue that considerations "of rhetoric are *necessarily* and *unavoidably* philosophical" and that "*no* theory of rhetoric can be premised on antiphilosophical claims" (1990, p. 76). Their position, which I will challenge below, suggests that a theory of rhetoric devoid of philosophical foundations would call into question the very legitimacy of the academic discipline of rhetoric, which gains its respectability through an adherence to the epistemological concerns characterizing philosophical discourse and analysis. Thomas Farrell offers a wonderfully frank and "sobering vision" of the debate on the epistemic nature of rhetoric, arguing that there "is no reason why the dispute about rhetorical epistemology needed to turn into a dispute between theory and practice" because "the real mission of rhetoric as a tradition and theory has always been to invent and to enrich rhetorical practice" (p. 84). Indeed, much of the contemporary debate concerning the epistemic nature of rhetoric has to do with its failure to manifest practical applications that arise out of its theoretical concerns.

Robert Scott sees the debate over rhetoric's epistemic status as beneficial for the continued growth of the rhetorical tradition (1990), and Allan Gross suggests that his own work in the rhetoric of science is "a continuation of a movement that had lost steam for . . . its unwillingness to test principles against practice" (1990, p. 304). Gross suggests that the epistemic approach to rhetoric continues to be viable and valuable for a variety of disciplines such as sociology, economics, composition, and philosophy. Rhetoricians of science he notes, regardless of discipline, emphasize the available means of persuasion scientists use to convince each other of the efficacy of particular paradigms for the discovery of reality. In *The rhetoric of science* (1990) he offers a thorough, critical application and explication of principles of rhetoric at work in scientific texts to illustrate how both scientists and their audiences are convinced of the truth and legitimacy of their studies. A similar approach is offered by Charles Bazerman who, in *Shaping written knowledge*, also illustrates the rhetorical aspects of scientific writing.

Bazerman offers an excellent discussion of physics in the tradition of the rhetoric of inquiry and epistemology, and draws some important connections between social interaction and conceptions of reality. Bazerman explores the dynamic interaction of texts and contexts in twentieth century physics in his discussion of the Compton Effect, "the first empirical validation of the quantum theory" (1988, p. 191), focusing on how Arthur Holly Compton effectively utilized available means of persuasion in the announcement of his discovery: "Compton creates a crispness of argument not only detailed by revision of the representation of the experiment and the results, but also by his careful control of epistemic level, authorial voice, and authorial judgments" (p. 234). Bazerman's case study is a practical consideration of the rhetoric of science as applied to contemporary quantum physics, and other rhetorical scholars have suggested that this is indeed an important area of rhetorical inquiry. For example, Donald McCloskey suggests that contemporary contributions to the philosophy and history of physics "represents a descent, accelerating recently, from the frigid peaks of scientific absolutism into the sweet valleys of anarchic rhetoric" (1985, pp. 33–34). This approach to the rhetoric of physics offers important insights into the argumentative foundations of scientific inquiry, but falls short in providing an understanding or the epistemological common grounds of rhetoric and physics.

Robert L. Scott brings us close to such an understanding when he observes: "In contemporary physics (Heisenberg) and mathematics (Gödel) as well as in politics, sociology, and psychology, uncertainty cannot be obviated. In such a world rhetoric has a genuine role" (1990, p. 302). Scott's observation suggests that a rhetorical exploration of physics should go beyond the argumentative structures and strategies which physicists use to communicate their findings with themselves and each other, and consider the implications of what quantum physics has to say about the nature of reality and our methods of understanding it. Rhetoric as epistemic calls into question the idea of a reality that exists separate and distinct from the persons who speak about it, and the arguments of its proponents range from the position that all reality is created through language, to the more attenuated discussions of the dynamic relationship that exists between rhetoric and an objective reality that exists independent of the human agents who perceive and discuss it.

Indeed, the rhetoric as epistemic position has been called into question by scientists, philosophers and rhetoricians who take issue with claims such as "science is rhetorical" or "rhetoric creates reality." Additionally, these writers argue that it is both incorrect and inappropriate to assert that the uncertainty and indeterminacy that characterizes reality at the subatomic level is actualized at the level of either macrophysics or human interaction. While these objections have been dealt with elsewhere,[6] it is important to point out that all of the participants in this debate agree that rhetoric does in fact create *attitudes* toward and about reality. I believe that the implications of those attitudes have prompted many writers to subscribe to constructivist and subjectivist notions of reality.

Both foundationist and externalist philosophical perspectives have traditionally resulted in epistemologies that privilege certain positions at the expense of others (the rhetoric/philosophy distinction being one example), while subjectivist and constructivist epistemologies have pursued a wholesale rejection of objectively determined and referential conceptions of reality. Both approaches, however, fail to recognize the dynamic interplay of material and perception that results in meaning, and thus forms the foundation of whatever we choose to define as reality. In short, both approaches fail to recognize how they work together to create a reality of competing and mutually exclusive positions. Yet these very positions illustrate the common thread which ties them together: that we can come to some understanding about the nature of reality through language, specifically through argumentative language. However, argumentative language perpetuates division and fragmentation because it assumes *that competing positions are in fact mutually exclusive.* With this in mind, we might view the debate concerning the rhetoric of inquiry as a manifestation of the human need to understand the interconnectedness of existence and the holistic nature of reality.

I believe that this debate is resolved by the rhetoric of physics, which offers a coherent view of reality as the result of a complex and dynamic interaction of mind, matter and language, as a process of creative communication and consciousness. The rhetoric of physics does not deny the existence of an objective material reality as much as it questions the existence of reality as *only* objectively material: it suggests that objective and subjective views of reality are complementary and interdependent. This view can be traced back to the origins of the worldview that gave rise to both rhetoric and science, the rationalism of Ancient Greece, as well as the contemporary discoveries of relativity and quantum physics. A consideration of contemporary physicists' views on language and the epistemological transformations initiated by the "new story of science" indicates that the calling into question of an exclusively objective and material reality is not only a preoccupation of rhetoricians, but of physicists as well.

Physicists on Language and Reality

We derive the term "physics" from the *physis* of the Greeks, and with it all of the assumptions about the nature of reality that have helped to maintain an antithetical relationship between language and science. This mutual exclusivity was based upon the "old story" of science, a science that distanced itself from human symbolic action and interaction. The "new story" of science, however, has recalculated the equation in terms of the human factor, and as a result "holds great promise for the future." Robert Augros and George Stanciu explain: "We have seen that the new story has already transformed modern physics. It is to be expected that the disciplines that have patterned themselves after the old physics will eventually adjust themselves to the *new* physics and all of its implications" (1986, p. 183). The most exciting implications of the new story are its reconstruction of an objective reality and the reconceptualization of language this reconstruction has initiated.

The discovery of the quantum nature of matter in the early part of this century changed the way that physicists talked about the world, and also the way they talked about language. The quantum world, we now know, is a world of uncertainty, probability and paradox; a world in which "reality" exists as much in the mind of the experimenter as it does "out there;" a world intimately connected to—and confronted by— language. Quantum physics calls into question not only the existence of an objective reality, but also the possibility of talking about it objectively: it suggests that the entities which physicists called "atoms" are in fact metaphors. Heisenberg writes in *Physics and philosophy* that "the problems of language here are really serious. We wish to speak in some way about the structure of atoms and not only about the 'facts.' But we cannot speak about the atoms in ordinary language" (p. 179). This ordinary language is the rational language of "facts" and things that exist in and of themselves, a language that merely reflects a singularly real and rationally conceived reality. Heisenberg, however, understood that the world of quanta was a world of metaphors and figures that offered a way of talking about dynamic qualities in terms of static quantities.

Despite the implications of quantum physics, language functions in scientific discourse primarily as a way of talking about the physical world through what Neils Bohr described as a "common language" (1963, p. 1). Yet both Bohr's theory of complementarity and Heisenberg's uncertainty principle implicitly call into question the existence of such a "common language," and of the environment it purports to describe in terms of rational interactions, at least at the subatomic level. Yet at the macro level, the rules of classical mechanical reality still apply, and language continues to be constrained by a deterministic rationality that pictures the world of words as so many positions competing with each other in a universe of discourse. This rhetoric of "rational" reality so strongly informs the language of science still, that many physicists are unable to make the quantum leap from the "old story" to the "new story:" at least in terms of language.

In *Science, order and creativity*, David Bohm and F. David Peat agree: "Even within the quantum theory itself there is a serious failure of communication between the various interpretations" (1987, p. 86), a failure of communication that occurs because physicists tend to view various approaches as mutually exclusive or antithetical, and thus are incapable of finding a common ground for discourse. This failure also occurs, Bohm and Peat suggest, because it is assumed by many physicists that informal language is incapable of playing any role in the process of scientific discovery and explanation, an assumption reflecting a resistance or perhaps an inability to apply the lessons of quantum theory to language. Perhaps the reasons run even deeper and, as N. David Mermin suggests, have "something to do with certain deterministic presuppositions that are built into our thought and language at some deep and not very accessible level" (1990, p. 202), presuppositions that limit our abilities to see the possibilities inherent in the word, and limit us to divisive and fragmentary visions of the world.

If we are to see those possibilities, I believe, the rhetoric of physics must move beyond agonistic and argumentative paradigms in exploring the epistemological connections between these two disciplines. David Bohm and F. David Peat seem to agree when they point to how the language of scientific discourse illustrates the assumptions of knowledge to which scientists subscribe, assumptions of knowledge that inhibit scientific development: as indicated above, they offer instead an approach based in dialogue. Like the quantum view of matter that goes against the common sense view of the world as fixed and static, dialogue, Bohm and Peat suggest, could facilitate both scientific discovery *and* social development through an emphasis on process and flexibility. Bohm and Peat's explication of the way physicists might communicate with each other illustrates an understanding of the epistemological foundations binding rhetoric and physics together: rhetoric, like physics, calls into question the existence of a fixed and static reality.

It is perhaps this aspect of quantum physics that has caused many physicists to suggest that a holistic understanding of the nature of reality is necessary in the search for an epistemic stance which corresponds with the quantum worldview. Ilya Prigogine and Isabelle Stengers offer one approach which seeks a common ground between quantity and quality, between human and physical existence (1984), and B. Alan Wallace suggests a similar synthesis when he argues for a centrist view which transcends the conflicting visions of scientific realism and idealism through an exploration of the relationship between mind and matter (1989). Wallace's work illustrates how mutually exclusive methods of analysis and theoretical perspectives can achieve the same results and "truths," and suggests that this aspect of quantum physics holds important implications for the way we think and talk about the world. Gary Zukav explains how complementarity and uncertainty offer insights into the epistemological considerations connecting physics and rhetoric. "The uncertainty principle rigorously brings us to the realization that there is no 'My Way' which is separate from the world around us. It brings into question the very existence of an 'objective' reality, as does complementarity and the concept of particles of correlations" (p. 136). Quantum physics has forced a re-cognition of the belief that human beings are separate from the world in which we live, and that the separation of the linguistic and the physical is useful and appropriate for our understanding of reality.

The quantum view, as evidenced by the writings of both Wallace and Zukav, is often paralleled with Eastern Buddhist and Taoist epistemologies, yet both the Eastern and Western traditions have only recently reintegrated language into the picture of wholeness. As Fritjof Capra explains in *The tao of physics*: "The problem of language encountered by the Eastern mystic is exactly the same as the problem the modern physicist faces" (1984, p. 33). What the physicist and the mystic have in common in this instance is an inability to accept the fact that language, like reality, is full of paradoxes and contradictions. This inability is undergirded by a belief that there is *one true reality*, that can be understood through physics or contemplation, that somehow exists outside of, or beyond, language. By rejecting language they attempt to understand unity by dividing it into pieces, some of which are important and some of which are not. But this method of negation cannot, by definition, ever achieve an understanding of the unity that is assumed to exist if language is, in fact, a part of that unity.

The reintegration of language is, however, anticipated in conceptualizations of reality that focus on extrapolating the wholeness and interdependence of the quantum world to the social order. David Bohm's concept of the "implicate order," for example, suggests that reality is *essentially* holistic and inter-connected. Bohm provides support for this view in *Wholeness and the implicate order* when he argues that social fragmentation arises out of a belief in the essentially separate nature of things, that is, *essentially*, an illusion. Bohm contends that this sense of separateness is both illusory and problematical. This "illusion," he argues, is grounded in "the process of division," an approach to understanding the world that defines and describes reality in terms of its elements considered in and of themselves. It is this same worldview, one which has historically denied language a role in the creation of a reality, that paradoxically has been maintained and perpetuated through language.[7]

And that language, agonistic and argumentative, tends to create physics in its own image: thus at the level of symbolic interaction physics remains in a Newtonian paradigm of determinacy and certainty while constructing a reality of indeterminacy and uncertainty. And yet, as one contemporary physicist suggests, the relationship between physics and language seems to correspond to the position taken by the most radical proponents of constructivist rhetoric: that rhetoric creates reality. Bruce Gregory writes in *Physics as language*: "The lesson we can draw from the history of physics is that as far as we are concerned, *what is real is what we regularly talk about*. For better or for worse, there is little evidence that we have any idea of what reality looks like from some absolute point of view. We only know what the world looks like from *our* point of view" (p. 184). Gregory's analysis points to the role of human action and inter-action in the construction of reality, and suggests that language plays a fundamental role in the determination of what we perceive and believe is real.

His conceptualization of physics *as* language is powerful precisely because it indicates that rational reality might be nothing more than an epistemic self-fulfilling prophesy. Because language influences that reality, it follows that rational premises of knowledge imbedded in language will construct a reality, *or at least the illusion of a reality,* that corresponds to those premises. The fundamental metaphysical question then becomes: does our language merely reflect a world of divisions and separations, or does our language create that world? Perhaps the answer is both. Gregory explains: "*The minute we begin to talk about this world, however, it becomes transformed into another world, an*

interpreted world, a world delimited by language" (1988, p. 183).
Gregory's analysis sounds peculiarly like Paul Watzlawick's contention that "communication creates what we call reality" (1977,
p. xi). Indeed the view of reality presented by quantum physics so
closely parallels Watzlawick's discussion of reality that we must
seriously consider it as a foundation for the rhetoric of physics.

Watzlawick argues that "our everyday traditional ideas of
reality are delusions which we spend substantial parts of our
daily lives shoring up, even at the considerable risk of trying to
force facts to fit our definition of reality instead of vice versa" (p.
xi). Our perceptions of reality are intimately connected to the
way we construct the world with words, and much of what we
have constructed, at least in terms of what we believe to be real,
is at best an illusion and at worst a delusion: "And the most dangerous delusion of all is that there is only one reality. What there
are, in fact, are many different versions of reality, some of which
are contradictory, but all of which are the results of communication and not reflections of eternal, objective truths" (p. xi).
Watzlawick's position, like Gregory's, offers an important connection between rhetoric and physics in its insistence on the
intimate relationship between communication and reality, and
points toward the possibility of a theory of language that recognizes the interconnectedness and holistic nature of both material
and symbolic reality. Such a theory can readily be discerned in
the reality of rhetoric, a reality which begins with the ancient
Greeks and continues to be transformed in our own time.

THE REALITY OF RHETORIC

The discovery of the quantum nature of matter disrupted the
view of reality that had been evolving in Western science since
the ancient Greeks, a view in which continuity had been the cor-
nerstone. Quantum physics put a rather large crack in that cor-
nerstone, not only in terms of reality at the subatomic level, but
all other levels as well. The discoveries of contemporary physics
caused scientific thinking to take a quantum leap back to its
very beginnings. Yet quantum physics unearthed an argument
that had presumably been settled but which it dramatically
refuted; the argument concerning the continuous nature of reality. Fred Alan Wolf explains in *Taking the quantum leap* when he

notes that the problem of discontinuity that arose in quantum physics initiated a look backward toward the past: "It would be this discontinuity that would lead two new physicists, Werner Heisenberg and Niels Bohr, back to that earlier Greek picture of wholeness" (1989, p. 59). The rhetoric of physics returns us to that picture of wholeness.

Perhaps the clearest articulation of that picture is offered by Parmenides of Elea, whose hexameter poem on the nature of Being suggests a conceptualization of essence very similar to David Bohm's "implicate order," or the Tao of Eastern philosophy. Parmenides is most often contrasted with Heraclitus, whose "logos" exemplified the interpenetration of opposites as a characteristic of the nature of existence. Yet Parmenidean "Being" is also full of the contradictory and paradoxical assertions of existence that are at the heart of the quantum theory. As Carl Friedrich von Weizsacker, in reference to the Parmenidean assertion of Being explains: "Unity by itself is not a principle; in being, unity is multiplicity, but at the cost of self-contradiction" (1987 p. 119). Parmenides' student, Zeno,[8] would continue in his teacher's footsteps, and articulate his own paradoxes on discontinuity that, although dismissed by philosophers for centuries, would re-emerge as central elements of the new physics. Zeno's student Gorgias likewise carried on the tradition, articulating a rhetoric that calls into question the foundational assumption of the rational worldview of the philosophers: the existence of an essential reality.

Gorgias is most well known for his participation in the Platonic dialogue bearing his name, and is credited with having defined rhetoric as "a creator of persuasion."[9] An examination of his extant writings, however, suggests that he viewed rhetoric *as a way of criticizing persuasion*: In the *Encomium on Helen*, for example, he argues that "persuasion by speech is equivalent to abduction by force," and goes on to discredit persuasive discourse as it is manifest in "arguments of the meteorologists," the "legal contests," and *"the philosophical debates, in which quickness of thought is shown easily altering opinion"* (Freeman, 1977, p. 132, emphasis mine). Gorgias' indictment of philosophy is seen in several other sections of the *Helen*, wherein he implicitly calls into question the Platonic Ideas and Forms and the notion of a prenatal confrontation with essential reality. His most evident denial of an essential reality is seen in his treatise *On Being* in which he uses dialectical argument to "prove" that nothing exists, and in the course of his explication illustrates the paradoxes created by self-legitimating assumptive grounds of dialectical argument.

Parmenides, Zeno, and Gorgias all articulated positions that were at odds with the philosophical explanation of the relationship between the one and the many through their emphases on paradox and discontinuity. The debate concerning the one and the many was for the ancient Greeks a very rational matter, for it was central to all intellectual inquiry concerning the essential nature of reality, including the *physis-nomos* controversy. The resolution of the debate was embodied in the rational premises of knowledge exemplified by the philosophy conceived by Plato and nurtured by his student Aristotle. Their rejection of rhetorical knowledge has created a double-standard of judgment that has privileged rational discourse, and created a prejudicial negative difference that has had profound social and historical implications. "This unequal relationship," notes Jean François Lyotard in *The postmodern condition*, "is an intrinsic effect of the rules specific to each game. We all know its symptoms. It is the entire history of cultural imperialism from the dawn of Western civilization" (p. 27). Rhetoric defined in terms of rational premises reifies a view of reality constrained by the assumptions and presuppositions of those premises.

In contrast to these rational premises, however, another view of knowledge was articulated, an epistemic stance which was fundamentally rhetorical and which called into question all of the underlying assumptions of rational reality: the epistemology of Sophistry. John Poulakos[10] explores the epistemic foundations of Sophistic rhetoric in "Rhetoric, the Sophists, and the possible" and explains that "the Sophists show no interest in a world of conceptual perfection or rational orderliness. Theirs is a constantly changing world, full of ambiguity and uncertainty, always lacking, never complete" (1984, p. 221). Jean-Pierre Vernant offers a similar explanation of sophistic rhetoric in his discussion of the "logic of polarity" which characterizes the *dissoi-logoi*. The *dissoi-logoi* suggest that competing discourses are *both* distinct *and* complementary, that "they are mutually exclusive, but you still cannot choose just one" (p. 289). The same notion occurs in Sophistic rhetoric in Gorgias' indictment of philosophical discourse in the *Helen* and Thrasymachus of

Chalcedon's "theory of the opposite party," to name only two examples which suggest why the Sophists were so thoroughly discredited by the philosophers of ancient Greece. The Sophists denied philosophy the privileged position it claimed for itself through a radically empirical conceptualization of language: they explicated the fundamentally complementary nature of the very vehicle through which philosophy claimed its distinctiveness.

The *dissoi-logoi* was an antiphilosophical rhetoric, and called into question the underlying assumptions of "true and false discourse." One sees this "logic of polarity" in the Zen notion of the "center of being" which is both beyond all opposites and within all opposites simultaneously (Suzuki, p. 80), and in the realms of uncertainty and indeterminacy that characterize contemporary physics. Such an antiphilosophical rhetoric, the objections of Cherwitz and Hikins notwithstanding, does not endanger the academic discipline of rhetoric, but in fact enriches it. One sees the same rhetoric in the "plural orchestration," and "perpetual cognitive dissonance" that Richard Lanham suggests are the essence of the "rhetorical ideal of life," and in the conceptualization of rhetoric as *aretē* which Robert Pirsig contemplates in *Zen*.

N. Katherine Hayles writes that Pirsig's *Zen* illustrates an attempt to articulate, for all intents and purposes, the rhetoric of physics: "Robert M. Pirsig's version of the field concept derives in part, as his title suggests, from the Zen concept of a fluid, dynamic reality that precedes and eludes verbal formulation. Yet it is also informed by the Western tradition that sees the Word as the ultimate reality" (1984, p. 63). While Hayles does not believe that Pirsig is successful in his attempt to synthesize field theory with language, his view of rhetoric as *aretē*, or excellence, suggests a conceptualization of rhetoric that goes far beyond the limitations imposed upon it by rational views of reality. With the triumph of philosophy, rhetoric becomes devalued, and its metaphysical and epistemic coherence is overshadowed by the truths of an objective reality that cannot resolve the paradoxes and polarities inherent in the symbolic elasticity of linguistic discourse.

But the rational premises which have historically been used to define rhetoric have resulted in theories of language that do not adequately reflect the empirical reality of linguistic interaction. If, for example, we apply objective criteria to an argumentative interaction, in order to be consistent with the underlying assumptions of objectivity, we must observe that the participants in the interaction are agreeing to hold mutually exclusive positions in relation to each other: that they are agreeing to disagree. Once we take a position by siding with one or the other of the participants, we are *by definition* no longer being objective. Objectivity assumes observation from outside of the discourse: by taking a position, *regardless of the criteria we use to justify our choice*, we have violated the most basic requirement of objectivity. The reality of rhetoric parallels Heisenberg's uncertainty principle: the more certain we are of the truth (i.e., the position), the further we are from the process that generates that truth (i.e., the meaning). The paradox which language creates for objective reality is the impossibility of being *truly* objective in terms of the very assumptions of objectivity; the more objective we are, the farther we are from grasping that *the truth of discourse is that we cannot be outside of it*, and thus cannot *by definition* be objective. This is the paradoxical view of reality that arises in the rhetoric of the Sophists, in the *dissoi-logoi*, the antiphilosophical logic that threatened the certainty of objective conceptions of the real and the true.

These rhetorical paradoxes, ostensibly resolved by the logic of rational objectivity, resurface in physics' calling into question the existence of an objective reality. Instead of descriptively accounting for the experience of discourse on its own terms by acknowledging that logical division and mutual exclusivity are embedded in assumptions of knowledge which are intimately tied to language, much of Western theoretical discourse concerning language has historically superimposed the formal structures of rational analysis and logic on the paradoxes of communicative interaction. In short, instead of acknowledging that on any one issue there can be any number of equally valid positions, Western theoretical discourse has attempted to transcend the paradox of polarity by privileging an objectivist logic to legitimate one position at the expense of others. The result has been a failure to either acknowledge or recognize the symbolic foundations of objective accounts of physical reality.

Gregory comments in *Physics as language*: "We have a strong penchant for maintaining that a statement must be either true or false. Indeed, there is a principle in logic, called the *law of the excluded middle, or bivalence*, which says that every statement must be either true or false." Gregory's conceptualization of physics as language, which I believe provides a powerful foundation for the rhetoric of physics, calls even this fundamental assumption of logic and theoretical discourse into question: "But how do we know the law of the excluded middle is true? In fact, of course, we don't. The law is a convention—a way to use language" (1988, p. 172). Our conventional way of thinking and talking about the world and ourselves has significantly influenced all areas of human linguistic, epistemic, and social discourse, and has created a fragmentary and antagonistic worldview. Quantum physics offers a new way of thinking about physical and linguistic reality that can initiate a "transition of language" capable of epistemological, and perhaps even social, transformation, one which offers the possibility of a "postmodern" rhetoric grounded in a holistic and transcendent understanding of the word and the world.

THE RHETORIC OF PHYSICS:
TOWARD A VISION OF TRANSFORMATION

The possibility of a "postmodern" rhetoric is not a new idea: it was anticipated in the classical tradition by the Sophists and has emerged in the contemporary notion of rhetoric as epistemic which, Brummett's later arguments notwithstanding, has by no means exhausted its critical and theoretical potential. In fact it is Brummett's early essay on "postmodern rhetoric" that offers the most powerful indication of that potential in its realization of the transformative possibilities of symbolic interaction: "The point here is that whenever meanings are shared they are shared only because discourse has the power to induce people to participate in that shared reality. The same power may be used to change that reality" (1976, p. 31). If we choose to view reality as the interconnected and holistic reality of the quantum microworld, we may be able to transform the disconnected and fragmented material and social realities of the macroworld in which we live: a simple case of mind and word over matter. The transformative power of the rhetoric of physics lies in its potential to transcend the vision of division which influences human consciousness and undermines human unity.

Michael Talbot makes the case for a rhetoric of physics that reflects a "transition of language" initiated by quantum physics

which he believes emphasizes just such a holistic vision of transformation, one capable of healing the divisions of human consciousness that undergird our fragmented conceptions of reality:
"The fact that the new physics contains within it powerful
metaphors of self-transformation and social transformation
should also not be ignored. Effecting such a shift in language and
consciously emphasizing that we humans and the universe we
inhabit are all part of a living, intelligent, and infinitely inter-
connected fabric might be a good first step toward trying to heal
those ills" (1988, p. 200). In addition to its social possibilities,
such a transition will have important implications for epistemology. Talbot continues: "Hand in hand with this last point is
the fact that such a transition of language may allow us to begin
to see qualities and relationships that we might otherwise have
overlooked" (p. 201). By looking for these qualities and relationships in the epistemological connections between physics and
rhetoric, we can facilitate a transformation of consciousness that
allows us to transcend the agonistic dualism of the past, and consciously consider the possibilities presented by the future.

Such a transformation of consciousness is, I believe, already
in the making. The rhetoric of physics exemplifies Argüelles'
transformative vision, a vision moving beyond the psychology
of dominance, which has characterized the rise of materialistic
science and technology in the modern period. Argüelles agrees:
"In order for us to transcend the combative dualism that is the
very essence of our condition, there must be a unitive experience of the world that can be achieved only through a major collective catharsis. And it may well be that we are already in the
throes of such an event" (1975 p. 292). The notion of rhetoric as
epistemic, when considered in terms of the epistemological
implications of quantum physics, offers communication scholars
an opportunity to facilitate that catharsis if we continue to
explore and nourish conceptualizations of language and symbolic
interaction that focus on wholeness and respond to our contemporary struggle with fragmentation.

Janice Hocker Rushing's essay "*E. T.* as rhetorical transcendence" represents a critical manifestation of just such an exploration. Like Argüelles, she integrates psychophysical aesthetics
and perennial philosophy as a methodological foundation for a
"rhetoric of wholeness," and explicates *E.T.* as a rhetorical
response to the "contemporary exigence of fragmentation."

Rushing points out how a holistic rhetoric functions as an organizing critical principle as well as providing the foundational assumptions of the film's message. She views *E.T.* as part of a larger contemporary social phenomenon that reflects a theme common to our time: the need to find wholeness and synthesis in a fragmented and divided world; the need to find a transformative vision. What Rushing's essay teaches is a recognition that rhetorical theorists need to consider a wider range of both methods and materials for understanding the dynamic complexity of reality. The lesson of *E.T.*, she suggests, is that human beings can, through a holistic vision of rhetoric, choose how we relate to, construct, and understand reality: "We must unite with the cosmos rather than possess it" (p. 200) to recognize the fundamentally unified and holistic nature of reality. This, I believe, is the same lesson that we learn from the rhetoric of physics.

It will be in the articulations and dissemination of that lesson that the rhetoric of physics can make its greatest contribution. Rhetoric has since its origins been recognized as a perfect vehicle for imparting an understanding to the many of the One: of what quantum physics tells us about our world, our role in it, and the potential each of us possesses as agents of transformation. The *ethos*[11] of a postmodern rhetoric of physics offers a more humanistic understanding of human action and inquiry, and allows for a revisioning of the past which recognizes the fundamental unity and wholeness characterizing reality. In anticipating such a transformative vision, we may wish to consider Fred Alan Wolf's challenge: "If we are 'hung up' on the past, we will choose to see the future as we saw the past. If we alter our perception of the now, then our altered view will change the future! The question is how far can we go?"[12]

The question has profound and powerful implications for our understanding of rhetoric, precisely because it pushes rhetoric beyond the contingent realm of the probable, and into the chaotic space of the possible, a space that, like the void of the Buddhists, is all encompassing yet encompasses nothing. As Michel Foucault observes: "When language arrives at its own edge, what it finds is not a positivity that contradicts it, but the void that will efface it."[13]

Rhetoric, having arrived at the edge of modernism, peers into the abyss of its postmodern unmaking: "Whatever, else the rhetoric of the postmodern era might be, writes Raymie

McKerrow, it cannot be 'argument' as that term is normally understood." McKerrow suggests that a postmodern rhetoric will help us see the future and the past in new and potentially transformative ways, and might help us recognize how they are implicated in each other. The promise of postmodernism is a reaffirmation of rhetoric's coherence, a coherence that incorporates preclassical, classical, modern, and postmodern tendencies in a discourse "at once multidimensional and non-reductive, keyed to the possibility of the transformation of power, yet finite and incomplete." Indeed, postmodernism's resituating of argument leans toward a coherentist epistemological strategy, for as McKerrow explains, it "does not necessitate the destruction of reason. What it does is to refocus the attention on reason as contingent and fallible. In its postmodern guise, argumentative discourse is perceived as it actually is—not as modernist ideals would have it be."[14] In the next chapter, I will take McKerrow's observation one step further to suggest that a coherent rhetoric offers an understanding of argument that is realized in both modernist ideals and postmodern praxis.

5

ONE HAND CLAPPING

> I believe one can learn much about Zen from any activity one is engaged in by remaining aware of one's inner reactions. The key is a constant exercise of awareness, vigilance of mind, and relaxation of the body. Applying the principles of Zen frees an individual from concern, tension, and anxiety about winning and losing.
>
> —Joe Hyams, *Zen in the martial arts*

A rhetoric that connects the past with the present in powerful ways points to the possibility of synthesizing traditional and contemporary concerns into a transformative vision of human knowledge and being.[1] As Warren Sandmann (1993) suggests in his integration of preclassical and postmodern thought, in rethinking our understanding of argumentation, we need to interrogate the assumptions of philosophical idealism and realism: "Argumentation should function as continuing skepticism, privileging no position (neither the thought nor the observation: neither the ideal or the socially agreed upon), and staking no ground of knowledge" (p. 99). We need, he suggests, to turn argument back upon itself, to interrogate its own assumptions, and to call into question the epistemic constraints that have kept the discipline "imperiled by the contradiction between objectivity and, at best, intersubjectivity, the idea of common and social agreements about reality" (p. 102). The issues raised by Sandmann and various other rhetorical scholars are perhaps best reflected in McKerrow's words: "Charting the course of rhetoric/argument in a postmodern world is a frustrating if not futile task."[2]

The terms "frustrating" and "futile," are often invoked by those confronted with the koan, "the famous device used by Zen meditation masters in both China (where it originated) and Japan. Its literal meaning is 'public statement' or 'saying.'" The koan, like postmodernism, is an attempt to challenge and undermine the essentializing consequences of rationality, to unmask them as constructions. But the rewards of the seafarer who attempts to navigate between the Scylla of idealism and the Charybdis of realism, like the rewards of the Zennist, are potentially great: "If the grueling, frustrating pursuit of the koan is carried on to the end, there comes a breakthrough to a realm of Truth far deeper than, far transcendent of, any intellectual statements," explains Winston King. "The intellect and its rationalities are seen as what they truly are — superficial reflections on the surface of the ocean of being, true and important only in the world of man-made distinctions and cultural perceptions."[3] Although many postmodernists might take issue with King's reference to "Truth," it nonetheless seems reasonable to assert that the relationship between rhetoric and postmodernism is something like the Zen koan, "what is the sound of one hand clapping?"

The debates that have emerged in response to the articulation of a "postmodern" rhetoric are somewhat paradoxical in that they seem to perpetuate the very problem that postmodernism calls into question: the privileging of discourse. Since the privileging of discourse is the domain of argument and analysis, the idea of postmodern criticism is somewhat of an oxymoron, a paradox that only seems possible if we can move beyond oppositional criticism to an actively non-argumentative discourse. Such a discourse appears both improbable and impossible, yet in light of the concerns of postmodernism seems somewhat necessary for a postmodern rhetoric to integrate theory and practice. This move beyond argument is something that is anticipated by a postmodern rhetoric in its emphasis on the relationship between language, power, and empowerment, yet only a few theorists have acknowledged such a move or what it might look like.[4] Raising the possibility of an actively non-argumentative discourse is, I believe, a legitimate end of postmodern rhetorical theory.

Postmodernism is primarily concerned with calling into question existing paradigms and exploring relationships between power and discourse. Stephen Tyler's "essays of the unspeakable" exemplify the postmodern agenda: "They speak the language of resistance to all totalizing ideologies that justify the repression of the common sense world in the name of utopia, or that seek to legitimize practice and judgment as the expression of theory" (1987, p. xi). Robert Harriman argues that postmodern rhetoric must explore "how we continue to be dependent upon conventions of modern discourse that suppress the very tradition with which we would think" (1991, p. 70). Blair, Jeppeson, and Pucci argue that postmodern rhetorical praxis must make the critic "an interventionist rather than a deferential, if expert, spectator" (1991, p. 283). If we consider that the dominant convention of modern discourse with which power is maintained and perpetuated is argumentative and critical language, the relationship between postmodernism and rhetoric becomes somewhat paradoxical, since the logic of postmodernism would seemingly call into question criticism as a modernist enterprise.[5] The postmodern rhetorical theorist or critic is like a student of Zen who is asked to give an answer to a question that is, by the very mechanisms with which it defines and is defined, unspeakable.

I return here to the Zen notion of "beginner's mind" as a starting point to explore the paradoxical tensions between modernism, postmodernism, and rhetorical theory and practice. The question of a postmodern rhetoric needs to be addressed with the "beginner's mind" characteristic of students of Zen, with a non-dualistic attitude that emphasizes the finding of similarities in differences as a way of understanding and managing diverse conceptions of reality. Such an approach is as old as the discipline itself, and not only illustrates coherences between rhetoric and postmodernism, but also suggests how rhetoric can provide a vehicle for a postmodern concern with transformation. I will explore connections between postmodern rhetoric in order to reconsider postmodernism's rejection of modernism, and suggest a critical explication of this rejection that illustrates how the finding of similarity in difference and the articulation of an actively non-argumentative conceptualization of discourse are important ends of a coherent postmodern rhetorical theory.

POSTMODERNITY AND THE RHETORICAL IDEAL OF LIFE

Over a decade ago, Barry Brummett explicated the principles and practices of a postmodern rhetoric, and defined its major concern as "the advocacy of realities."[6] His exploration of the implications of process and intersubjectivity in science and philosophy for rhetorical theory illustrated a key concern of postmodern thought: the calling into question of dominant paradigms and perspectives. Brummett's consideration of a postmodern rhetoric is also echoed by McKerrow, who argues that "a critical rhetoric celebrates its reliance on contingency, on doxa as the basis for knowledge, on nominalism as the ground of language meaning as doxastic, and critique viewed as performance."[7] Critical rhetoric suggests that the relationship between modernism and post-modernism is in many ways a rehearsal of the debate between philosophy and rhetoric, between "serious" and "rhetorical" ways of knowing, that has been waged for centuries.

The debate between philosophy and rhetoric is at its root, grounded in the politics of power which preoccupy postmodern critics. Contemporary writers such as Lanham and Valesio have explored the epistemological and ideological implications of the debate, and the complementary relationship between rhetoric and dialectic. For Lanham, rhetoric represents a calling into question of the privileged discourse of philosophy, and for Valesio it offers a strategy for demystifying ideology and reopening closed discursive formations. Both of these positions echo the concerns of postmodernists, and find their early articulations in the history of rhetorical theory in the rhetoric of the Sophists. Indeed, the questioning of privileged discourses was a basic concern of sophistic rhetoric, and the political and epistemological implications of this concern were, and still are, central to the debate between rhetoric and philosophy. Sophistic rhetoric also recognized the two-sidedness of language, and within this two-sidedness situates the possibility of transformation as an end of a post-modern rhetoric. The rhetoric of the Sophists emphasized possibility and recognized the complementary nature of opposites as a foundation for judgment.

This approach to judgment challenged the political and intellectual conventions of the time, and not only offered a strategy for calling into question existing power relations, but also offered access to the means—language— by which they were constructed and legitimated. I. F. Stone, in *The trial of Socrates*, demythologizes the portrait of the father of philosophy received from his students, and suggests that the antagonism which existed between the Sophists and the philosophers was undergirded by a struggle for power which addressed fundamental questions of equality. "A basic reason for the antagonism to the

Sophists in Socratic and Platonic circles is that among those teachers were thinkers who for the first time affirmed the equality of man" (p. 43). Undoubtedly, the Sophists saw an equality of discourse as the vehicle through which social equality could be achieved, and thus provided their students with the argumentative skills necessary to achieve political access, access which threatened existing class stratifications and privileges. Stone concurs: "There is a strong element of class prejudice in the Socratic animosity toward the Sophists," he notes, because the Sophists' students consisted of a class of individuals who "wanted to be able to challenge the old landed aristocracy for leadership by learning the arts of rhetoric and logic so they could speak effectively in the assembly" (p. 41). Sophistic rhetoric, unlike Socratic dialectic, was an *aretē* of which all were capable, which did not discriminate on the basis of birth, heritage, or social status.

The assumptive grounds of Sophistic rhetoric are reflected in Protagoras' dictum that humans are "the measure of all things," by the antilogic of the *dissoi-logoi*, and by Thrasymachus' "theory of the opposite party." These three themes of the Sophistic enterprise provided powerful interrogations of the essentialist positions of epistemology and ontology defended by the philosophers, and illustrate the earliest manifestations of rhetoric's postmodern sentiments. As Werner Jaeger notes, "their great invention, rhetoric, was to meet powerful opposition and competition in science and philosophy when they became independent of it." Although the Sophistic movement was made up of a number of individuals with differing strategies and methods, the democratization of social and symbolic interaction was a characteristic end of their project.[8] Perhaps the most well-known of the Sophists, Protagoras, believed that the training of the mind involved an acceptance and understanding of the paradoxical nature of language and reality. Edward Schiappa observes that "evidence of Protagoras' importance can be provided by noting his contributions to the politics and philosophy of his time. His human-measure tenet was at the heart of the sophistic movement to democratize aretē and knowledge" (p. 13). He suggests that Protagoras and some of the other Sophists played a powerful role in facilitating the emergence of democracy in ancient Greece:

The sophistic contribution to this process of democratization was two-fold. First, some Sophists helped to provide a theoretical justification for education and democracy itself. Second, on a practical level the Sophists' secular theories and highly developed prose aided the break from the mythic-poetic tradition and the elitism associated with it. Protagoras was a pioneer with respect to both the theoretical and practical aspects of advancing democracy. (p. 170)

For Protagoras in particular, the nature of difference depended upon the nature of the measurement taken, the choice of perspective. His position offered an important alternative to the idealism of Plato and the realism of Aristotle, one which escaped the essentializing consequences of bivalence. Schiappa explains that "Both Plato and Aristotle argue from an either/or logic, whereas Protagoras' used a 'both/and' logic. To him experience was rich and variable enough to be capable of multiple—and even inconsistent—accounts" (p. 193).

The importance of this approach is its relation to the larger Sophistic concern with the democratization of social and symbolic action. Like Protagoras' both/and strategy, the *dissoi-logoi* transcend the problematical divisions created by dialectical thinking. The *dissoi-logoi* call into question all of the fundamental assumptions of essential philosophy: singular transcendent truth, the privileged position of the dialectic, and change-lessness in the realm of human affairs. The *dissoi-logoi* articulate the reality of language as it is observed, as *theoria*, and as it functions in social reality, as praxis. Anticipating the emergence of "true discourse and false discourse," and the political and epistemological privilege which it would create, some of the Sophists articulated a destabilizing rhetorical strategy which offered some protection against the *terror* of rational discourse. They found it in the *dissoi-logoi* and in the logic of polarity. It is within the context of this logic of polarity that Thrasymachus of Chalcedon, in his "Public orations" articulates his "theory of the opposite party." This is a powerful refutation of the essentialist presuppositions of philosophical dialectic, precisely because it exposes an underlying agreement to disagree. Thrasymachus, like many of the other Sophists, counters the philosophical privileging of dialectical discourse with the empirical observation that all arguments are presupposed by *a choice* to see positions as mutually exclusive and *essentially* at odds with one another.

That choice suggests a direction for a postmodern rhetoric that can facilitate "an understanding of discourse in a fragmented world."⁹ It offers the possibility of a constructive critique that challenges modernist assumptions not by rejecting them, but by illustrating their coherence with postmodern perspectives. The rejection of modernism by postmodernism problematizes criticism precisely because it suggests the replacement of one oppressive discourse with another. Harriman makes this argument, well aware of his own complicity, in response to McKerrow's definition of postmodern rhetoric. He describes McKerrow's enterprise as "modernist" in its assumptions and in its acceptance of the discriminatory tendencies of rationalism. In defining postmodern rhetoric as a distinct approach, McKerrow not only rejects the assumptions of modernism but also differentiates it from other approaches to rhetoric that, from Harriman's perspective, seem entirely consistent with it.

The same issues are being raised outside of rhetorical theory in the debate between Jean François Lyotard and Jürgen Habermas, and a consideration of the underlying assumptions and similarities of both sides might prove useful in illustrating how the debate is indeed a rehearsing of the conflict between rhetoric and philosophy. The Habermas/Lyotard debate is especially useful because it illustrates some major points of disagreement between modern and postmodern perspectives, and also considers the rhetorical implications of these perspectives. Frederick Jameson in his foreword to Lyotard's *The postmodern condition* touches upon the two key issues with which I am concerned: the role of language and its relation to legitimation.¹⁰ Jameson explicates Lyotard's articulation of the postmodern condition in a manner which suggests that we might profitably view the Habermas/Lyotard debate as a contemporary manifestation of the perennial conflict between philosophy and rhetoric. "The rhetoric in which all of this is conveyed is to be sure one of struggle, conflict, the agonic in a quasi-heroic sense," notes Jameson, and he relates this to Lyotard's consideration of the conflict between Sophistry and essentialist philosophy (p. xix). Instead of focusing on the evident differences between Habermas and Lyotard, I want to consider how Habermas' concern with an ideal speech situation and Lyotard's emphasis on the non-hegemonic Greek philosophers provide a common ground for a postmodern rhetoric. I wish to view Lyotard's perspective as a continuation of

Habermas' in order to illustrate how postmodern and modern conceptualizations of knowing and being can be viewed as inter-dependent and complementary.

RHETORICAL IDEALS AND DEMOCRATIC REALITIES

Lyotard argues in *The postmodern condition* that "it seems nei-ther possible, nor even prudent, to follow Habermas in orienting our treatment of the problem of legitimation in the direction of a search for universal consensus through what he calls *Diskurs*, in other words, a dialogue of argumentation" (p. 65). This refuta-tion illustrates the underlying problematic of the Lyotard/Habermas debate: a *consensual* agreement to disagree. As Phillips correctly observes, Habermas' position "does not itself force him to adopt any particular position so far as the just soci-ety is concerned" (p. 88). This aspect of Habermas' theory, which can be seen as a weakness, can also be seen as a *meta-ethical* commentary on Lyotard's position. Lyotard's rejection of Habermas' "dialogue of argumentation" *is a practical affirmation of a theoretical problematic which strengthens Habermas' posi-tion in two ways:* first, it assumes the necessity of argumentative discourse, and second it points to assumptive inconsistencies in Lyotard's allegiance with the Sophistic agenda. Lyotard's opposi-tion to Habermas' position reflects a *complicitous* agreement to disagree, and is an affirmation of the very dialectical assumptive grounds of essentialist epistemology—the very terror— that Lyotard is attempting to call into question.

This problematic is recognized in *The differend*, in which Lyotard deals with the paradox of speaking into being a genre of discourse that transcends essentialist presuppositions.[11] Lyotard pursues the notion of the differend through an exhaustive explo-ration of the paradoxes presented by logic and its relationship to language as they are articulated in the conflict between philoso-phy and rhetoric. Beginning with Sophistic and ancient Greek conceptions of symbolic and social action, Lyotard explicates the differend from the pre-Socratics to postmodernism. Central to his analysis are issues of justice, and he explores their many man-ifestations in relation to the problematic of judgment initiated and sustained by essentialist epistemology, the problem of nega-tive difference. "Proof is negative, in the sense of being refutable.

It is adduced in debate, which is agonistic or dialogical if there is a consensus over the procedures for its being adduced" (p. 54). Ultimately, for Lyotard, this consensus is self-legitimating, an illusory "Idea" that carries with it all of the terroristic implications of any "Idea." The *differend* is the play of possibility which always calls into question the Idea that is totalizing, that asserts its own primacy and mastery over language.

The differend articulates a calling into question of privileged discourse from within, which situates itself at the *stasis* of argument, the point of conflict. It is the point at which both/and converge, at which either/or judgments collapse in upon themselves like black holes or quantum equations. "In the matter of language, the revolution of relativity and of quantum theory remains to be made" (p. 137). Perhaps Lyotard's differend represents the event horizon of that revolution in the making: "The differend is reborn from the very resolution of supposed litigations. It summons humans to situate themselves in unknown phrase universes, even if they don't have the feeling that something has to be phrased" (p. 181). The differend offers the subtle promise of the potential of judgment unencumbered by essentialism, and grounded in the possibilities of language unhindered by dialectical constraints. It suggests a fulfillment of what Habermas describes in *Knowledge and human interests,* as an "ideal speech situation."

The ideal speech situation illustrates Habermas' concern with communicative action and its implications for social discourse. The concern with communicative action also leads Habermas to an explication of the liberating function of critical activity. "In self-reflection knowledge for the sake of knowledge attains congruence with the interest in autonomy and responsibility. The emancipatory cognitive interest aims at the pursuit of reflection as such" (p. 314). This leads Habermas to suggest in *Theory and practice* that theory which "obligates one to militancy" cannot be meaningful, but that theories can be distinguished in terms of the degree to which they anticipate the possibility of emancipation (p. 32). Habermas' concern with emancipation is central to his positions on the role of theory and its limitations in relation to agonistic social contexts and realities. "No theory and no enlightenment can relieve us of the risks of taking a partisan position and of the unintended consequences involved in this." Habermas clearly suggests that argumentation is a necessary vehicle for critical analysis, and argues that rational knowledge and self-reflection are necessary for social praxis and transformation. "Attempts at emancipation, which at the same time are attempts to realize the Utopian contents of the cultural tradition, can, under certain circumstances be rendered plausible as *practical* necessities" (*Theory and practice*, p. 32). Through an explication of Freudian and Marxist psychological and social theory, Habermas argues that emancipation is the end product of the self-reflective activity that is central to critical inquiry. His articulation of the *emancipatory interest* synthesizes both the Hegelian and Kantian transcendentalist presuppositions of the modernist enterprise, and best exemplifies his belief in the constructive potential of practical reason in the realms of human symbolic and social reality.

Within these realms of activity Habermas isolates three "specific viewpoints"—work, interaction, and power—which he sees as *essential* aspects of human existence. Each represents an *a priori* or, as Habermas contends, "transcendental" aspect of the human condition. All human beings, he notes, must confront the material realities of work, the symbolic realities of language, and the political realities of power, regardless of the historical or cultural contexts which circumscribe their interactions. Habermas' use of the term transcendental is pivotal to an explication of his views on communication and its role in the creation of a "just" society. Following Kant, he writes in *Communication and the evolution of society*: "to the extent that we discover the same implicit conceptual structure in any coherent experience whatsoever, we may call this basic conceptual system of possible experience *transcendental*" (p. 21). Habermas asserts that transcendental philosophy provides an essential strategy for approaching and understanding the "presuppositions of argumentative speech" (p. 23), presuppositions which he believes are imbedded in the "ideal speech situation."

This situation is defined by the normative forces grounded in language, and provides a foundation for rational inquiry:

> The *design* of an ideal speech situation is necessarily implied in the structure of potential speech, since all speech, even of intentional deception, is oriented toward the idea of truth. . . . Insofar as we master the means for the con-

struction of an ideal speech situation, we can conceive the ideas of truth, freedom, and justice, which interpret each other—although of course only as ideas. (1970, p. 372)

Habermas' ideal speech situation is the essential ground of rational discourse, and provides an arena free from domination, in which communicative interaction is open, equal, unconstrained, and which calls into question, through the emancipatory interest, inauthentic or distorted power relations.

The emancipatory interest is both grounded in, and anticipates, the ideal speech situation, and together they constitute the essential elements of a just society, a society premised upon the classical philosophical ideal of the "good life." Thus, the ideal speech situation provides the theoretical anticipation of Habermas' concern with the practical realization of social justice. Derrick Phillips, in his discussion of the relationship between Habermas' ideal speech situation and ideas concerning social justice, argues that "Habermas must be almost completely silent in regard to" articulating "principles of justice that would characterize a just society" (p. 84). Habermas himself argues that "we are quite unable to realize the ideal situation; we can only anticipate it" (*Recent sociology*, p. 120), an admission which runs counter to the synthesis of theory and practice which he advocates in his writings.

Phillips' critique of the ideal speech situation offers an important point of departure for a consideration of the common grounds of agreement which link Habermas with Lyotard. He notes that "although in an ideal speech situation participants are bound only by the power of argument, the ability to argue is also a power. It is difficult to see how *this* power could ever be distributed equally" (p. 85). The equal distribution of power seems a likely end of postmodernism's attempt to transform the idealism of modernism into a realized democratic praxis. In arguing that this necessitates the rejection of modernism, however, postmodern criticism reinforces argument's discriminatory and dualistic tendencies. Beyond those tendencies one can see that both approaches complement each other's concerns and analyses.

For example, like Habermas, Lyotard is concerned with the problem of domination in discourse, and its relationship to legitimation and justice in social praxis. His treatment of language games echoes Sophistic conceptions of discourse in the sense that he argues against the privileging of one discourse at the expense of another, a position which is, in principle, fraught with paradox and potential contradictions. "The question then is whether it is possible to achieve the same level of refinement, if I may call it that, and the same power in several games. And this, without privileging any of them, without saying: This is the good one" (p. 62). Lyotard grounds his thinking in the Sophistic or "pagan" tradition of rhetoric, and asserts that ancient Greek society in the transitional period between Homeric and Platonic culture witnessed a similar approach to symbolizing and conceptualizing social reality.

Lyotard's position suggests that this pagan conception of justice is grounded in Lanham's "plural orchestrations" of rhetorical reality. He sees language as central to the evolution of philosophical thought, and thus argues that justice is situated in the practical reality of linguistic interactions. He envisions a justice situated in a language game of obligation and consequence, one which recognizes that "those who conform the most can be perfectly unjust, and those that conform the least, perfectly just. Both obtain" (p. 65). This situates justice outside of its traditional essentialist ontology, replacing the guiding principle of the existing rule of justice, intent, with another: consequence. For Lyotard an ideal justice is manifest in plurality, in the capacity to move between discourses with a conscious awareness of the unity of their underlying differences. He asks

> Can there be a plurality of justices? Or is the idea of justice the idea of a plurality. That is not the same question. I truly believe that the question we face now is that of a plurality, the idea of a justice that would at the same time be that of a plurality, and it would be a plurality of language games. (p. 95)

Lyotard views the rule of justice as a "rule of divergence," a rule which characterizes the critiques of political judgment presented by the "minority": "Basically minorities are not social ensembles; they are territories of language. Every one of us belongs to several minorities, and what is important, none of them prevails. It is only then that we can say that the society is just. Can there be justices without domination of one game upon the others?" (p. 95).

Lyotard's rhetorical question touches on the issue that is most at stake in the debate between modernism and postmodernism: *judgment*. And it is in terms of judgment that we must reconstruct the conflict between rhetoric and philosophy. Lyotard takes up the positions articulated by the Sophists and the practical philosophy of Aristotle to call into question the legitimacy of the philosophical enterprise in its search for determination in the last instance in the realm of the normative and prescriptive. "There is no knowledge in matters of ethics. And therefore there will be no knowledge in matters of politics. That is also the Sophists' position. And also Aristotle's, who, in matters of ethics and politics, follows the Sophists' problematic completely. In other words, there is no knowledge of practice."[12] It is this position which he explicates in terms of the conflict between narrative and scientific (i.e., *rhetorical and philosophical*) knowledge, and which he brings to bear in this refutation of Habermas.

And in that refutation resides the paradox of postmodernism. While Lyotard attempts to transcend the fundamental dualism of Western thought through postmodernism, he cannot resist the temptation to subscribe to the fundamental duality of argumentative language. "So we are caught between two unacceptable choices: Habermas' defensive position in relation to the old Enlightenment project and Lyotard's Euro-centered celebration of the postmodern collapse," observes Stuart Hall. "To understand the reasons for this oversimplified binary choice is simple enough, if one starts back far enough."[13] In postmodernism we see theory proclaiming the end of theory to achieve the ends of theory: a demand for the democratization of discourse. Yet its demands are cast in the same language of negations and divisions that characterize the modernist enterprise it calls into question. It is evident that both modernism and postmodernism subscribe to argumentative and critical principles of language in making their respective cases: in this sense the difference between the two rests upon different strategies of epistemic justification. Yet, while the strategies are different, the tactic—epistemic justification that assumes that the positions are mutually exclusive—is the same. This is the critical assertion of a postmodern rhetorical theory: *that they can be both the same and yet different at the same time.* And this simple observation provides a vehicle for integrating modern and postmodern perspectives and synthesizing their concerns with emancipation and transformation.

RHETORIC AND NEGATIVISM

Both Lyotard and Habermas perceive a transformation of educational practices as necessary to the achievement of pluralistic and emancipatory discourses, and both recognize the need for change and the strategies necessary for its execution. Habermas writes "that in advanced capitalism changing the structure of the general system of education might possibly be more important for the organization of enlightenment than the ineffectual training of cadres or the building of impotent parties" (*Theory and practice*, pp. 31–32). Lyotard, in *The postmodern condition*, concurs, and notes that the epistemic stance adopted must transcend the traditional divisions which compartmentalize and categorize realms of inquiry.[14] The procedures characteristic of such an epistemic stance have traditionally fallen squarely in the realm of rhetoric, and this art offers the best opportunity for fulfilling the agendas of both modernism and postmodernism, and resolving the differences between them.

One question that a postmodern theory of rhetoric potentially raises is the necessity of criticism and argument, and the possibility of moving beyond them. It questions whether a way of knowing premised upon the legitimacy of differential standards of judgment can be transformed. This premise is an accepted convention of modern and postmodern discourse: the negative judgments of critical analysis. A postmodern rhetorical theory, I believe, offers the possibility of a higher affirmation. And so we are returned to the place that we began, for this is the basis of Zen. D. T. Suzuki explains: "Negativism is sound as method, but the highest truth in an affirmation."[15] A postmodern rhetorical theory might emphasize similarities as a basis for judgment: such an emphasis, while potentially transformative, is nonetheless quite traditional. It evidently informs the rhetoric of the Sophists, whose emphasis on possibility and judgment resurfaces in the rhetorical ideal of life, and again in postmodern rhetoric.

It also emerges in Perelman and Olbrechts-Tyteca's "rule of justice." As a principle of judgment, the rule of justice emphasizes common grounds and qualities as a way of knowing and being. It allows for a recognition of the complementary relationship between different positions, which Lanham suggests is the basis of the rhetorical ideal of life. The rhetorical view teaches that we, "and others—may not only *think* differently, but may *be* differently." The price we pay for this, notes Lanham, "is "religious sublimity, and its reassuring, if breathtaking, unities" (p. 5). The rhetorical ideal of life is consistent with both the rule of justice and the Golden Rule, and emphasizes the finding of similarity in difference as a way of understanding and managing diverse conceptions of reality. It is an important principle for considering the conflict between modernism and postmodernism and its implications for rhetoric because it illustrates how, just as we may *choose* to view them as mutually exclusive and antithetical to one other, we might also choose to see them as *essentially* the same.

Such a choice induces us, like the Zennist, to ask why we need speak of anything as distinct, as having an identity? Postmodernism emerges most forcefully in the "unspeakable." It is an assault on identity that identifies itself, a negation of the negations of the tribe, that like the sound of one hand clapping challenges rhetoricians in old and new ways. It connects us with the past and projects us toward the future, and at the same time denies us any distinct identity at all. If some strands of postmodernism threaten to settle the struggle between identity and difference by doing away with identity, then we need to consider the possibility of having both, the possibility of realizing in symbolic action a transcendence of dualisms. And just as in the Buddhist tradition transcendence arises out of embracing dualism, the rhetorical ideal of life offers the possibility to do the same by persistently pointing to the underlying unity and coherence of human existence. Modernism and postmodernism, like rhetoric and philosophy, exist in relation to each other, and a postmodern rhetoric—if we can indeed speak of one—might be usefully understood as actively non-argumentative discourse.

By this I mean an understanding and experience of language that begins with the assumption that all things are essentially the same, and uses this assumption as a foundation for judgment. It illustrates an application of the rule of justice to the process of judgment, and the emergence of principles of nonviolence in symbolic action: it is thus consistent with the rational demands of modernism and at the same time fulfills the transformative interrogation of power relations anticpated in a number of postmodern theories. It recognizes that which postmodernism privileges most, difference, and also fulfills modernism's demands for rational emancipation. Argumentation is the discourse through which both modernism and postmodernism are sustained: it is essentially the way we speak our world into being. Rejecting argument, however, can only perpetuate the same tendency to privilege one discourse at the expense of another. Actively non-argumentative discourse does not reject argument: it simply represents a choice not to argue.

An actively non-argumentative discourse is conditioned by the rule of justice. It offers the opportunity to explore, in theory, the coherences and complementarities of meaning that might emerge in a transformative and unifying praxis. Such an approach to judgment transforms how we think and how we talk about each other and our world: it is an active rhetorical strategy that emphasizes similarities in order to create common places. It seeks to find a way not to do away with argument, but to provide the possibilities it offers to as many as possible so that the power of argument will be distributed equally. It posits that the realization of an ideal speech situation as the democratization of discourse begins with the belief that such a realization is indeed possible, and this is a leap of faith. The leap is best made possible through an assumed unity of reason and faith, of success and truth.

This was the agenda of the ancient Greek Sophists,[16] is the rhetorical ideal of life, and suggests an important end of a postmodern rhetorical theory. It offers an end of theory which is, in the classical sense of theory—the rapture of *theoria*—an equally viable and potentially transformative contemplation of the reality and possibility of language. It offers a realization of the possibility of *emancipatory plurality*, an awareness of the possibility that all positions and privileges are illusions of negative difference, what Zen practitioners call *maya*, and what Pirsig sees as "ghosts, immortal gods of the modern mythos which appear to us to be real because we are *in* that mythos" (p. 337). To be in that mythos and yet beyond it at the same time is to see in the ghosts of the past the possibilities of the present, and to view the ends of theory from the perspective offered by a "beginner's mind." A postmodern rhetoric raises the possibility of transcending argument by democratizing it, by giving as many as possible access to the mythos. Perhaps it offers an answer to the classic koan, "what is the sound of one hand clapping?" Zen in the art of rhetoric?

From its earliest articulation in the philosophical tradition rhetoric has been understood and practiced almost exclusively in terms of argument and persuasion. While postmodern conceptualizations of rhetoric have helped to transcend these boundaries in theory, the limitations of this understanding become evident when we consider how the belief in the necessity of argument influences intellectual and social praxis. In our educational and economic institutions the primacy of essential knowledge continues to contribute to social fragmentation and alienation, yet we have at our disposal the means for articulating coherent conceptualizations of difference and identity capable of meeting the postmodern challenge. It is the paradoxical two-ness of those means, the double-edged nature of rhetoric, which we will turn to in the next chapter in order to return to a question that has preoccupied the Western mind since classical times, has influenced this "inquiry into coherence," and which prefaces Pirsig's *Zen:* "And what is good, Phaedrus, and what is not good—Need we ask anyone to tell us these things?"

6

COHERENCE

Only a few initiates attain its ultimate goal, finding in the Tea Way the path to the true Self. They become free of concern for the transitoriness of all earthly things; they partake of the eternal; they rediscover nature, because they are in harmony with all living things.

—Horst Hammitzsch,
Zen in the art of the tea ceremony

The epigraph from the Platonic dialogue *Phaedrus* with which Robert Pirsig prefaces his "inquiry into values" confronts us with an issue that has plagued Western culture since the time of the ancient Greeks: the possibility of the teaching of *aretē*, a term which we in modern English translate as "virtue," but which, as H. D. F. Kitto remarks, is more properly translated "excellence."[1] Today, like Plato and Pirsig, we continue to confront the challenge of teaching our students a holistic excellence, one which combines the pragmatic specificity of technical knowledge with the humanistic generality of artistic understanding. Thus, Ernest Boyer's explication of the American experience of higher education calls for a balanced, socially responsible educational experience.[2]

Boyer's concern is not so much with knowledge, but with the attitudes with which knowledge is governed and attenuated. His study, like Alan Bloom's, both implicitly and explicitly suggests that the college experience, while successful in some areas, has not adequately fulfilled this charge. Indeed, Boyer's assertion that American colleges "have been successful in responding to diversity and in meeting the needs of individual students" yet at the same time "much less attentive to the larger, more transcendent issues that give meaning to existence and help students put their own lives in perspective,"[3] sounds suspiciously like Bloom's critique of American higher education. While both are concerned with making the ideals of education real, their concerns are reflected in different analyses of the causes and consequences of the shortcomings of American education. These differences reflect, in its modern guise, the age-old debate between serious and rhetorical views of the world.

Like Bloom, Boyer argues that while we look toward an undergraduate body that can synthesize professional and civic concerns, today's students are torn between material gain and social commitment, between me and we, between the one and the many. Unlike Bloom, however, in response to this situation of uncertainty and equivocation, Boyer envisions not a return to perennialism, but a reconstructive transformation of the undergraduate experience, one that emphasizes language skills, critical thinking, a wholesome respect for knowledge, and a sense of empowerment. This transformative vision is as old as the educational experience itself, as old as the assumptions of knowledge out of which that experience has evolved. It is part of a philosophical problematic which begins with the ancient Greek experiment in the complex self, the warring ideals of social and central selves, the dialectic of philosophical and public discourses. It is a vision that places us squarely in the realm of rhetoric.[4]

Boyer explicitly suggests a return to a rhetorical curriculum, including a senior project equivalent to the declamations of classical and colonial education. But the importance of rhetoric for education today and into the twenty-first century does not end there. A rhetorical education provides students with an understanding of how to live in a constantly changing world in relation to others as well as themselves. It provides a knowledge of the various means of definition available in any social situation, and an understanding of the positionality of human interaction. A rhetorical education not only provides students with the technical knowledge necessary to communicate effectively, but also offers a critical sensibility which facilitates a healthy respect for knowledge and knowing. Most importantly, a rhetorical education gives students an appreciation of the importance of having a voice, and the ability to tolerate the opinions of others. It is these faculties of

empowerment and tolerance that lie at the root of a true democracy. As Lanham points out, the importance of a rhetorical education was that it offered the possibility of individual empowerment as well as the ability to tolerate difference.

Perhaps the most important aspect of Lanham's discussion is
the light it sheds on the assumptive grounds of educational practices. The dominant educational philosophy in Western culture is
essentialism, and yet rhetorical education implicitly calls essentialism into question. Historically, essentialism has dominated
Western notions of knowledge, notions consistently called into
question by the processes of rhetorical inquiry. Thus, in contemporary philosophical and critical circles, rhetoric has resurfaced as
the critical method *par excellence*. Academia offers numerous
examples. In literary studies, deconstruction has indicted the
legitimacy of criticism itself, and in social and political theory
reconstruction has forced an examination of many of the prevailing assumptions of contemporary thought in these areas of
inquiry. Even in law, the most essential of our institutional studies, there is presently a "legitimation crisis" occurring, called
forth by the critical legal studies movement.

These critical perspectives, however, fail to find their way
into the arena of undergraduate education, ostensibly because
our students are not equipped with the tools of inquiry necessary for them to understand and apply them. Yet there is, I
believe, another reason which has to do with the assumptions
and practices to which we, as educators, subscribe. We all view
education as a serious business, and therein lies the dual-pronged
dilemma: education as serious, and education as a business. It is
the seriousness of our assumptions which paralyzes rhetorical
education, and it is the serious premises of intellectual inquiry
which are illustrative of what Martin Carnoy refers to as "colonized knowledge." He argues that education in Western culture
perpetuates inequality and injustice through the legitimation of
hierarchical ontological and epistemological ideologies and systems of interaction.[5] Rhetorical inquiry, even in its most traditional forms, facilitates the breaking down of these systems of
interaction precisely because it places the *responsibility for
knowing with the knower*. In rhetoric, human motive is the substance of human action, and all beings have knowledge of motive.
Referential reality is naught without the human factor to shape it
toward certain ends.

A rhetorical education confronts us with the possibility that the knowledge which we impart to our students and share with each other, the knowledge of which we are often so certain, is self-legitimating, has no essential validity other than that which we give it. It demands that we provide them with the tools to achieve this view of the "true" and "real" on their own, in deference to the authority of essential knowledge. As educators we have a responsibility to our students to help them achieve some level of self-sufficiency, yet we must also persuade them (and ourselves) that there is something more to the educational experience than economic gain. The empirical relationship between economy and education, however, undermines the legitimacy of this persuasive position, as both the historical positioning of rhetoric in the academy and business illustrates. While educators and business leaders emphasize the importance of valuing diversity, adapting to change, and appreciating difference, the rhetorical means that might facilitate these goals remain undermined by a continuing commitment to essentialized conceptions of knowledge, and an educational system that is first and foremost, a business.

RHETORIC AND THE BUSINESS OF EDUCATION

The link between business and education is most clearly seen in essentialism's insistence that objects have value "in and of themselves." In terms of education, essentialism has been the guiding force of Western pedagogical practice since the ancient Greeks, applying the theoretical presuppositions of perennialist idealism to the practical realm of human affairs. Herein lies the basis of the pragmatic materialist position that presently guides the means and ends of educational experience. In terms of business, essentialism provides the assumptive grounds which legitimate materialist interaction. One must assent to the belief that essential valuation exists outside of the realm of human symbolic action, that things exist "in and of themselves," before a system of monetary exchange can function as the basis of human interaction. Yet, as contemporary communication scholars, social theorists, and even physicists convincingly argue, "essential" reality is constructed through language, through human symbolic action. Thus, the legitimacy of economy resides in the assumptions of language which are adhered to by individuals, since material has no value other than that negotiated and defined by consensual agreement.

Essentializing reality dissociates the locus of authority from the human agent and places it within the object (without equal emphasis on the process) of discourse. This dissociation undermines the position that language constructs reality by assuming that reality is referential, out there, existing apart from the human agents who interact within its contexts. This assumption, which is called into question by rhetorical means, provides the ground for the legitimacy of essentialist systems of knowledge, the "serious" realities of economy and its compatriots, science and technology. The praxes of essentialist education support these serious realities, provide the assumptive grounds for a rhetoric of business that asserts an *a priori* legitimacy for economy as the basis of human interaction and exchange. Yet prior to the valuation of material essential for the functioning of economy is the process of language, and at the heart of language there is rhetorical reality. It is within the realm of rhetorical inquiry that one finds the critical tools which bring forth what Habermas has termed a "legitimation crisis," a crisis characterized by the calling into question of previously accepted assumptions and beliefs.[6]

I believe that we do not teach these tools primarily because they have the potential of calling into question the legitimacy of both the educational and economic systems from which we, as educators, derive our own legitimacy. Both education and economy are grounded in rationally determined hierarchical orders, orders which we like to assume are "natural" as opposed to "invented." Ultimately, however, these natural inventions gain their legitimacy on the basis of essentialist justificatory strategies, and as such, can best be interrogated epistemologically, at the assumptive level. In the past, the means for interrogating such strategies were provided only for the few, while the many accepted the representations of reality provided for them by "the best and the brightest." Today, however, many of our academic disciplines and economic organizations are beginning to address the problems of social and psychological fragmentation characteristic of a postmodern condition that undermines both intellectual potential and material productivity. The emphases on cultural diversity and communicative competence in schools and businesses reflect these concerns.

Two of the most pressing issues in educational and professional institutions today are the need for improved communication and a recognition of the importance of appreciating cultural and ethnic diversity.[7] The point at which these two issues converge provides an important direction for rhetorical theory and practice precisely because it offers an opportunity to further explore the extent to which such institutions are socially constructed through consensually determined rules of discourse. What constitutes "effective communication" or "valuing diversity" in business and education is determined by the rules and conventions developed by the individuals interacting within the contexts of these social realms, yet much of the research which explores these areas of inquiry, I believe, is grounded in assumptions which undermine both communicative and cultural cooperation. While the rhetoric of business emerges in calls for improved communication skills and the appreciation of differences, the practical realities of educational and professional institutions mitigate against the achievement of these very objectives.

While many organizations have sought to address the issues of communication, class, gender, and race that are central to the contemporary concern with human difference, few have attempted to explore the underlying assumptions which give rise to the discriminatory attitudes and practices that create the need to improve communication and interaction in the organizational arena. Those attitudes and practices are grounded in the hierarchical structures that define these institutions, and the belief that they are "natural" and not determined by symbolic interaction. The classical approaches to organizations and communication that continue to dominate both theory and practice are grounded in epistemological assumptions that perpetuate the communicative and cultural divisions within organizations and institutions that these approaches are attempting to resolve. A coherent conception of rhetoric offers an alternative perspective for examining the extent to which educational and organizational realities are socially constructed and reflect an understanding of language grounded in the legitimacy of negative differences. Rhetorical coherence, which utilizes an approach to judgment that emphasizes the application of common principles and standards, can be instrumental in facilitating both improved communication and the appreciation of diversity.

Such an approach to judgment has been recognized in the literature in business communication, and its application would seem to be necessary to achieving both improved communication and an appreciation of diversity in both business and education. Mohan Limaye and David Victor's (1991) analysis of research in cross cultural business communication suggests that "new paradigms and redefinition of some concepts to include non-Western worldviews and effectiveness criteria, we think, would greatly strengthen the catholicity and diversity of approaches in this field" (p. 293), and I agree. I think we need to consider also, how some old paradigms of Western knowledge might be useful for expanding the field by suggesting a redefinition of rhetorical inquiry that addresses underlying issues of negative difference that emerge in educational and professional arenas. An examination of contemporary business communication as it relates to issues of valuing diversity suggests that the unexamined justificatory strategies at work in these areas of inquiry perpetuate the very problems of judgment that valuing diversity attempts to address, and that efforts geared toward both improved communication and the appreciation of differences could benefit from a reconceptualization of rhetoric as coherence.

THE RHETORIC OF BUSINESS

The need for effective communication in business environments has become an increasingly important priority. Herta Murphy and Herbert Hildebrandt (1991) observe that "managers and top-level executives of American business, industry and government have repeatedly expressed their concern regarding the need for better communication" (p. 4). They indicate that contemporary business communication is rooted in rhetorical principles, and illustrate extensively throughout *Effective business communication* that the types of communication skills sought by businesses are persuasive and argumentative. While the theoretical concerns of business communication may be diverse, its practical concerns are clearly delineated as pragmatic and utilitarian, and thus rhetorical in the traditional classical and contemporary senses.

Because the essentializing consequences of foundationist and externalist justificatory strategies circumscribes argumentative and persuasive language, they are implicated in the perpetuation and legitimation of judgment based on negative difference. Yet it is these traditional rhetorical skills, communication and criticism, that business leaders seek and business communication scholars emphasize.[8] Communication, as it has been practiced and continues to be practiced in Western culture, is geared toward social control and the maintenance of existing ideological and epistemological structures. Grammar, rhetoric, and logic all represent ways of knowing that define existence in terms of separate and distinct entities, and conceptualize relationships in terms of negative differences. All of these understandings of the word illustrate the privileging of *technē* in discourse, language as a tool for achieving an end, and all are geared toward persuasion and argumentation. These ends of language, which for centuries were considered "natural," are only now being recognized as socially constructed, and that recognition calls for a reconceptualization of rhetoric that has been anticipated by theorists who have called into question existing paradigms of communication and knowledge. Yet this calling into question of existing paradigms itself poses some paradoxical problems, for it too subscribes complicitously to principles of negative differences in judgment. Indeed, some of the research that has been done that explores the relationship between communication and diversity continues to subscribe to assumptions which emphasize essential differences and distinctions.

THE DILEMMA OF DIVERSITY

The importance of valuing diversity has become recognized in both popular and scholarly journals and magazines, and it represents what one writer calls "the New American Dilemma" (Coleman, 1990, p. 2). Both scholars and journalists tend to agree that valuing diversity is not simply an expression of ethical benevolence, but a practical necessity: Lennie Copeland (1988) notes that business leaders "know this is not just a moral or social responsibility, but a competitive advantage. Indeed, some executives and trend analysts consider valuing diversity to be a matter of survival" (p. 38), and Jim Kennedy and Anna Everest (1991) agree when they contend that a "company's success may depend on its ability to compete for tomorrow's multicultural work force. Communication is a key" (p. 50). The relationship between communication and valuing diversity is clear, and just as it is being considered in terms of its practical application, so too are its theoretical implications being explored.[9]

One of the most extensive considerations of this relationship is Marlene Fine's (1991) explication of research directions for multicultural communication. Her analysis focuses on what she describes as "two core processes: (a) resisting privileged discourse, and (b) creating harmonic discourse" (p. 263), concepts which she acknowledges emerge in the works of other scholars, especially postmodern and feminist perspectives. These two concepts correspond with what I have defined as complicity and coherence, and thus Fine's analysis offers an excellent way of illustrating how rhetorical inquiry provides a thread between the two. Fine suggests that research in multicultural communication should be fourfold: it should document different organizational discourses; document discourse that asserts privilege; document discourse that resists privilege; and document multicultural organizational discourse. Her insights on the last of these provide a starting point for my own research agenda. She explains: "Documenting multicultural discourse is the most difficult of the research tasks, and may, in fact, be impossible to do now. I am unaware of any organizations that are truly multicultural, in which no one voice is privileged over any other." The privileging of discourse, Fine suggests, presents an important challenge to communication scholars and practitioners. "Our task, as researchers may be to help create such organizations, so that we have the group harmony that Follett so eloquently describes" (p. 271). Fine explains that Follet's description of "harmonic discourse" is one in which there are "no differences" (p. 266), and one that emphasizes interconnectedness and coherence.

Fine synthesizes feminist and postmodern perspectives as the foundation of multicultural communication because both subscribe to ontologies that accept diversity.[10] She observes that a postmodern perspective "requires multiple discourses and multiple interpretations of reality" (p. 263), and explains that "a feminist perspective sets a research agenda in which human beings are seen as proactive creators of meaning" (p. 267). Postmodernism, she argues, is essentially "nihilistic," and thus must be complemented by a feminist perspective which is essentially "affirmative." Both positions share in common the calling into question of privileged discourses, either patriarchal or modern, and the replacement of those discourses with alternative paradigms. Ultimately, both negate existing epistemologies in favor of these alternatives, and it is in this negation that they fulfill those paradigms at the assumptive level. Here, Fine's position exemplifies a complicitous acceptance of the underlying assumptions of modernist and patriarchal discourses, and thus her emancipatory agenda calls for an justificatory strategy that resolves the problem of negation without rejecting it. Such an approach is found in coherence.

Coherence assumes a unified ground of existence in which divisions are constructs of thought and language. It is, in this sense, completely consistent with both feminist and postmodern perspectives, and offers a fulfillment in praxis of the theoretical principles of both positions. Both feminism and postmodernism, as they are articulated, are grounded in negations: male and female, modern and postmodern, and so forth. These negations are themselves presupposed by basic principles of logical analysis, bivalence being the most prevalent, and while they are eschewed theoretically they are invoked methodologically. Indeed, both feminism and postmodernism assert themselves as distinct fields of inquiry, an assertion that is at its root consistent with the very paradigms they reject. This paradox leads to an approach to language and epistemology that allows for something to be itself and something else at the same time, and which challenges our dominant approaches to inquiry and understanding by positing a holistic ontology. We come close to such an approach both in symbolic and systemic approaches to knowing, but these too are viewed as discrete processes of understanding. The challenge for multicultural communication is finding a way in which similarities can lead to an understanding of the coherence of existence and the inseparability of all phenomena.

I suggested above that we might look to quantum physics as a medium for conceptualizing this challenge, and have maintained throughout these essays that we likewise consider Eastern conceptions of reality for an epistemic stance which resolves the problem of negative difference. Both of these parallel preclassical rhetorical theories, specifically Sophistry, and emerge quite clearly in Lanham's rhetorical ideal of life, which teaches that we can both think and be differently, and that our ability to do so may lead to the enlightened unities of "religious sublimity." It is within such unities that we find an understanding of coherence that allows for the recognition of similarities in difference. While contemporary research in multicultural communication suggests that we need to focus on differences, I wish to contend that we might also consider similarities: just as we look toward non-Western approaches in order to understand the distinctiveness of cultures, we might also look backwards in Western thought to discover that our own traditions offer insights that could help us understand how those cultures are also bound together. In short, because our dominant paradigms emphasize distinctions, I would like to suggest as a direction for future research an explication and understanding of the coherences that transcend those distinctions. This, I believe, is the business of rhetoric.

THE BUSINESS OF RHETORIC

The rhetoric of business, like the rhetoric of academic inquiry, is grounded in methods and practices which reflect essentialist ontological and epistemological assumptions, and thus the inherent hierarchical structures that circumscribe interactions in educational and work environments are grounded in approaches to judgment that legitimize negative differences. The reality of these environments continues to be one in which individuals are judged by distinguishing factors such as rank and position, ability and intelligence, class and classification. One's place in an educational institution or organization is determined by classification of some kind: administrator and faculty member, teacher and student, management and labor, supervisor and worker. It is within the contexts of these divisions that those individuals who find themselves at lower levels often are disempowered by the assumptions and practices of essentialist thought and language.

Ultimately, such disempowerment has a negative impact on both individuals and organizations as a whole, yet no approaches of which I am aware aimed at improving communication or valuing diversity address the significance of essentialism in the social construction of difference. Most existing approaches deal with issues in terms of structural, institutional, or attitudinal barriers, but few emphasize the underlying epistemological assumptions that serve as the foundation to these barriers, nor the extent to which these barriers are socially constructed through communication. At both the linguistic and institutional level difference is defined primarily in negative terms. The dominant theory of communication and knowledge in Western culture remains referential, understanding difference in terms of individual entities that are separate and distinct from one another and that are defined by essential characteristics. This essentialism legitimates the hierarchical structures of educational institutions and businesses and at the same time represents these structures as "natural."

Contemporary approaches to business communication and valuing diversity are grounded in essentialist assumptions, and this is where the rhetoric of business is problematized on two levels. First, in terms of developing communication strategies that facilitate the valuing of diversity, researchers are confronted with what I like to refer to as a "civil liberties dilemma:" if one asserts that everyone deserves access to a particular discourse, how can one integrate even those who assert that some people don't deserve access? This is, of course, the dilemma of post-modernism and the major difficulty faced in generating a multi-cultural communicative praxis. The second emerges in terms of the impact that improved communication skills will have on businesses. Lanham suggests that whenever we speak of rhetoric we are in fact speaking of rhetorics: rhetoric as a *technē*, as persuasion and argumentation, and rhetoric as an *aretē*, as a way of knowing and being. Rhetoric represents a double-edged sword of the word, one which both empowers and disempowers depending upon its conceptualization. The emphasis on persuasion and argumentation in business communication, on *technē* alone, I believe will continue to perpetuate problematic communication and discriminatory practices and attitudes precisely because these approaches to language are grounded in essentialism, and emerge within the existing hierarchical structures of academic and professional institutions as privileged discourses.

Yet those same institutions, by equally emphasizing rhetoric as *aretē*, might also facilitate the type of transformation that will make the type of multicultural communication which Fine envisages a reality. The synthesis of rhetoric as *technē* and *aretē* offers the opportunity to recognize the coherence of symbolic and material realities because it points to the extent to which they are each manifestations of a singular ground of being: this

insight ultimately will lead to a transformation of human interaction through a transcending of negative difference. This could
mean, for both businesses and educational institutions, a paradigmatic shift that will call into question the legitimacy of the hier-
archies inherent within them, both linguistic and material, that
we assume to be "natural." This would mean *the end of such
institutions as we know them*, for the praxis of coherence is ultimately the creation of social realities grounded in an equality of
discourse that transcends the discourse of inequality. Through
an emphasis on rhetoric as coherence we will be able to create
institutions within which all individuals have a voice, and consequently within which no one voice is privileged.

FROM PRIVILEGE TO PARTICIPATION:
THE RHETORIC OF CONTEMPORARY CRITICISM

In contemporary critical studies of language, science, social and
political theory, and law, there has been a significant reassessment of the legitimacy of existing epistemological systems. The
positionality of essentialist knowledge has been called into question by deconstruction, reconstruction, postcritical philosophy,
and constructive argumentation. At the heart of each of these
disciplines is the re-emergence of a rhetorical approach to knowledge that for twenty-five centuries has languished in the shadow
of the word. In language studies, deconstruction has initiated a re-
examination of how texts are situated within various realms of
discourse. The "deconstructive turn" calls for a cross-disciplinary
assessment of meaning which calls into question the positionality of any particular discourse. Christopher Norris writes:
"Deconstruction explores the transformative potential of treating
texts as *undecidedly* situated between 'literature,' 'criticism,'
and 'philosophy.' It generates questions which cannot be resolved
(much less dismissed) within the purely institutional bounds of
any one discipline" (1984, p. 6).

Norris' analysis questions the privileged position held by
philosophical discourse as advanced by essentialist epistemology, suggesting that philosophical texts are "literary." It is
through deconstructive analysis that philosophy "comes up
against the problems implicit in its own status as written or textual discourse" (p. 7), and is undermined by the dialectical posi-

tion (here meant in the methodological sense) of the inadequacy of language. Philosophy's status as a privileged discourse is seen as indefensible in light of its own dialectically derived and directed assumptive grounds. Philosophy has historically gained its privileged position from essentialist assumptions, assumptions which construct a clear and distinct separation between the realms of belief and knowledge, or rhetoric and philosophy. Yet contemporary philosophers of science point to the fact that belief both undergirds and informs knowing. Michael Polanyi writes in *Personal knowledge*: "The learner, like the discoverer, must first believe before he can know. But while the problem solver's foreknowledge expresses confidence in himself, the intimations followed by the learner are based predominantly on his confidence in others, and this is an acceptance of authority" (1962, p. 208).

This acceptance of authority is the basis of our system of education, and it provides educators with a privileged position, one which we rarely call into question. This would seem to be the logical end of the skills which we believe are essential for our learners, critical skills, the ability to question. Yet we draw the line, for our knowledge provides us with a privileged position within the socioeconomic system, and the authority which it affords us provides the ground for the legitimacy of our vocation. The implications for our students, for ourselves, for the polity, are powerful. Bernstein bears witness to the point in the realm of social and political theory: "But we do know—or ought to know—that if we fail to attempt the power of critique—if we do not seek an in-depth understanding of existing forms of social and political reality; if we are unwilling to engage in the type of argumentation required for evaluating the conflict of interpretations; if we do not strive to realize the conditions required for practical discourse—then we surely will become less than fully human" (1982, p. 367). The teaching of rhetorical inquiry is a prerequisite to any realization of practical discourse as a productive social praxis.

To teach a critical sensibility that calls our own authority into question may not sound rational, might be considered by many to be unthinkable, but as Argüelles argues in *The Mayan factor*, "the moment has come when the rationally unthinkable may be the only solution remaining in order to allow safe passage beyond the treacherous onslaught of nuclear militarism and environmental poisoning which now threatens the existence of this planet" (1987, p. 15). Rational essentialism dismisses Argüelles' "transformative vision" immediately, yet that dismissal is based upon a self-legitimizing system of knowledge, a system of knowledge that has brought us to the very point that Argüelles believes we can move beyond. Thus, we must unleash a critical sensibility that calls into question the legitimacy of existing social and political institutions and arrangements, including the very system that offers the keys to that sensibility. As Allan Bloom has illustrated quite convincingly in *The closing of the American mind*, while ostensibly we purport to teach our students open-mindedness and respect for difference and diversity, our efforts have in actuality fostered individuals who believe that they are open-minded and respecting of difference, but who have failed to achieve a social praxis reflective of those beliefs.

Yet Bloom's critique falls short of an assessment of the assumptive grounds of our educational practices. In fact, Bloom suggests an even greater acceptance of the essentialist presuppositions of Western pedagogical practices, and argues that students need to be further educated along these lines. His belief that the "Great Books" will rectify the problems of American education is a position that, within the context of contemporary critical theory, deconstructs itself. He ultimately defends the same system of knowledge which he indicts, and although recognizing the privileged position of educators, fails to address adequately the assumptive grounds of the privileged position of rational essentialism. Perhaps Carnoy's explication of colonized knowledge explains the nature of Bloom's dilemma.

> We argue that even though changes in educational philosophy had influence on educational reform, in practice the philosophies that were most influential were those that were consistent with economic and social changes taking place at the same time. We argue that the way a society organizes formal schooling is a function of the economic and social hierarchy and cannot be separated from it. We contend that the schools function to reinforce the social relations in production, and that no school reform can be separated from the effect it will have on the hierarchical relations in the society. (p. 343)

We have in essence created a self-legitimating, self-protective discourse of privilege through the privileged discourse of essentialism. The students who leave our universities, whom we bemoan as being bent on materialism and without social conscience, have learned their lessons well. This is the endpoint of essentialist education, the social construction of privileged discourses, of realities presupposed by the legitimacy of negative difference, and the violation of the rule of justice, the like application of like criteria to like objects or beings. It is this notion of privileged discourses which has been a catalyst for much contemporary critical thought. Nowhere is this more evident than in critical legal studies and its assessment of the role of the institution of law in society. The critique advanced by critical legal theorists echoes that advanced by the Sophist Thrasymachus in Plato's *Republic*: that "Justice" is the interest of the stronger, and law a system predicated upon the defense of privilege.

Within the context of this position, democracy becomes dependent upon seemingly radical transformation. As Unger observes: "To imagine and establish a state that had more truly creased to be a hostage to a faction, in a society that had more truly rid itself of a background scheme of inadequately vulnerable division and hierarchy, we might need to change every aspect of the existing institutional order. The transformed arrangements might then suggest a revision of the democratic ideal with which we had begun" (1986, p. 30). The bringing about of such a transformation can be accomplished through an emphasis on rhetorical inquiry. As evidenced by the first democracy of Western civilization, the Athenian *polis*, democracy is socially constructed by a situation in which "everyone" has a voice, in which "all" are empowered.[11]

To a certain extent, we are told, this was the case with the ancient Greeks, and we have yet to see a similar situation since. It was, of course, the rhetoricians who believed that individuals should have the capacity to speak for themselves, and the philosophers who advanced the belief in privileged discourse. Yet today the philosophers have turned to rhetoric for an answer to the question "what is good and what is not good?" And the rhetoricians respond that only the knower can know that he knows nothing, that all knowledge is contingent upon position, and position is the beginning of privilege. Rhetoric exposes the positionality of privileged discourses, so calls them into question, creates debate, empowers. That is the basis of democracy, and democracy is the business of rhetoric.

THE STRUCTURE OF SCIENTIFIC REVOLUTIONS

John Dewey in *Democracy and education* calls for a reconstructionist educational philosophy to empower learners, to close the gap which he perceived to exist between the individual and society, between the knower and the known. His "logic of inquiry" was an early manifestation of what Wayne Booth calls a "rhetoric of inquiry." Booth's insights are illustrative of the transformation of knowledge that will resituate essentialism within the greater universe of epistemic discourse as one of many positions, as part of a much broader realm of knowledge than we have yet been able, or willing, to realize. The seeds for this transformation are there, germinating in so many of our academic disciplines, waiting to be planted in the fertile minds of tomorrow. What we await is the equivalent of an Einsteinian scientific revolution, a new paradigm of knowledge, a reordering of our universe of discourse, enriched by a leap of imagination, and perhaps premised upon a leap of faith.

As educators we defend the privileges which our belief in an essentialist system of knowledge affords us. It is time to reconsider the implication of that belief if we are truly concerned with the integrity of education for the future. The teaching of *aretē*, of excellence, must begin at home. Such a beginning will inevitably occur within the context of a clash of opinions, a dialogue of debate, will invoke many available means of persuasion, and will facilitate a rhetoric of coherence. I conclude with Thomas Kuhn:

> At the start a new candidate for paradigm may have few supporters, and on occasions the supporters' motives may be suspect. Nevertheless, if they are competent, they will improve it, explore its possibilities, and what it would be like to belong to the community guided by it. And as that goes on, if the paradigm is one destined to win its fight, the number and strength of the persuasive arguments in its favor will increase. (1970, p. 159)

This paradigm, the possibilities of which we shall explore in the final chapter, is characterized by a way of teaching and learning that draws on Eastern and Western, ancient and modern philosophies and practices. It pursues a way of knowing and being that, like Zen, recognizes in the word a double-edged sword, and sees in the forms of rhetoric the potentials of disciplined dialogue and coherent compassion, and the possibility of finding in the Way of the word a symbolic equivalent to the martial arts.

7

HONORING THE FORM

> This state, in which nothing definite is thought,
> planned, striven for, desired or expected, which aims
> at no particular directions and yet knows itself capable
> alike of the possible and the impossible, so unswerving
> is its power—this state, which is at bottom purpose-
> less and egoless, was called by the Master truly "spiri-
> tual."
>
> —Eugen Herrigel, *Zen in the art of archery*

Thomas Kuhn's description of the transformations that accompany a paradigm shift offers a somewhat paradoxical challenge for
the field of rhetoric, for if we accept the traditional view of
rhetoric as an art of persuasion, a paradigm shift might suggest
the development of a understanding of rhetoric incommensurate
with the prevailing conceptualization.[1] Like Lao Tzu we might be
forced to conclude that "[g]ood words are not persuasive; persuasive words are not good. He who knows has no wide learning; he
who has wide learning does not know";[2] we might equate persuasion with violence, persuading against persuasion and arguing
against argument; we might attempt to broaden the scope of
rhetoric beyond persuasion, recapturing its aesthetic dimensions
and exploring its narrative and dramatic possibilities. All of these
are viable and important options, and suggest a reclaiming as
well as a reframing of rhetoric, but something more is needed,
something that goes beyond the rational and the material, and
engages our most coherent sensibility: the spiritual.

I believe that we need to reflect on the ethos which we bring
to rhetorical scholarship and pedagogy, and the alternative possibilities that a spiritual sensibility might bring to our under-

standing and practice of rhetoric.[3] While we recognize the ethical implications of discourse, the teaching of rhetoric still focuses on argumentative and persuasive paradigms that posit an amoral essentialism in which positions are aligned in relation to rational foundations legitimized by intellectual inquiry. Thus, "the force of the stronger argument" is still determined by reference to an essentialist conceptualization of knowledge, and rhetoric is seen as the first line of defense in the clash and conflict of opinions that constitutes public discourse. While this perspective is, I believe, indispensable in a world in which words are used as weapons, it cannot alone create discursive spaces in which difference is tolerated and diversity valued. Something is missing from our discipline, and I believe that it is time that we offered a persuasive argument for that which, for too long, has been missing from rhetoric: love.

This is, of course, not a new idea. Socrates spoke of it in the *Phaedrus*, and Wayne Brockriede reiterated it in the aftermath of the turbulent 1960s.[4] The Socratic lover argues that dialectical interaction constitutes the love relationship between two knowers that culminates in the true love of wisdom and the understanding of essential reality that it engenders. While well-intentioned, the historical consequences of this perspective have exposed its narcissism, its elitism, and its tendency to suppress and deride difference. In rethinking rhetoric we need to find a way to acknowledge and accept those aspects of dialectical inquiry that contribute to self-reflection and the appreciation of Otherness, and at the same time cultivate an awareness of those aspects that perpetuate symbolic violence.

Brockriede illustrates the need for just such an awareness when he notes that the "epistemic truth of a transaction may be determined unilaterally by the argument of forcible rape or the argument of deceptive seduction, or it may be achieved bilaterally through the free assent of lovers."[5] Brockriede's rendering of argument exemplifies, like the Socratic conception, an "ideal speech situation," one in which the power that accompanies argumentative inquiry does not enter the equation. But power does fit into the equation, and has profound implications that we cannot ignore. As Jerry Farber (1990) explains:

As teachers, we tend to grab power, to exercise it far beyond what is necessary; we get hung up on it, we misuse it. Too often we keep for ourselves the power that we should be helping others to develop (the way literature typically has been taught provides an excellent example of this). And all of this power tripping, unfortunately, fits into larger patterns of social oppression. (p. 140)

Farber recommends love as a remedy for the "disease of power" with which teachers, like other human beings, are afflicted.

Farber dialogues in this essay with Mary Rose O'Reilly, whose own struggles in the classroom around issues of love and power caused her to find Farber's position "disquieting." Farber quotes her contention that "nothing messes up my classroom faster than love," and concludes his own essay with the response: "If love messes up your classroom, O'Reilly, then you're probably going to have to learn to live with the mess" (pp. 140, 141). This is the question that confronts contemporary rhetorical scholars and teachers: can we can live with the mess that love creates? The question becomes even more difficult to answer when, as O'Reilly notes, issues of power come into play. Can we create spaces, pedagogical and discursive, in which love and power can coexist without enmity, can facilitate emancipatory action, can realize the ideal of a rhetorical praxis that from Socrates to Brockriede has somehow escaped us? I believe that we can, and that a revolution in rhetoric, a paradigmatic shift from dialectic to dialogue, will bring us there.

Perhaps "shift" is not the appropriate term, for as Bohm and Peat indicate, this reading of Kuhn's theory gives the impression that "a fundamental dislocation of ideas must always accompany a scientific revolution." Instead, Bohm and Peat suggest that "the whole issue is far more subtle than that of opposing two incommensurable paradigms. Indeed, there is a potential for a continuously creative approach in science so that any abrupt discontinuity of ideas is not inevitable" (p. 27). In re-examining the structure of scientific revolutions, they illustrate how the "tacit infrastructure of scientific thought," its epistemic norms and assumptions, perpetuate the intellectual fragmentation and breakdown of inquiry that characterize scientific revolutions. Their analysis suggests "there is nothing inherent in science which makes such breaks in communication and fragmentation inevitable. Indeed, whenever, fragmentation and failures in communication arise, this clearly indicates that a kind of dialogue

should be established" (p. 240). As indicated above, Bohm and
Peat see dialogue as an alternative to argumentative forms of discourse: here I wish to suggest that it also provides the basis for a
scientific revolution in rhetoric.

In light of the weight of this phrase, let me address each of
its terms in turn. The notion of science that I shall draw on
emerges in B. Alan Wallace's *Choosing reality.* Wallace suggests
that the principles of Buddhism and those of science are both
commensurate and coherent, and ultimately seek the same goals.
Science, he suggests, can learn from Buddhism, not simply epistemologically but ethically as well. Both contemporary physics
and classical Buddhism come to many of the same conclusions in
regard to what "essential reality" is. But Buddhism also offers a
sense of self and Other that physics, despite its intellectual understanding of the inseparability of the two, has yet to appreciate.
Buddhism achieves its understanding through the four "divine
states," which "are of enormous benefit in attenuating a broad
range of mental distortions and in providing protection from
external hindrances" (p. 176). The four steps offer a disciplined
and compassionate way of inquiring into the nature of the "real."

The first of these four steps is *loving-kindness;* the second is
compassion; the third is *sympathetic joy;* and the fourth is *equanimity.* These are the basis of the Buddhist way, and offer for
Wallace a vehicle for realizing the ideals of scientific inquiry:

> In all of human experience two types of aspiration bear an
> integrity and nobility beyond all others: the yearning for
> understanding and spiritual awakening, and the longing to
> be of service to others, to dispel suffering and bring joy.
> Modern science, as developed and expressed by the greatest of its exponents, is motivated by both these aspirations.
> Intellectually and practically it stands, at its best, as a model
> of freedom of inquiry and ingenuity; and if put into active
> balance with religion and philosophy, it may well serve us
> long into the future. (p. 179)

Wallace notes that these aspiration are central to Buddhism as
well, and suggests an integration of science and Buddhism that
exemplifies a "spirit of awakening" that "acknowledges the interdependence of self and others and the kinship of all that lives, and
is the sole motivation with which one can attain the full spiritual

awakening of a Buddha" (p. 179). Wallace is calling for a state of mind that recognizes the coherence of phenomena and persons, a state of mind that in our time is nothing short of revolutionary.

And for this term, our second, I turn to Freire's recognition that "true revolutionaries must perceive the revolution, because of its creative and liberating nature, as an act of love" (p. 77). Like Wallace, Freire sees love as a key sensibility in the realization of political liberation, and like Bohm and Peat suggests that dialogue can facilitate social and intellectual transformation. Indeed, Freire recognizes the inseparability of love and dialogue in any emancipatory project: "The naming of the world, which is an act of creation and re-creation, is not possible if it is not infused with love. Love is at the same time the foundation of dialogue and dialogue itself" (pp. 77–78). Freire, whose life work has been committed to the questioning of power and the creation of empowerment, reminds us that power and love not only commensurable, but are powerfully implicated in our "naming of the world," in our practice of rhetoric.

For this, our last term, I turn to Thomas Farrell: "And now to rhetoric. For all of the varying senses of rhetoric we might employ, the coherence of discursive form in rhetoric seems to derive from a tension between the exterior and interiorized domains of influence."[6] Between the extremes of idealism and realism, between foundationism and conventionalism, there is the middle way of rhetoric, the path to dialogue which when envisioned as a vehicle for coherence, offers the possibility of an actively non-argumentative approach to discourse. That possibility emerges most powerfully not in the simple rejection of argument, but in a rethinking of the assumptions at work in how we teach and use it.

THE WAY OF THE WARRIOR:
RECONTRUCTING RHETORIC AS COHERENCE

Rhetoric, when defined in essentialist terms, can be viewed as an oppressive and dehumanizing way of teaching language skills, one which undermines students' creative abilities and energies. This I believe is why many composition teachers and students hold rhetoric to be suspect: it reflects a language "tainted" by the quality of a society in which power and empowerment are constrained by predefined coordinates. Teaching rhetoric is sometimes equated with teaching the very system of language which Adrienne Rich and many other scholars call into question. Nonetheless, rhetoric offers much more, and in viewing it as *aretē* we can understand its capacity to empower, not only in terms of self-reflection but also in terms of creating spaces in which we can transcend our differences and empathize fully with one another. Rhetoric offers an opportunity to bring the two halves of the human experience together by emphasizing both serious and rhetorical ideals of life, and understanding how they complement each other.

Like a double-edged sword, language can empower or disempower depending upon who is using it, and the purposes for which it is used. Students and teachers of rhetoric have always been acutely aware of this double-edged aspect of language, and have often sought ways to balance this and other related concerns encountered in the composition classroom. As a teacher of writing I have often reflected upon the fact that the very language which provides students access to the privileged discourse of academic communication at one and the same time denies them access to that discourse. I have tried to address this paradox by synthesizing seemingly disparate views of rhetoric into a coherent pedagogical strategy that helps students understand the importance of forms and mannerisms in terms of their participation in social and intellectual discourse, yet that also teaches students a respect for the word and each other that offers an awareness of how language can be used to move beyond discourses of domination.

In short, I teach students argument so that they do not need to argue, and emphasize those elements of language that facilitate identification as well as division. I begin by defining rhetoric as the symbolic equivalent of the martial arts, emphasizing the importance of discipline, commitment, and the practice of basics as a prerequisite to mastery. I believe that a technical mastery of language offers individuals the opportunity to achieve two complementary objectives: discipline and compassion. An approach to language training which synthesize these objectives provides essential strategies for imparting to students the possibility of empowerment through the power of words.

Pirsig's *Zen* emphasizes this approach by focusing on the concepts of quality and caring and their influence on judgment and action. Pirsig's text considers rhetoric in both its classical and contemporary senses, and explores the relationship between "classical thinking," which deals with scientific or technical inquiry, and "romantic thinking," which deals with artistic or creative activities. The complementary relationship between these two ways of thinking provides the context for his discussions of quality, rhetoric, and power in the composition classroom. Here I wish to explore how *Zen* facilitates both discipline, in terms of the technical and formal aspects of rhetoric, and compassion, in terms of how it provides a point of reference for students to connect with experiences that reflect some deeply humanistic—and perhaps even spiritual—elements of the study and practice of rhetoric. Through an examination of two student essays written about Pirsig's text I will show how *Zen* offers students and teachers an excellent vehicle for exploring the rhetorical ideal of life.

Pirsig's journey is physical, psychological, and spiritual, and is grounded as much in ways of thinking as it is in ways of speaking and writing. Ultimately, Pirsig's contribution to the canon of Western literature and criticism is, like Aristotle's, squarely grounded in the realm of rhetoric. N. Katherine Hayles writes in her essay "Drawn to the web": "Contrary to what the 'Author's Note' implies, rhetoric is not peripheral to this enterprise; it is at its center" (1984). In his author's note Pirsig relates that *Zen* "is based on actual occurrences," but goes on to state that "much has been changed for rhetorical purposes" (p. 1). Here, Pirsig seemingly uses the term to imply a strictly literary meaning, and in fact, one can quite easily substitute the term "stylistic" for "rhetorical." But *Zen* is about much more than style. Pirsig's web stretches out in several directions, touching upon his past, his present, and his future, and we are drawn into and often snared by the layers of meaning, experience and knowledge that he strings so subtly together. Rhetoric is for Pirsig much more than an art of persuasion: it is an art of coherence, one which influences how we make and remake our worlds in much the same way that Pirsig has made and remade his own.

Just as Pirsig suggests that the book is not about "rhetoric," he also notes that it is not about "Zen" (or motorcycle maintenance for that matter!) either. But clearly, Pirsig's concern with moving beyond dichotomous thinking reflects the underlying principles of Zen Buddhism, the perception of the fundamental nature of reality that is beyond all dualism. Hayles suggests that, while Pirsig does not himself achieve this level of enlightened synthesis in the book as a whole, *Zen* "gives powerful expression to the harmonies that the cosmic web can suggest": harmonies that produce peace of mind, and which echo the Buddhist path to enlightenment (p. 83). Other writers have also commented on this aspect of *Zen*. Tim Crusius notes that the "value of *Zen*, the primary reason it deserves praise, is the 'co-operation of form and content.'" Crusius sees the book as both a vehicle for the synthesis of form and content , and for the synthesis of self and environment: "The content of *Zen*, to risk a convenient oversimplification, has importance 'outside' the book, insofar as it induces us to reassesses ourselves and our world; the form of the book is an 'inside' function, a value found primarily when we consider the thing in itself."[7]

I wish to further explore this complementary function of *Zen* in terms of two pieces of student writing. The first is an assessment exam taken by an entering freshman to determine his placement in a writing program. The essay was scored by two readers based on global or holistic considerations, as well as ideas and arguments, rhetorical (in this case organizational) control, and language control. Each of these elements is ranked on a score from one to six, one being the lowest and six the highest, and scores of five and six result in the student being exempted from the university's freshman writing requirement. This essay scored fives and sixes when originally assessed, and continued to score in the upper level when used for standardizing in subsequent readings. The second essay was written by a student in a writing practicum who performed a section from *Zen* in class, and whose experience illustrates how the book indeed "induces us to reassess ourselves and our world."

These essays illustrate how *Zen* establishes a space in which, at least these two students, were able to integrate formal and substantive rhetorical strategies for writing, as well as opportunities to connect with issues that are grounded in the more creative and intuitive experience of encountering a text. I believe that these two approaches to the teaching and learning of writing parallel what Pirsig refers to as "classical" and "romantic" modes of understanding. "A classical understanding sees the world primarily as underlying form itself. A romantic understanding sees it primarily in terms of immediate appearance" writes Pirsig. We associate classical thinking with traditional views of rhetoric as a strategy of persuasion or argument, and romantic thinking in terms of rhetoric as a phenomenological or experiential process. Classical thought "proceeds by reason and by laws," while romantic thinking is "primarily inspirational, imaginative, creative, intuitive" (p. 61). The best writing brings these two together, for they are ultimately implicated in each other.

Central to Pirsig's discussion of classical and romantic thinking is the concept of "Quality." Indeed, *Zen* cuts directly to the core of what is perhaps the most difficult issue with which teachers of writing are often confronted: *How do we judge the quality of good writing?* Certainly, we use "classical" principles of rhetoric (or principles of classical rhetoric if you will), but we also look for something more, some sense of how writing illustrates a personal encounter that goes beyond the formal and substantive elements of argumentation. We look for thinking which is both intelligent and expressive, which illustrates analytical abilities and empathic abilities as well, which is both "classical" and "romantic."

In some instances we look for the "classical" traces of what Jack Meiland in *College thinking* calls "dialectical argument." The "dialectical argumentative essay," he writes, "exhibits a back and forth movement from argument to objection to reply to objection to reply, and so on. The dialectical argumentative paper does not stop short after giving an argument. It tests various positions on a question to see which is stronger. It does not necessarily try to persuade or prove: it inquires" (1981, p. 68). In other instances we look for the "romantic" traces of self-knowledge and dialogic understanding emphasized by expressivists, that help students achieve, in Donald Stewart's words, "a new level of self discovery," and the emergence of "an authentic voice."[8] Both of these traces, dialectical and dialogical, exemplify the two-ness of rhetoric, and each of these samples of student writing illustrate the dialogical possibilities that emerge even in dialectical inquiry.

THE QUALITY OF INQUIRY:
REFLECTIONS OF A DIALECTICAL RHETORIC

These possibilities are realized in the first essay I want to consider, an essay written by a first-year student titled "Progress."

The essay illustrates what one community of writing teachers consistently agrees constitutes "quality" thinking and writing. The essay was written in response to the following prompt: "There is always disagreement within a society about what constitutes 'progress.' Frequently, progress in one aspect of life may mean deterioration in another. For example, industrialization has led to increased convenience, but also to environmental damage. Computerization has led to an information explosion but also to intrusion into privacy. Clearly, different generations and social groups hold unlike definitions of progress. In fact, one of the challenges of the next decade will be to evaluate the results of 'progress' in the last century and chart new directions of technical, scientific, educational and social development that will be in keeping with emerging views of what is to constitute 'progress' in the next century."

The prompt asks students to "consider the issues related to 'progress.' Establish and explain your own point of view about progress; discuss what values should be pursued in the name of progress and what the desired results of progress should be. Take into consideration that others may have different views of what constitutes progress, and show how society might balance conflicting views in working toward the future." They are then admonished to remember that their work "will be read and judged by college writing instructors who expect to find that you have thought critically about the complexities of the subject, have developed your ideas and supported them with evidence or examples, and have organized and presented your essay clearly."

In response to these directions, the student composed the following essay in a period of fifty minutes:

It is said that one man's meat is another man's poison. Similarly, what may seem like progress to one man may appear as a step backward for another. While it is true that mankind has always striven for progress and development, it is also true that historically, the human race has demonstrated a pronounced inability to agree on exactly what progress is. This disagreement is manifested every twenty years as a "generation gap": the nation's youth rises up and tries to correct the "errors" of their parents. But the differences in opinion transcend mere generations; it is a split that runs directly through society. Fundamentally, the difference is not one of philosophy; it is a basic difference in ways of thinking.

In *Zen and the art of motorcycle maintenance*, Robert Pirsig describes the two ways of thought as "Classical thought" and "Romantic thought." The Classical thinker, says Pirsig, sees the world in terms of underlying form and function. A Classicist sees and understands the way various parts and elements interact to produce a net result. When a Classical thinker sees a factory, he perceives the way the different divisions interact to create a positive net result. Those who work the factories serve a vital function to improve the quality of life for all of us. This, to a Classicist, is progress.

On the other hand, a Romantic views the world in terms of surface appearance and "essence." He understands the way things look, seem, and feel. When a Romantic looks at a factory, he sees an ugly brick-and-steel monster obstructing a beautiful view and polluting the air with dark black smoke. He sees the workers as robots performing unintelligible acts for uncaring machines, slaves to a mechanical master. This, to a Romantic, is anything but progress.

To a Classicist, the Romantic is a throwback and a parasite. To a Romantic, the Classicist is an egghead and a "square." To a Classicist, the Romantic is superficial and out of touch with reality. To a Romantic, the Classicist has lost touch with what's really important.

A Classicist sees a computer as a useful tool in aiding man's life. A Romantic sees it as an alien, incomprehensible menace. A Classicist sees poetry or music as a waste of time, or, at best, an amusing diversion. A Romantic sees it as the magic that makes life worth living.

Who is right? The answer, of course, is neither—and both. What both Classicists and Romantics fail to understand is that either view, taken alone, is insufficient. True progress can only arise from a unification of these two methods of thought.

There is, in fact, a need for "Classical" progress—but the goal of such progress has got to be the enhancement of the quality of life in a Romantic way. A factory may provide an essential part of the economy, but if it makes people miserable, it can hardly be called progress. But the solution is not to tear the factory down; nor is it to paint the factory in bright, cheerful colors in a half-hearted attempt to "paste on" quality. Quality—in Pirsig's sense of the word—can not be added on after the fact. It must be an inherent part of the structure.

If progress is designed to enhance the quality of life, then we have no choice but to seek a definition of quality. Quality, in Pirsig's view, is the event that occurs at the interaction of subject and object. When the "doer" really cares about what he is doing, there is Quality. When the motorcycle repairman is so intent on his task that the line between man and machine blurs, there is Quality.

This is the heart of true progress. Building for the sake of building is ridiculous if the building does not enhance people's lives. Making life faster, easier, more convenient and longer is pointless if people don't have something to live for. It is the union of Classicism and Romanticism that leads to true progress, and to true Quality. Until we learn to see what we do and make as a reflection of ourselves, true progress is impossible.

The essay exemplifies both the back-and-forth movement which characterizes dialectical argumentation and the clarity valued by "serious" critics of rhetoric, but the most impressive aspect of the essay is its synthesis of classical and romantic thinking into a position which considers the complementary relationship between them. The notion of synthesis is a central theme of *Zen*, and its importance is—at least for this writer—both understood and addressed. The vehicle for this synthesis is quality, and it is in the discussion of quality that Pirsig grounds his consideration of rhetoric.

An important part of Pirsig's journey in *Zen* is his search for quality, a search which he pursues with a vengeance. He explains to his composition students that quality could not be defined, but that they knew what it was. To prove his point he selects two samples of student writing and asks the students to rate them: twenty-eight of thirty students agree that one piece exhibited a higher degree of "quality" than the other. "'Whatever it is,' he said, 'that caused the overwhelming majority to raise their hands for the second one is what I mean by Quality. So *you* know what it is'" (p. 185), Pirsig recalls. He then connects rhetoric with quality by illustrating how the forms and figures of classical rhetoric represent a *technē*, a set of strategies that can be used to achieve this thing called "quality" that cannot be defined. "What had started out as a heresy from traditional rhetoric," he explains, "turned into a beautiful introduction to it" (p. 186). Actually, Pirsig's connection between rhetoric and quality is not a heresy from traditional rhetoric, but a fulfillment of it in terms of its classical origins.

Pirsig's quality represents a synthesis of forms, a movement beyond divisions: this is clearly what the student suggests when he notes that quality results "when the line between man and machine blurs," and this same consideration can be extended to the lines which divides human beings from each other. Rhetoric as a *technē* is thus directly connected to rhetoric as an *aretē*, as a vehicle for the achievement of "excellence." The essay, I would argue, emphasizes the best of what rhetorical *technē* has to offer: an understanding of the complementary nature of opposites which "is achieved in part by teaching the willingness and the wit to argue both or for that matter all sides, never avoiding the advocacy of the very side the dogmatics would suppress."⁹ The next essay that I wish to consider emphasizes rhetoric's *aretē*, its capacity to facilitate a dialogic connection between self and Other that complements the dialectical emphasis we see above.

TO FACE THE SELF AND DIE:
ZEN IN DIALOGIC RHETORIC

I had assigned a performance from *Zen* in my writing practicum as a way to teach critical reading. Most of the students read aloud from the text, without thinking about what they were reading, although some had taken the time to memorize the texts and performed quite well. One student, however, engaged the text dialogically when she encountered her own experiences within it. The young woman, a science major, gave a performance which so clearly illustrated the self-reflexive power of critical reading and its facilitation of both self-knowledge and self-expression, that I asked her to write an essay on her experience. What follows are several excerpts from her essay.

I began to cry so hard I could not remember the lines nor read my notes. I was not nervous to speak in front of these people but I was not speaking, I was opening up to them. I grew up as an "army brat." I went to 3 different middle schools and 2 different high schools. I have never lived in the same state for more than 3 years. In the years I have made many friends but they never knew the real me. It was very hard to get close to people and have to move away and leave my friends. I put up walls and throughout the years the walls have gotten thicker and stronger. Once in a while I will let the walls down for a very special friend but I can honestly say that this has only happened twice.

So now here I am in front of 20 classmates speaking about anxiety and letting my walls crumble little by little. My crying became uncontrollable. I had to sit down and let someone go ahead of me while I composed myself. I of course made a joke and made everyone laugh, which I do so well. This helped me to relax and put me at ease and (I hope) made everyone think that it was no big deal to me. It was my turn again—so [I] stood up and began one more time. This time I thought I would read the section following the lines on anxiety; this section was about boredom. I felt that I could calm down and get my act together before I had to read the section about anxiety.

I stumbled over the first few lines on boredom but I managed to pull through. I finished the section and took a deep breath and started one more time on the tough part. As I read my lips quivered (the first sign that I was going to cry). My eyes filled up and my mind went blank. I could not see anything nor think straight. I thought to myself, "these words I am reading are not Pirsig's they are mine. There were written by me!!" I had felt this way for so long about anxiety but I could never really put the right words together to express myself!

Actually I had never had any reason to even say these words to anyone—that would mean I would have to open up! So for the first time, I saw all my feelings down on paper. I have never been able to express my feelings this way and now in front of my English class I had to. I have built the walls so strong that I almost forgot I was hiding something or someone—*ME*!! I fooled everyone so well that I fooled myself, but now I was being reminded that I was not the secure and confident [person] I usually pretended to be. I continued to cry and I remember the professor saying that it was okay. I looked up at him and said that these words were so true and real to me:

> anxiety, which leads to over motivation, can lead to all kinds of errors of excessive fussiness. You fix things that don't need fixing and chase after imaginary ailments. You jump to wild conclusions and build all kinds of errors into the machine because of your own nervousness. These errors, when made, tend to confirm your original underestimation of yourself. This leads to more errors, which lead to more underestimations.

The above passage was so hard to read. I felt the whole time, "Yes, this is how I feel!" I was so upset and frustrated by those words. I couldn't believe that my thoughts were put into words, and the first time I really felt the meaning of the passage was when I read those lines in my English class.

I continued to read even though I cried the entire time. With every line I was telling my classmates about me and how I feel about myself. This was probably the hardest thing I have ever had to do. I have learned a lot about myself after that day. I feel like I can open up to people a lot more and I am not as hard on myself. I am even handling my problem with anxieties and I feel more relaxed and at ease.

From what I can remember, the narrative is a very accurate description of her experience with the exception of one detail: I remember asking if she wanted to stop.

"No," she said, "I'm going to make it through this."

This student's essay was one of the best that she had written during the semester. It illustrates an important aspect of what Lanham sees as a central aspect of the two-ness of rhetoric: the struggle between the social and central selves. "The Western self has from the beginning been composed of a shifting and perpetually uneasy combination of *homo rhetoricus* and *homo seriosus*, of a social self and a central self," he explains. "It is their business to contend for supremacy. To *settle* the struggle would be to end the Greek experiment in a complex self" (p. 6). As I read this student's experience, her "central" or serious self, knows that the words are Pirsig's and not her own: yet her "social" or rhetorical self identifies so strongly with the language that the difference between her reality and Pirsig's is blurred. She experiences the tension between the internal and external that Farrell connects with rhetorical coherence, becomes one with the text, and exhibits what I believe is a dialogic understanding of self and Other.

Indeed, both of these essays exemplify such an understanding, though in different yet complementary ways. The first illustrates how an understanding of interrelatedness can be arrived at through dialectical inquiry, through the application of very traditional terms of rhetorical argument. The second illustrates how rhetoric can facilitate identification and consubstantiality,[10] and how the "curative or healing rationales of therapeutic rhetoric attempt to unify the self."[11] Each essay on its own interrogates the necessity of duality and questions the need for separation that so powerfully defines how we think, how we feel, and how we speak the world into being. Taken together they illustrate the transformative possibilities of an understanding of rhetoric that recognizes the coherence of language, life, and method, that understands the inseparability of division and identification, that celebrates both the dialectical and the dialogical, and sees even in conflict the possibility of cooperation.

RHETORIC AS A MARTIAL ART: TOWARD A DIALOGIC COHERENCE

This connection between conflict and cooperation returns us to the martial arts. As Shigeru Egami explains in *The heart of karate-do*, the "essence of the art is mutual cooperation. This is the ultimate in Karate-do." The popular view of the martial arts is that they are used aggressively, that their emphasis on self-defense is secondary to their offensive capabilities. As a set of techniques, this may well be true: but as an art, this is far from the case. Egami continues: "The relevance of this to karate training and practice is that they are in reality ways of pursuing and exploring the essence of being human. . . . To know yourself, to know your opponent, to understand the relationship between the two: these are the true objectives of training" (1976, p. 14).

Training in rhetoric, like training in the martial arts, can teach self protection as well as a sense of self that promotes harmony and peace through understanding and empathy.

Such an approach to the teaching of rhetoric does not, however, simply reject argument: indeed, a rhetoric of dialogic coherence cultivates argument and persuasion in the same way the martial arts cultivate self-defense. The issue, in my mind, is not so much what we teach as how we teach it. Whether preclassical, classical, modern, or postmodern, rhetoric offers a way—the Way of the word—that can help us realize the enlightened ideal of the "good life," with which we in the West have been preoccupied since the birth of reason. By honoring its *many* forms we will initiate an inquiry into coherence capable of interrogating, and perhaps transforming, the dualisms and divisions that have contributed to the symbolic and social fragmentation that we today encounter. What could be more traditional, more in line with Aristotle's observation that "if it is a disgrace to a man when he cannot defend himself in a bodily way, it would be odd not to think him disgraced when he cannot defend himself with reason [in a speech]"?[12] Indeed, what could be more revolutionary in an age when form has become so insistently associated with the terror of reason, has become the object of postmodern scorn and poststructuralist deconstruction, than to honor the form?

I am here in agreement with Charles Johnson, who argues in favor of the discipline of "formal virtuosity" and at the same time recognizes that form is never "neutral" by indicating how the concept emerges in the arts of self-defense: "In the traditional, Asian martial arts, we say of a student after he has brilliantly executed a kata, or prearranged set of fighting moves, or done them *con brio*, that he has 'honored the form.'" Johnson explains that, while the form retains its sameness, it also evolves over time in the personal encounters of each individual: the form exhibits both permanence *and* change. "These forms predate the student in many cases by two or three centuries, have been executed over and over in Asia, America, and European countries, and by thousands of practitioners, old and young, Occidental and Oriental," explains Johnson. "Each student is obliged to respect his predecessors, the spirit or meaning of each form, and, he one day realizes, he must interpret the ancient form in terms of the strengths and limitation of his own body." Johnson explains that the form represents an ideal that the student realizes only after constant repetition and practice: "During rare moments, the student will lose himself in the form," will become one with it, and in even rarer moments, will be performed by it.[13]

That this approach to form parallels traditional notions of rhetoric, with their doctrines of imitation and translation, is readily apparent. What it not apparent, however, is the difference between the sensibility that is created in the *dojo*, and that which is created in the classroom. The dojo is a sacred space. Often incorrectly translated as "school," the dojo is literally "a place for causing, predicting, or observing transformations that occur from or while following the pathway."[14] It is a space that is, in many ways, similar to the traditional Western essentialist classroom: the teacher is at the center of what occurs here. But that is often where the similarity ends. The *dojo* is defined by ritual and respect, and these forms and practices are followed precisely because the teacher offers instruction in a Way that the student must eventually make her own, one which promises betterment and empowerment if sincerely honored. This is a metaphor that, I believe, can facilitate a transformation of rhetorical inquiry and pedagogy that integrates the best of what our ancient tradition offers with the concerns with power and empowerment that circumscribe contemporary theory and practice.

The best of what our tradition offers is the recognition that rhetoric is deeply implicated in democracy, and plays an important role in defining and determining the political possibilities of human existence. The vision of rhetoric that I offer has implications that go far beyond the classroom and is, I believe, one that is sorely needed today, in a time when our "present international legal and political systems are overwhelmed by processes which are beyond determination of the 'truth,' who is right and who is wrong," as Arnold Mindell suggests. Mindell's concept of "deep democracy" is an integrative and coherent approach to addressing social and individual fragmentation that draws on both ancient and modern ways of knowing to synthesize transpersonal and pragmatic goals.[15] He concludes *The leader as martial artist* with the following challenge and insight:

> There is no succeeding or failing with deep democracy. It knows neither winning nor losing, neither inside nor out, neither Yin nor Yang, but is deeper and more fundamental. Its focus is upon the swirling cycles that create the whole-

ness we call the world. Some hope that this focus will emerge in the figure of a new elder who has been missing in our global tribe. Others experience such focus as their own capacity to love, which appreciates and facilitates all the elements of change. (p. 160)

Because I am less confident of negation as method, I would complement Minnel's insights, in the spirit of Zen, with the affirmation that there is *both* succeeding *and* failing, winning *and* losing, inside *and* out, Yin *and* Yang in the deepest democracy. I am confident, however, that it will be warriors of the word—leaders, teachers, and others—who will bring that which lies within that depth to the surface. Still, we will do well to recognize, in the teachings of one of the world's greatest martial artists, the sense of uncertainty characteristic of Zen: "There is no fixed teaching," explains Bruce Lee. "All I can provide is an appropriate medicine for a particular ailment."[16]

Following Lee, I shall like the ancient philosopher Plato, connect rhetoric to medicine, though not to deny their likenesses, but instead to suggest that the two are implicated in each other. Rhetoric may, today, be just the medicine needed by an unhealthy polity, though I am not sure that we can be content, as Plato was, with a rhetoric that is limited in its range or focus. Instead, I offer a rhetoric that reminds us that the classical and the romantic, the serious and the rhetorical, the dialectical and the dialogic, discipline and compassion, can and must coexist if we are to share with each other our knowledges and experiences, to share ourselves without fear and with a sense of empowerment that only language can provide. By theorizing rhetoric in light of dialogic coherence, we can reclaim the emancipatory promises of language that emerged, albeit imperfectly, in the depths of an ancient democracy. By teaching rhetoric using the metaphor of the martial arts, we will facilitate a way of looking at the world that combines discipline and compassion, that allows for both debate and discussion, and that recognizes Zen in the art of rhetoric.

NOTES

INTRODUCTION

1. Richard Lanham in *The motives of eloquence* explains rhetoric's relationship to traditional Western conceptions of the word: "The rhetorical view thus stands fundamentally opposed to the West's bad conscience about language, revels in what Roland Barthes (in 'Science vs. Literature') has called 'the Eros of Language'" (p. 5).

2. Chögyam Trungpa offers the following characterization of the Eastern view of reality in *Cutting through spiritual materialism:* "Then what can we say about mind or reality? Since there is no one to perceive a mind or reality, the notion of existence in terms of 'things' and 'form' is delusory; there is no reality, no perceiver of reality, and no thoughts derived from perception of reality" (p. 196).

3. Quoted in Helmut Brinker's, *Zen in the art of painting.* Brinker prefaces his quotation with a reference to the claims of Zen masters that the teachings are transmitted not through verbal communication, but through direct experience: "It is for this reason that the Zen masters never tire of reiterating that, in the last resort, Zen is neither teachable nor transmittable; and in this light, concepts such as 'teaching, transference, transplantation' are to be seen as less than satisfactory attempts at designating a process which cannot really be grasped conceptually or intellectually" (p. 5).

4. According to Geoffrey Parrinder's *World religions,* Buddhism, as it is called in the West, is known in Asia alternately as *Buddha-Dhamma,* which roughly translates as "'the eternal truth' of the Awakened One" and *Buddha-sasana,* "the way of life, or discipline of the Awakened One, the Buddha," (p. 262). Buddha is the epithet best known in the West for the sixth century B.C.E. Indian prince Gotama Siddhattha, who achieved enlightenment after six years of spiritual discipline. Also known by the names Sakyamuni and Tathagata, Gotama Buddha is said to have given up the promise of an inherited earthly kingdom in order to find some solution to the problems of human exis-

tence and suffering. After exploring the various religious practices and doctrines of his time, he chose meditation as his way, "and after a night of spiritual struggle, all the evil factors which, in the Buddhist view, tie men to this imperfect, mortal existence were overcome, and he became the Awakened, the Buddha, and entered a transcendental, eternal realm of being" (p. 264). Over the next twenty-five centuries the Buddha's teaching spread throughout Asia and the rest of the world, producing countless sects and schools within the two major divisions of the tradition, the *Hinayana* or "Little" or "Lesser" Method, Way or Vehicle, and the *Mahayana* or "Great" or "Greater" Method or Vehicle, in which Zen is included. Tibetan Buddhists claim a third *yana*, the Vajrayana, which is viewed as a continuation of the other two vehicles. For overviews of the history and cultural significance of Buddhism, see Daisaku Ikeda's *Buddhism the first millennium*, Richard A. Gard's *Buddhism*, Walpola Rahula's *What the Buddha taught*, or Heinrich Dumoulin and John C. Maraldo's *Buddhism in the modern world*. For a discussion of Tibetan Buddhism, see any of Chögyam Trungpa's writings.

5. Zen was introduced to the West by abbot Soyen Shaku in 1893 at the World's Parliament of Religions in Chicago. A transcript of his presentation is contained in *The dawn of religious pluralism: Voices from the World's Parliament of Religions, 1893*. For accounts of the introduction of Zen to the West see Ernst Benz's "Buddhist influences outside Asia" in Dumoulin and Maraldo, or chapter seven of Perle Besserman and Manfred Steger's *Crazy clouds: Zen radicals, rebels and reformers*.

6. The irony of Zen's rejection of language can be seen in the juxtaposition of section 21 of the *Diamond Sutra*, "Words cannot express Truth, That which Words Express is not Truth," and the phrase "Thus I have heard," which begins this and many other Buddhist sutras.

7. Thomas Merton concurs in *Zen and the birds of appetite:* "The language used by Zen is therefore in some sense an antilanguage, and the 'logic' is a radical reversal of philosophical logic" (p. 48).

8. Suzuki explains the role of language in relation to Zen: "First, Zen verbalism is quite characteristic of Zen, though it is so completely differentiated from the philosophy of linguistics or dialectics that it may not be correct to apply the term 'verbalism' to Zen at all. . . . But Zen verbalism has its own features, which violate all the rules of the science of linguistics. In Zen, experience and expression are one. Zen verbalism expresses the most concrete experience" (p. 6).

9. "Sila," *Being here: Poetry 1977–1980.*

10. The phrase is taken from Chögyam Trungpa's book, *Journey without goal*, which offers an understanding of the word as Way from the perspective of Vajrayana Buddhism: "At the level of speech, there is much more movement, much more shiftiness and dancelike quality than in our experience of the body. The vajra mandala of speech refers to the mandala of letters, which are traditionally seen as symbols and seed syllables. Relating to the mandala of letters does not mean being literate, or being an educated person. Instead it is the notion of seeing the world in terms of letters: A-B-C-D. The phenomenal world actually spells itself out in letters and even sentences that we read, or experience" (p. 73).

11. There is an impressive amount of scholarship in the field of communication that explores similarities and differences between Western and Eastern conceptualizations of rhetoric and communication from various perspectives. Perhaps the seminal work in communication is Robert Oliver's *Communication and culture in ancient India and China*, which has had an important influence on research in the field. The "Asian challenge," as Mary Garrett describes it, has impacted almost every area of the field, from organizational and performance studies, to rhetorical theory and criticism. Research in this area has explored relationships between Western and Chinese, East Indian, and Japanese approaches to communication, as well as examining indigenous cultural influences on the shaping of communicative interaction within the cultures themselves. For examples of research on Chinese rhetoric and communication, see Guo-Ming Chen and Jensen Chung, "The impact of Confucianism on organizational communication"; Mary Garrett, "*Pathos* reconsidered from the perspective of classical Chinese rhetorics," "Wit, power, and oppositional groups: A case study of 'pure talk,'" and "Classical Chinese conceptions of argumentation and persuasion"; J. Vernon Jensen, "Rhetorical emphases of Taoism," and "Values and practices in Asian argumentation"; Xing Lu and David A. Frank, "On the study of ancient Chinese Rhetoric/Bain"; Robert Scott, "Dialectical tensions of speaking and silence"; June Ock Yum, "The impact of Confucianism on interpersonal relationships and communication patterns in East Asia." For research relating to East Indian culture, see Robert Allen Bode, *Mohandas Karamchand Gandhi's rhetorical theory: Implications for communication ethics*; A. Cheree Carlson, "Gandhi and the comic frame: 'Ad bellum purificandum'"; Anjani Gandal and Craig Hosterman's "Toward an examination of the rhetoric of ancient India"; William J. Starosta and Anju G. Chaudhary, "'I can wait 40 or 400 years': Gandhian *Satyagraha* West and East"; William Kirkwood, "Shiva's dance at sundown: Implications of Indian aesthetics for poetics and rhetoric," "Truthfulness as a standard for speech in ancient India," or "The turtle spoke, the donkey brayed: Fables about

speech and silence in the *Panchatantra."* For research relating to Japanese culture, see William R. Cupach and T. Imahori, "Managing social predicaments created by others: A comparison of Japanese and American facework"; Richard Fiordo, "Debate, pedagogy, and the Japanese RAM"; Judith Hamera, "Silence that reflects: Butoh, *Ma* and a crosscultural gaze"; Satoshi Ishii, *"Hyaku-nin Isshu* (Single poems by a hundred poets): A Japanese text-performance tradition"; Donald W. Klopf, "Japanese communication practices: Recent comparative research"; Leslie Di Mare, "Ma and Japan"; John L. Morrison, "The absence of a rhetorical tradition in Japanese culture"; Gordon Nakagawa, "'What are we doing here with all these Japanese?': Subject-constitution and strategies of discursive closure represented in stories of Japanese American internment"; Roichi Okabe, "The impact of Western rhetoric on the East: The case of Japan"; Andrew R. Smith, "Mishima's *Seppuku* speech: A critical-cultural analysis" and "Seeing through a mask's confession"; Lea P. Stewart, William B. Gudykunst, Stella Ting-Toomey, and Tsukasa Nishida, "The effects of decision-making on openness and satisfaction within Japanese organizations." For recent essays that draw connections between Zen and Western communication practices, see Doreen Geddes' "Using Zen principles in interpersonal communication," or Jean Brown's "Zen: The Eastern counterpart of cynicism."

12. I advance and develop this argument in *The rhetoric of racism,* suggesting that a rhetorical conception of coherence provides a viable strategy for addressing and moving beyond the dualistic theories and practices of contemporary race relations.

13. In addition to those included in this book there are others that bear mentioning, for example Brendan Kehoe's *Zen and the art of the Internet,* Jennifer Machiorlatti's "Zen and the art of the documentary: Resolving the attachment of self to subject," and Ed Parker's *The Zen of kenpo.*

14. David Tukey suggests that we re-examine "the rhetorically familiar" and examine "the rhetorically unfamiliar," such as "the rhetoric of Zen masters" (p. 71). Reflecting concerns similar to mine, Tukey notes that "spiritual writings can be read to discover what they have to say about words and rhetoric; Lao Tze's *Tao te Ching,* is an often used text in this regard, especially Chapter 1, and part of the Buddhist 'eightfold path' includes Right Speech. But there is more that rhetoric can gain from these texts" (p. 72).

15. Robert Branham uses this phrase as the subtitle of his textbook on academic debate. Branham examines different cultural perspectives on debate, and draws an explicit connection between the practice and the martial art aikido: "Some of the Asian martial arts, such as

aikido, offer unusual advice on how one might deal with an attack or thrust from an opponent. In Western style boxing, one might dodge, deflect, or simply absorb the adversary's blow. In other martial arts, however, the adversary's own power is used against him or her. Instead of meeting the blow, the expert will use the adversary's own momentum in the attack to carry him or her off-balance" (p. 117). Branham uses aikido as an analogy to the traditional rhetorical tactic of using an opponent's words against him or her, and I will extend the analogy to suggest that one should use argument, as one would use a martial art: only as a last resort.

16. In Kirk and Raven, *The pre-Socratic philosophers*, p. 296.

17. *Zen*, p. 342.

CHAPTER 1. TO GRASP THE WORDS AND DIE

1. An earlier version of this chapter, entitled "To grasp the words and die: Power, empowerment and Zen in the art of rhetoric," was originally presented at the 1990 University of Iowa Conference on narrative in the Human Sciences.

2. *The ideals of the samurai: Writings of Japanese warriors*, p. 127.

3. In *Methods of rhetorical criticism*, Bernard L. Brock and Robert Scott write that "the primary purposes of rhetorical criticism are to describe, to interpret, and to evaluate. These purposes tend to merge into one another. One purpose prepares for the next; the one that follows reflects back on the one that has been explicated" (1982, p. 19).

4. "Criticism in the Jungle," p. 6. While Gates is profoundly aware of the relationship between rhetoric and race in Western culture, he is also suspicious of charges of essentialism, and thus his comments on the relationship between ethnocentrism and logocentrism should not be seen as entirely consistent with the position I have taken here and elsewhere.

5. Referring to Memmi by way of a footnote, Crapanzano offers this explanation of the complicity of racial interaction: "Although racist and other essentialist categories—when the exist—enter the rhetoric of domination and subordination in hierarchical societies, they are not as freely manipulated by the dominant, the possessors of power, status, and wealth, as is popularly thought. . . . To be dominant in a system is not to dominate the system. Both the dominant and the dominated are equally caught in it" (pp. 20–21).

6. Foundationism and externalism represent two of the three dominant epistemological strategies in Western thought. Keith Lehrer explains in *Theory of knowledge* the assumptions of justification at work in each. Foundationism assumes "that some beliefs, basic beliefs, are completely justified in themselves and constitute the foundation for the justification of everything else" (p. 39). "The central tenet of externalism is that some relationship to the external world accounting for the truth of our belief suffices to convert true belief to knowledge without our having any idea of that relationship" (p. 153). Lehrer supports the third approach to epistemology, coherentism, in his works, arguing that "complete justification is a matter of coherence within a system of things a person accepts, which is a subjective fact about the knower but with some features adapted from the foundation theorist and the externalist. From the former, we shall take the insight that some beliefs are justified without being conclusions of argumentation and, from the latter, we shall incorporate the idea that a system yielding coherence may contain correct representations of how our beliefs are connected to reality" (p. 15). Lehrer's coherentism, I believe, offers a "middle way" between the extremes of idealism and realism, and provides a viable justificatory strategy for critiques of foundationism and externalism pursued by oppositional critics whose positions are advanced as "anti-essentialist." It also reflects the epistemic stance at work in what I refer to here and elsewhere as "rhetorical coherence," which extends the internalist concerns of philosophical coherence to the realm of discursive interaction.

7. Terry makes the observation in his essay "The negative impact on white values." In *Impacts of racism on white Americans*, p. 120

8. St. Aubryn discusses the fallacy of special pleading in the chapter entitled "Prejudice" in *The art of argument*: "To use an argument when it supports our preconceptions and reject it in another context when it fails to do so is known as 'special pleading'" (p. 40). St. Aubryn uses the specific example of racial prejudice to exemplify the inconsistencies and absurdities that arise when special pleading is used to justify privilege gained by applying principles to others differently than they are applied to oneself.

9. See *The new rhetoric: A treatise on argumentation*, p. 218.

10. See *Wholeness and the implicate order*, pp. 1–2, xi.

11. See Bohm's *Noetic Sciences Review* essay "On dialogue," p. 18.

12. *The rhetoric of Aristotle*, p. 7.

13. Bohm offers an interesting insight into this problem in his discussion of dialogue groups, in which there are no "leaders."

14. Jerry Farber makes this observation in *The student as nigger*, p. 14.

15. Susan Miller's analysis of the teaching of composition in American universities based on Harvard's "dual curriculum in English" lends support to this notion. "Composition is clearly a site for the 'low,' in all its senses. As an intrinsic portion of the new American educational system, composition shared in the same tendencies to institutionalize 'pure' systems that characterized the entire nineteenth century. Its organized inclusion in the new curriculum was an example of enclosing formerly 'undiscoursed' or domestic societal functions in new, rigid definitions of them as established practices, a movement that has been described in many studies by Michel Foucault. Asylums, hospitals, schools, barracks, prisons, insurance and finance houses—and among these, the quickly prominent new discipline of English—arose in the late nineteenth century to assure the maintenance of bourgeois reason" (pp. 53–54).

16. The Phaedrus that survives as Pirsig, Geoffrey Galt Harpman explains, is "a master of rhetoric's devices, including the device by which he appears as a speaker within his own text, addressing the reader, projecting himself as a character. . . . Sanity and survival in *Zen*, and elsewhere, can be purchased only through a full participation in the totality of language, its marks of mortality as well as its intimations of immortality" (1988, pp. 80–81).

17. The reference here to is Lanham's positioning of the "rhetorical ideal of life" in contrast to those "serious" views of knowledge, for instance idealism and realism, when they are characterized by foundationist assumptions.

18. Georges Poulet, "Criticism and the experience of interiority," p. 42, emphasis mine.

19. See *Knowledge and human interests*.

20. See chapter 2 of Freire's *Pedagogy of the oppressed*. The paradox that the student encounters in her reading of Freire is his own dialectical depiction of the oppressiveness of the banking concept and the need for its rejection by those committed to emancipatory action: "Those truly committed to liberation must reject the banking concept in its entirety, adopting instead a concept of men as conscious beings, and consciousness intent upon the world" (p. 66). The paradox again emerges in Freire's argument in favor of dialogue as an alternative to "'depositing' ideals in another," and it is this paradox with which I am concerned primarily in this and the next two chapters.

21. The reference here is again to Lanham's "rhetorical ideal," in which he translates Aristotle's *Rhetoric* 1357a as "We think . . . about those things that offer alternative possibilities" (p. 2).

22. Vernant explains in "Greek tragedy: Problems of interpretation": "The Sophists, as you know, invented what are called the *dissoilogoi*. The idea is that on any question tragedy considers, on any human problem, it is possible to compose two strictly contradictory arguments. Discourse implies polarity. There is not yet any Aristotelian logic because, for the Sophists, one discourse is as good as the other. The discourses are not mutually exclusive. If I take up one from the right I cannot take the one from the left. This is no longer Hesiod, where you had both at the same time. Now they are mutually exclusive, but you still cannot choose just one. Such are the *dissoi logoi*. There is a polarity in every problem of human life. And later, with the great movement of classical philosophy, there will be truth and error, and with truth and error, with true discourse and false discourse, we see the triumph of philosophy but the end of tragedy" (p. 289). For alternative interpretations of the Sophistic *dissoi-logoi*, especially the notion that "one discourse is as good as the other," see Kerferd's *The Sophistic movement* or Schiappa's *Protagoras and logos*.

23. Vernant, p. 289.

24. See Habermas' "Towards a theory of communicative competence."

25. Sharon Crowley echoes this sentiment in her analysis of the debate between traditional and ideological critics in contemporary rhetoric when she notes that "[a]ll criticisms are exclusive of someone, somewhere. This means that ideological criticisms are inevitably exclusionary as well. Ideological critics must remember that their acknowledgment of partiality does not guarantee that their criticism will be inclusive" (p. 463). The same, I submit, holds true for radical pedagogues and critics as well.

26. My thoughts here parallel those of the Marxist film critic Hans Magnus Enzenberger, who argues that there "is no such thing as unmanipulated writing, filming or broadcasting. The question is therefore not whether the media are manipulated, but who manipulates them. A revolutionary plan should not require the manipulators to disappear; on the contrary, it must make everyone a manipulator" (p. 104).

27. From "The Way to the Way," in *Zen antics: 100 stories of enlightenment*, translated and edited by Thomas Cleary.

28. "Reinventing invention," p. 472.

CHAPTER 2. BEGINNER'S MIND

1. An earlier version of this chapter appeared as "New Beginnings: Rhetoric, race and the reopening of *the American Mind*" in the 1989 *Michigan Association of Speech Communication Journal*.

2. Bloom's educational philosophy is best described as "perennialism," a position that combines the essentializing tendencies of both realism and idealism. George F. Kneller explains: "Against the progressive emphasis on change and novelty, perennialists call for allegiance to absolute principles. Despite momentous social upheaval, permanence, they say, is more real than change. It is also more desirable as an ideal. In a world of increasing precariousness and uncertainty nothing can be more beneficial than steadfastness of educational purpose and stability in educational behavior" (p. 42). Kneller notes that perennialism's "philosophical foundations are embedded in classical realism," and characterizes its approach as "the 'Great Books' Theory" (p. 45).

3. Almost fifty years before Bloom's critique of American education, Mortimer Adler offered a similar critique in which he articulated the essentialist epistemic assumptions of perennialism. George Kneller explains Adler's position in the following manner: "Knowledge, too, is everywhere the same. If it were not, learned men could never agree on anything. Opinion, of course, is different. Here men may disagree. (But when they do agree, opinion becomes knowledge). Admittedly, the acquisition of knowledge is not easy and some children are apt to resist it" (1971, p. 43).

4. In his analysis of Richard Rorty's "postfoundationist" critique of philosophy, Ernest Sosa observes the following: "The foundation is thus always provided by assertions with direct authority. The superstructure is built by argument or inference on that foundation. This is outright foundationism, even if what provides authority at the foundation is not the taking of the given but the approval of society, and even if what permits the erection of the superstructure is social legislation." He further goes on to argue against Rorty that "if traditional foundationalism were refuted by the charge of confusing causation (mirroring Nature) with justification, conventionalist foundationalism would seem equally well refuted by a charge of confusing convention (direct social approval) with justification" (p. 93). As Janet Horne (1989, p. 256) argues, "Rorty rejects epistemology altogether," but this reading of Rorty points to a paradox that confronts theorists and critics offering "postfoundationist" perspectives. Such perspectives are grounded in epistemic assumptions that, if not interrogated, can lead to the same essentializing consequences of foundationism. Indeed, many of these positions, like

Rorty's, anticipate a coherentist conception of knowledge. As Rorty claims in *Philosophy and the mirror of nature,* "nothing counts as justification unless by reference to what we already accept, and . . . there is no way to get outside our beliefs and our language so as to find some test other than coherence" (p. 178). Rorty's substitution of conventionalism for foundationism, however, maintains the oppositional tendencies of the latter, thus reifying the essentialist assumptions of foundational philosophy. I believe that Sosa's critique of Rorty can be applied to the critiques of essentialism I discuss in this and the next chapter, and I am extending his analysis to suggest that conventionalism is a type of externalist justification that can potentially result in the substitution of one form of essentialism for another.

5. Bloom's position is directly at odds with research on symbolic or modern racism, which posits that traditional forms of racism have been replaced by more subtle anti-black feelings characterized by, as Robert Entman (1990) explains, "a general emotional hostility toward blacks," by "resistance to the political demands of blacks," and by "a belief that racism is dead and that racial discrimination no longer inhibits black achievement" (pp. 332–33). The most extensive work on symbolic racism has been done by Teun van Dijk, whose *Communicating racism* offers an examination of the linguistic strategies characteristic of symbolic racism. Symbolic racism is not without its critics. The most sustained critique has been advanced by group-conflict theorists such as Lawrence Bobo (1988), and cultural critics such as Thomas Fitzgerald (1992), who argues that van Dijk in particular "invokes the nebulous notion of 'symbolic racism' when he finds insufficient support for *actual* racism" (p. 117).

6. Hirschorn quotes Bloom's position in an interview that reveals his conception of relativism as one reflecting nihilistic and anti-intellectual tendencies. "I still think the issue is this profound relativism, where most people in universities don't believe in anything" (p. A22).

7. This is one of the most common critiques of perennialism, as Kneller explains: "Perennialists may be accused of fostering an 'aristocracy of intellect' and unreasonably restricting their teaching to the classical tradition of the Great Books. They fail to appreciate that, although many children lack the particular intellectual gifts perennialism emphasizes, they nevertheless become good citizens and productive workers. To subject them to the same sort of rigorous academic training as that given to students of university caliber is to ignore this difference and perhaps injure their personal growth" (p. 46).

8. For an excellent explication of the debate between rhetoric and philosophy see Samuel Ijselling's *Rhetoric and philosophy in conflict: An historic survey.*

9. This is the role that Michel Meyer gives to rhetoric, a role that suggests its potentially coherent properties: "When seen as based on the use of questioning, rhetoric ceases to be a 'weak' form of reasoning. This view transcends the classical opposition between the rhetoric of figures (or literary rhetoric) and the rhetoric of conflict (or argumentation, legal or not)" (pp. 155–56.)

10. For a recent and diverse selection of essays that illustrates the continuing existence of racism from both quantitative and qualitative perspectives, see *Race in America: The struggle for equality*. For a similar treatment written at the time of Bloom's analysis, see Bowser and Hunt's *Impacts of racism on white Americans*.

11. One example that indicates Bloom's failure to consider or provide empirical evidence when it is clearly called for is the following: "There is now a large black presence in major universities, frequently equivalent to their proportion in the general population. But they have, by and large, proved indigestible. Most keep to themselves. White students act as though their relations with black students were just as immediate and unself-conscious as with others (including Orientals). But although the words are right, the music is off-key" (p. 91).

12. See above, chapter 1, p. 24.

13. *Elite discourse and racism*, p. 98. For Bloom's specific observations on affirmative action, see page 96 of *The closing of the American mind*. Doris Y. Wilkinson's (1991) review of Bloom's book, points to the lack of substantive evidence provided for claims of black intellectual inferiority when she argues that "the claim by neoconservative critics that degrees granted to Afro-American and white students from first-rate private colleges and leading research universities are not equal warrants careful documentation" (p. 552).

14. The problematic nature of race relations goes beyond its symbolic dimensions, however, and even on college and university campuses has often escalated to violence. As Robert Carter (1993) explains: "In the 1980s, and increasingly since 1984, we have been faced with continual incidents of violence and confrontation—Howard Beach, Bensonhurst, the Citadel, Brown, Dartmouth, the University of Michigan, and the University of Massachusetts are the most publicized, but there are thousands of others. Indeed, there are almost daily newspaper reports of fights or hostile encounters having their genesis in racial antagonisms" (p. 83).

15. Bloom's past experiences with African-Americans have not been particularly positive. As Maureen Taylor observes: "Many of the references are to Bloom's experiences at Cornell, where he taught during

the 1969 student takeover. This incident appears to have had a profound effect on Bloom that pervades his writings" (1988, p. 1136). Perhaps it was this extremely emotional experience that colored Bloom's views on race relations in the university, but he also presents other arguments against feminism and contemporary literary criticism that seem more informed, if one chooses to draw such an essentialist distinction, by emotion than by reason.

16. Doris Wilkinson summarizes the justificatory strategies at work in Bloom's argument in terms of its contrasting of foundationist and reliablist assumptions: "Bloom asserts that the integrity of the university and academic freedom has been severely damaged by campus tensions and escalating demands for rapid and innovative changes. He especially disapproves of earlier protests by Afro-American students and the arguments of those who have exposed sexism in the organizational culture of the university—i.e. the system of tenure and promotion and the subject matter of courses" (p. 551).

17. Hook's review, "*The closing of the American mind*: An intellectual best seller revisited" appeared in the *American Scholar*.

18. Foster's reading of Dewey's theory, in my opinion, leans toward a coherentist conceptualization of inquiry: She concludes her review of Bloom's book in the following manner. "In sum, the foregoing is an argument that scientific reasoning and logic are applicable to philosophy and to the social studies as they are to chemistry and biology. The scientific reasoning and logic advocated in this reconstruction of philosophy is not culture bound; neither does it renounce moral judgment. But is it not that of Plato's ultimate reality, changeless and unalterable, or that of Kant's a priori conceptions that arise outside of experience. Logic, to Dewey . . . is a clarified and systemic formulation of procedures of thinking that will permit the deliberate reorganization of experience. Conceptions, theories, systems of thought are always open to development through use. They are tools. The test of their validity resides in their capacity to accomplish the predicted result, as shown in the consequences of their use" (p. 265).

19. Crapanzano suggests that the critical consideration of racism can mask its epistemological grounds: "Racism is, of course, one of the most blatant and potentially evil forms of essentialist thought, but often its critical consideration masks other classifications that have the same epistemological roots and permit the same social and psychological tyranny. When we isolate racism we risk the perpetuation of the *status quo* by letting one weasel category substitute for another" (p. 20).

20. See, for example, Jeff Smith's essay on comparisons between Bloom's book and Mike Rose's *Lives on the boundary*. Smith explains

that "*Closing* and *Lives* are worth considering together if only because they mark two poles in the present education debates—two sets of arguments and assumptions that those in our field generally, I think, feel they must choose between. Indeed, the books are superficially so at odds that they would seem to have little to say to each other. But in fact, comparing them is illuminating in several surprising ways. Each book was inspired by its writer's personal experience with students; each works from that experience toward a systemic critique of American higher education. The points of contact between those critiques tell us some important things about how the education debate is shaped by perceptions of the university's failures, and why that debate is as polarized as it is." Smith specifically attempts to find "the makings of a third view, something that breaks through the ossified positions into which the debate so often hardens" (p. 721) in the writings of Paul Goodman, which he suggests offers "a coherent answer to many of the concerns that today animate both left and right" (p. 729).

21. Thomas Cleary, *Zen antics*, p. ix.

Chapter 3. Otherness

1. An earlier version of this chapter appeared as "Complicity: The theory of negative difference" in the Summer/Fall 1991 *Howard Journal of Communications*.

2. *If Beale street could talk*, pp. 64, 65.

3. Earlier versions of this essay used the term "radical" instead of oppositional, and while I think that the two are interchangeable, the latter provides a clearer rendering of my position as it relates to criticism in particular and language use in general.

4. In Kathleen Freeman's *Ancilla to the pre-Socratic philosophers*, p. 141.

5. As Memmi explains in *The colonizer and the colonized*: "All racism and xenophobia consist of delusions about oneself, including absurd and unjust aggressions toward others. Included are those of the colonized—the more so when they extend beyond the colonizers to everything which is not strictly colonized. When, for example, they are carried away by enjoyment of the misfortunes of another human group simply because it is not in slavery, they are guilty of xenophobia. However, it must be noted at the same time that the colonized's racism is the result of a more general delusion: the colonialist delusion. Being considered and treated apart by colonialist racism, the colonized ends up

accepting this Manichaean division of the colony and, by extension, of the whole world" (pp. 130–31).

6. See chapter 1, above, p. 22.

7. "The *Phaedrus* complex." "The term for this kind of metaphysics is phallogocentricism," notes Whitson, "the primacy of the phallus and the philosopher's word as law" (p. 18).

8. See also Laclau's *Politics and ideology in Marxist theory*.

9. Laclau and Mouffe offer an extended analysis of "feminist essentialism" that points to the necessity of recognizing the coherence of discursive and material influences on the construction of gender. "The difficulty of this approach, however, arises from the one-sided emphasis given the moment of dispersion—so one sided that we are left with only a heterogeneous set of sexual differences constructed through practices which have no relation to one another. Now, while it is absolutely correct to question the idea of an original sexual division represented a posteriori in social practices, it is also necessary to recognize that overdetermination among the diverse sexual differences produces a systematic effect of sexual *division*. Every construction of sexual differences, whatever their multiplicity and heterogeneity, invariably constructs the feminine as a pole subordinated to the masculine" (pp. 117–18).

10. For another consideration of how oppositional rhetoric can problematize notions of identity, see Dobris and White's essay "A chorus of discordant voices: Radical feminist confrontations with patriarchal religion" in *The Southern Communication Journal*.

11. This is how Pirsig characterizes Aristotelian rhetoric in *Zen*.

12. In "Theoretical and research issues in Black communication," p. 139 (emphasis Smith's). Smith later changed his name to Molefi Kete Asante, and continued in his work to illustrate the distinctiveness of Afrocentric thought in contrast to Eurocentric thought. For an analysis of this distinction and its epistemological implications see my "Afrocentricity and complicity: An ethnophilosophical analysis."

13. Smith writes in "Markings of an African concept of rhetoric" that "African society is essentially a society of harmonies, inasmuch as the coherence or compatibility of persons, things, and modalities is at the root of traditional African philosophy. . . . In fact, Adesanya, a Nigerian writer, declares 'this is not simply a coherence of fact or faith, nor of reason and traditional beliefs, nor of reason and contingent facts, but a coherence of compatibility among all disciplines'" (pp. 367–68). He goes on to note the dialogic tendencies inherent in discourse: "The sta-

bility of the community is essential, and public speaking, when used in connection with conflict solution, must be directed toward maintaining the community harmony. As a microcosmic example of the traditional African society's base in the harmony of all parts, the meaningful public discourse manifests rhetorical agreeableness in all its parts" (p. 369).

14. Richard Johannessen, for example, indicates its coherentist assumptions when he notes that "dialogue manifests itself more as a spirit, orientation, or bearing in communication rather than as a specific method, technique, or format. We can speak of an attitude of dialogue in human communication. As categories, these characteristics are not mutually exclusive, not completely separate from each other; there may be margins of overlap. And other writers might choose different language to describe essentially the same characteristics. Furthermore, the categories are not intended in any particular rank of importance" (1983, p. 50).

15. See Bohm's *Noetic Sciences Review* essay, "On dialogue," p. 16.

16. "On dialogue," p. 18.

17. For a recent critique of Rogerian rhetoric and its dialogic possibilities, see Doug Brent's essay "Young, Becker and Pike's Rogerian rhetoric: A twenty-year reassessment." Brent observes that the "sense of threat created by Socratic probing and refutation is precisely what Rogers points to as a barrier to communication in everyday life, and what Young, Becker, and Pike's rhetoric is designed to circumvent. This does not mean, of course, that a Rogerian rhetoric must be set against classical rhetoric. The recent movement to search classical rhetoric for dialogic elements . . . can be complementary, not antithetical to modern perspectives such as Rogers'" (p. 463).

18. Freeman's *Ancilla to the pre-Socratic philosophers*, p. 132.

19. I draw this term from Kenneth Burke's writings, and argue elsewhere that Burke's conceptualization of rhetoric anticipates a coherent philosophy of language. See my "Coherence as representative anecdote in the rhetorics of Kenneth Burke and Ernesto Grassi."

20. Lanham, p. 6.

21. Chisholm, *Theory of knowlege*, p. 113.

22. David Bohm offers a similar view in *Thought as system*. Bohm contends that "thought is a system. That system not only includes thoughts, 'felts' and feelings, but it includes the state of the body; it includes the whole of society—as thought is passing back and forth

between people in a process by which thought evolved from ancient times" (p. 19). Bohm suggests that our contemporary systems of thought are subject to a "systemic flaw," for example, "fragmentation," and that this flaw results in our mistaken belief that the world exists as, and can be explained in terms of, separate and distinct entities. See also *Wholeness and the implicate order.*

23. This insight comes from Christopher Norris' *The deconstructive turn: Essays in the rhetoric of philosophy,* p. 22.

24. Schulke and McPhee explain that "Both men had a lasting influence on King's lifelong belief in a personal God and in the sacredness of the human person." Much later he was to write, "This personal idealism remains today my basic philosophical position. Personalism's insistence that only personality—finite and infinite—is ultimately real, strengthened me in two convictions; it gave me metaphysical and philosophical grounding for the idea of a personal God, and it gave me a metaphysical basis for my belief in the dignity and worth of all human personality" (pp. 21–22)

25. *Satyagrahis* are individuals who direct campaigns against injustice in a nonviolent manner.

26. *Choosing reality: A contemplative view of physics and the mind,* p. 153.

CHAPTER 4. EMPTINESS

1. An earlier version of this essay appeared as "Quantum inferential leaps: The rhetoric of physics" in the 1992 *Southern Communication Journal.*

2. See N. Katherine Hayles' *The cosmic web: Scientific field models and literary strategies in the twentieth century,* and *Chaos bound: Orderly disorder in contemporary literature and science.*

3. See for example R. A. Harris' "Rhetoric of science," Charles Bazerman's, *Shaping written knowledge: The genre and activity of the experimental article in science,* Kenneth Bruffee's "Social construction, language, and the authority of knowledge: A bibliographical essay," and, Greg Meyers' "Writing research and the sociology of scientific knowledge: A review of three new books."

4. J. E. McGuire and Trevor Melia's, "Some cautionary strictures on the writing of the rhetoric of science," offers this observation: "The proliferation of papers, programs, and now a journal issue dedicated to

the 'rhetoric of science' is eloquent testimony to the vitality of what may be called the 'rhetorical turn.'" The issue in which their essay appeared was devoted to the rhetoric of science and also contained Wilda Anderson's, "Scientific nomenclature and revolutionary rhetoric," John Angus Campbell's "The invisible rhetorician: Charles Darwin's 'third party' strategy," Carolyn Miller's "Some perspectives on rhetoric, science and history," Jean Dietz Moss', "The interplay of science and rhetoric in seventeenth-century Italy," and William Wallace's, "Aristotelian science and rhetoric in transition: The Middle Ages and the Renaissance." Nelson, Megill, and McClosky (1987) provide this explanation of the rhetoric of inquiry: "Rhetoric of inquiry studies what Abraham Kaplan has called 'logics in use.' But it does not combine them into some general 'reconstructed logic.' Instead it works within projects of research, to give them greater awareness of their practices and assumptions, and across fields of inquiry, to put them in better communication. It does not replace logic or inquiry as an authority over research in substantive fields; nor can it become an academic discipline in its own right. It seeks merely to increase self-reflection in every inquiry, and already it proceeds as a part of current research in several fields" (p. ix). Also see McClosky (1985) or Simons (1989).

5. The *physis-nomos* antithesis is an important starting point for any discussion of the rhetoric of physics because it illustrates the underlying assumptions which have defined the relationship between these disciplines for centuries in terms of the understanding of reality as either fixed or dynamic, as existing separate from human interaction or intimately connected to it. Kerferd (1981) explains: "The term *physis* is usually translated by 'nature.' It was the term which the Ionian scientists came to use for the whole of reality, or for its most abiding material source or constituents. But it also came early to be used to refer to the constitution or set of characteristics of a particular thing, or class of things, especially a living creature or person, as in the expression 'the nature of man'" (p. 111). "The term *nomos* and the whole range of terms that are cognate with it in Greek are always prescriptive and normative and never merely descriptive—they give some kind of direction or command affecting behavior or activities of persons and things" (p. 112). Guthrie (1971) also illustrates this connection: "The meaning of *physis* emerges from a study of the Presocratics. It can safely be translated 'nature,' though when it occurs in conjunction with *nomos* the world 'reality' will sometimes make the contrast more immediately clear. *Nomos* for the men of classical times is something that *nomizetai*, is believed in, is apportioned, distributed or dispensed. That is to say it presupposes an acting subject—believer, practitioner or apportioner—a mind from which the nomos emanates" (p. 55). Guthrie explains that while the antithesis emerges in the fourth and fifth centuries, prior to

this point in time *physis* and *nomos* were not viewed as mutually exclusive. Cornford concurs: for the early Greeks, before the birth of philosophy, "the 'nature' or 'essence' is the social function. The *physis* is the *nomoi*" (quoted in Degrood, 1970, p. 4).

6. Several writers outside of the discipline of rhetoric have explored relationships between quantum physics, indeterminacy, and interactions within systems. Both Roger Penrose's *The emperor's new mind* and Daniel Dennett's *Elbow room* consider how indeterminacy reveals itself in the operations of the human mind, and Ilya Prigogine and Isabelle Stengers' *Order out of chaos* explores how indeterminacy manifests itself in a number of systems, both quantum and classical. Stanley Jaki objects to this view, but does not develop his objections beyond a reaffirmation of modernist views of the value of science (1990). Also, within the field of rhetoric, however, a number of scholars have suggested that the claims of the rhetoric of inquiry need to be attenuated, and have cautioned against rhetoricizing science. Both James Hikins and Michael McGuire caution rhetoricians against equating science with rhetoric (1990), and Hikins and Zagacki view the "value-laden hypothesis" of physics as it is developed in the rhetoric of inquiry as a "non-sequitur" (1988, p. 209). In a similar vein Trevor Melia and J. E. McGuire question the validity of equating rhetoric with science because science is extra conventional in that its objects of analysis exist prior to human observation (1989, p. 99). Roger Trigg's defense of realism *Reality at risk* makes many of the same arguments in its rejection of subjectivist and constructivist views of knowledge (1980).

The justificatory weaknesses of realism and objectivism are, in my view, three fold: first, neither are able to move beyond the "brute fact" hypothesis (i.e., "this is a brick wall, I cannot walk through it, therefore it is real unto itself"), an hypothesis which is itself the product of realist and objectivist ontology and epistemology: thus, the theories fail to reflect on their own assumptions. Second, because realism and idealism cannot explain a link between non-essential realities at the micro level and their manifestation in the macro world of phenomena, the relationship is simply rejected. Hikins and Zagacki's claim that the extension of the value laden hypothesis of physics to language is a non-sequitur simply invokes realist and objectivist conceptions of language (logical fallacies) to reify realist and objectivist conceptions of reality. Finally, the political consequences of these theories cannot be ignored: Both realism and objectivism have been used to privilege some positions, and some societies and cultures, at the expense of others. Hikins' attempt, in response to this criticism, to separate the theory of realism from its consequences sounds peculiarly like the arguments offered by some gun control opponents: guns don't kill, people kill. All of these examples suggest the legitimacy of at least one position advanced by the proponents of the rhetoric of inquiry and epistemic rhetoric: that the separation of human beings from the intellectual methods of their own making may be less productive than we have traditionally assumed it to be. Instead of only attenuating the claims of the rhetoric of inquiry, I would suggest an attenuation of the claims of both positions in order to find some common grounds.

A useful discussion of this approach is outlined in Celeste Condit Railsback's essay "Beyond rhetorical relativism: A structural-material model of truth and objective reality" (1983). Railsback explores the prevailing issues in the debate and offers a "bounded network theory of language" that suggests a more integrated and holistic approach to "the interaction of rhetoric, objective truths, and objective reality, and allows a re-cognition of the role of consensus in truth-seeking" (Abstract). Railsback's position is perhaps closest to the view which I present in this essay: that all of these positions function together to create a dynamic, complex, and sometimes incomplete conception of reality. This view, I believe, exemplifies a coherentist approach to knowledge, and is compatible with constructivist, subjectivist, objectivist, and realist views of existence in terms of its recognition of the systemic and implicatory nature of these views. Indeed, even Trigg acknowledges that what we call reality presents us with paradoxes and uncertainties which make any attempt to define it in fixed or static terms problematical: "Reality is indeed far stranger than our developing conceptions of it at any one time suggest" (p. 182).

7. Richard Gregg cites Bohm in *Symbolic inducement and knowing* to support the idea that scientific knowledge "provides us with ever evolving and changing conclusions rather than immutable truths" (p. 11). He also makes a point similar to Bohm's discussion of the social problems which arise from fragmentation of consciousness when he discusses how the perceptual practices of "bordering" and "distancing" encourage "the universal human tendency to divide and categorize others into kin and non-kin, members and non-members, friend and foe. We tend to fear the actions of those who are not like us, and to respond in unreasoning ways to external threats. We elevate ourselves and those like us to positions of superiority, and reduce those unlike us to an inferior status" (p. 120)."

8. See Livio Rossetti's "The rhetoric of Zeno's paradoxes" for another perspective on Zeno's rhetorical implications.

9. Hamilton and Cairns, *Plato: Collected dialogues*, p. 234.

10. See also Poulakos' "Toward a sophistic definition of rhetoric," and "Hegel's reception of the Sophists."

11. LaRae M. Donnellan's essay "Examining the Ethos of Science" is worth mentioning here. Donnellan recounts the prevailing arguments about the rhetorical nature of science, but goes one step further by designating the ethos of science and technology as primarily masculine. Argüelles makes the same claim in *The transformative vision*, and also suggests that a stronger feminine epistemological sensibility would benefit both science and society through its humanizing and balancing influence. Donnellan writes: "Sociologists and rhetoricians of science are reconceptualizing the *ethos* of science to demonstrate that science is a human activity and scientific writing often does (and should) reflect that fact. As in the theory of cultural lag, however, theory and practice do not always coincide. It will take years for the revised *ethos* to be widely reflected in scientific rhetoric and to be identified by the public (both the general and the scientific publics) as a new and acceptable *ethos*. Indeed, it will take what many feminists urge: a rethinking and reshaping of society. What is necessary is not a feminist society or a feminist science, but rather a more fully human society from which a more complete science can emerge" (pp. 18–19).

12. *Space-time and beyond*, p. 166.

13. Quoted in Frank Macke, "The end of modernity and the ends of argumentation: A discourse on the notion of advocacy as rationality."

14. McKerrow, "Overcoming fatalism: Rhetoric/argument in postmodernity," p. 121.

Chapter 5. One Hand Clapping

1. An earlier version of this essay appeared as "One hand clapping: Postmodern rhetorical theory" in the 1994–95 *Speech Communication Annual*.

2. McKerrow, "Overcoming fatalism," p. 121.

3. Winston King, *Zen and the way of the sword*, pp. 16, 19–20.

4. David Cratis Williams offers a perspective similar to, and in my opinion, congruent with mine in "Approaching the Abyss: Argumentation theory and postmodernism." Williams argues that rhetoric is "'essentially, an act of affirmation, an affirmation that becomes constitutive of identity, and ultimately, being." He goes on to suggest that "'rhetorical criticism' might be understood as an oxymoron; that rhetoric contains within it an impulse toward affirmation (identification) while criticism contains within it an impulse toward negation (deconstruction). I see strains of postmodernism which echo 'criticism's'

negative, poststructuralist posture. And in a manner parallel to 'criticism's' need for the affirmation of rhetoric to provide it with the 'ground' from which to speak, so too do I see a need for aspects of postmodernism to recognize it lives in a rhetorical world in which, to cite Burke's famous description, we build our 'cultures by huddling together, nervously loquacious, at the edge of an abyss'" (p. 89).

5. The complexities and contradictions of the relationship between rhetoric and postmodernism have been thoughtfully and thoroughly considered in McKerrow's *Argument and the postmodern challenge.* Several of the essays included in this volume offer approaches consistent with those presented in this chapter, but others offer alternative perspectives on the relationship between modern and postmodern approaches to argument. I leave it to the reader to absorb what is useful from each, and suggest for points of comparison and contrast Barbara Biesecker's "Rhetoric, postmodernism, and desire," Frank Macke's "The end of modernity and the ends of argumentation," Warren Sandmann's "Gorgias and his postmodern cousins," and David Cratis Williams' "Approaching the abyss."

6. "Some implications of 'process' or 'intersubjectivity,'" p. 31.

7. "Critical rhetoric: Theory and praxis," p. 109.

8. In *Paideia: The ideals of Greek culture,* Werner Jaeger indicates the democratic agenda of the Sophists when he notes that "what was common to them all was that they all taught political aretê , and all wished to instill it by increasing the powers of the mind through training—whatever they took that training to be" (p. 293). For more on the emancipatory project of Sophistic rhetoric, see John Poulakos' "Sophistical rhetoric as a critique of culture."

9. "Critical rhetoric in a postmodern world," p. 78.

10. Jameson frames the debate between modernism and postmodernism in terms of the following contrast between Habermas and Lyotard: "Habermas's vision of an evolutionary social leap into a new type of rational society, defined in communicational terms as 'the communication community of those affected, who as participants in a practical discourse test the validity claims of norms and, to the extent that they accept them with reasons, arrive at the conviction that in the given circumstances the proposed norms are "right,"' is here explicitly rejected as the unacceptable remnant of a 'totalizing' philosophical tradition and as the valorization of conformist, when not 'terrorist' ideals of consensus. (Indeed, insofar as Habermas will invoke a liberatory rhetoric as well, there is a sense in which, for Lyotard, this philosophical position unites everything that is unacceptable about both traditions and myths of legitimation)" (p. x).

11. Lyotard defines the differend in the following manner: "The differend is the unstable state and instant of language wherein something which must be able to be put into phrases cannot yet be. This state includes silence, which is a negative phrase, but it also calls upon phrases which are in principle possible" (p. 13).

12. *Just gaming*, p. 79. Lyotard equates the privileged position of the Idea, from Plato to Kant, with "Terror in the name of freedom" (p. 92).

13. "The problem of ideology: Marxism without guarantees," p. 46.

14. In *Just gaming*, Lyotard argues that "the transmission of knowledge should not be limited to the transmission of information, but should include training in all of the procedures that can increase one's ability to connect the fields jealously guarded from one another by the traditional organization of knowledge" (p. 52). Lyotard's argument suggests that a coherentist approach could offer a powerful alternative to the essentializing tendencies that characterize traditional hierarchical models of knowing and being.

15. *An introduction to Zen Buddhism*, p. 39.

16. For a discussion of the complementary relationship between success and truth in Sophistic rhetoric, see Edward Schiappa's "Rhêtorikê: What's in a name? Toward a revised history of early Greek rhetorical theory."

CHAPTER 6. COHERENCE

1. An earlier version of this essay appeared as "Zen and the art of rhetoric: Empowerment and the teaching of excellence" in the 1988 Spring/Summer issue of *Spectrum*.

2. In *College: The undergraduate experience in America*, Boyer offers an emancipatory agenda for American education: "When all is said and done, the college should encourage each student to develop the capacity to judge wisely in matters of life and conduct. . . . The goal is not to indoctrinate students, but to set them free in the world of ideas and provide a climate in which ethical and moral choices can be thoughtfully examined and convictions formed" (p. 284).

3. *College*, p. 7.

4. Boyer indicates the importance of rhetorical inquiry for incoming students. "While stressing writing, we also urge that oral communication be an important part of the freshman language course. Historically the study of the spoken word, or rhetoric, as it was once

called, has been an essential element of education. The importance of speech is reflected in the classic works of Aristotle and Cicero. In the colonial period declamation was required of every student every year. Sophomores had a course in forensics and, before they graduated, seniors were expected to pass an oral examination" (p. 8).

5. Carnoy illustrates how colonized knowledge function in the educational system in his explication of how schools perpetuate the ideologies of development and equality. "If schools are to help in maintaining this *concept* of development as well as increasing the efficiency of the economic system, they have to be good political role teachers. Schools must help convince or reinforce children in believing that the system is basically sound and the role they are allocated is the proper one for them to play. Through such 'colonization' the society avoids having to redistribute the increases in national product and reduces the necessity for direct repression of the populace" (p. 13).

6. Habermas, *Legitimation crisis*. This calling into question is described by Habermas as *reflexive learning*. "Reflexive learning takes place through discourses in which we thematize practical validity claims that have become problematic or have been rendered problematic through institutionalized doubt, and redeem or dismiss them on the basis of arguments. The level of learning which a social formation makes possible could depend upon whether the organizational principle of the society permits (a) differentiation between theoretical and practical questions and (b), transition from non-reflexive (prescientific) to reflexive learning" (p. 15).

7. Herta Murphy and Herbert Hildebrandt observe: "Communication—written or oral—consistently receives one of the highest rankings for competencies that managers should possess to achieve excellence in business" (p. v.), and Marlene Fine, Fern Johnson, and Sallyanne Ryan (1990) note that the "changing gender and color of the United States' workforce have forced employers to confront issues of cultural diversity in the workplace" (p. 305). Fine (1991) further observes that this change "means that corporations must hire and promote employees who are different—different from the white males who have traditionally inhabited the corporate world, and different from each other" (p. 260).

8. See, for example, David T. Kearns, chairman and CEO of Xerox Corporation, who explicitly emphasizes the importance of traditional rhetorical skills. Kearns notes that "American business needs workers who not only are proficient in basic skills, but who know how to think and can communicate what they're thinking." Kearns' remarks were made in response to a report entitled "Learning to be Literate in America," which suggested the "back to basics" movement of the last two decades failed to accomplish its goals "because teachers tended to stress the mechanics of writing, but often neglected the reasoning and subject mat-

ter behind it" explains Lee Mitgang (1987, p. C1). The report suggests a movement from grammar through rhetoric to logic as a means of remedying America's literacy problems and improving the quality of communication both in schools and in business. This suggestion, however, fails to recognize the epistemological implications of such a move, and the extent to which it subscribes to essentialist principles of judgment.

9. Many writers have commented on the connection between communication and diversity. Marlene Piturro and Sarah Mahoney (1991) note that many businesses are "discovering that the opportunity for person-to-person misunderstanding is so great it threatens productivity" (p. 45), and Marilyn Loden and Ronnie Hoffman Loeser (1991) contend that institutions that have been successful at dealing with diversity are characterized by executives who "seek additional knowledge about the issues, speak the language of diversity, and attempt to 'walk the talk' as they set policy and provide guidance" (p. 22).

10. For an interesting consideration of several of the issues raised by Fine presented from a different perspective, see Margaret Zulick's "Standpoint, praxis, and postmodern argument."

11. This is, of course, an over-romanticized version of this era. Participation in the polis was limited to men of specified wealth, and women, slaves, and foreigners were excluded from the privileges of democracy. Nonetheless, in the context of the time the rhetorical education offered by the Sophists was revolutionary. As Susan Jarratt argues: "Sophistic teaching practice fueled a new political engine forged in the sixth and fifth centuries. The sophists redirected the emphasis in higher education, balancing instruction in aristocratic behavior and skill in arms, central to the status of the warrior/aristocrat at least from the Dark Ages to the mid-fifth century, with a much greater attention spent on the new arete essential for democracy: the ability to create accounts of communal possibilities through persuasive speech. In the case of the sophists, we see the very first education for empowerment, as their teaching-for-fees allowed anyone with the money access to power in the assembly, council, and courts" (p. 98).

Chapter 7. Honoring the Form

1. An earlier version of this essay appeared as "Discipline and compassion: Teaching rhetoric as a martial art," in the October 1994 *Ohio Speech Journal.*

2. *Tao te ching,* p. 143.

3. By "spiritual " I mean an attitude that recognizes first and foremost our common humanity, and privileges affirmation and peaceful interaction. It is the attitude exhibited by Martin Luther King and Mahatma Gandhi, and is characterized in discourse I believe by dialogic coherence.

4. Brockriede, "Arguers as lovers," p. 9.

5. Brockriede offers a rendering of argument as love that incorporates the intellectual ability for self-reflection with the emotional capacity for understanding when he quotes Douglas Enhinger's depiction of argument: "To enter upon argument with a full understanding of the commitments which as a method it entails is to experience that alchemical moment of transformation in which . . . , in the language of Buber, the *Ich-Es* is replaced by the *Ich-Du*; when the 'other,' no longer regarded as an 'object' to be manipulated, is endowed with those qualities of 'freedom' and 'responsibility' that change the 'individual' as 'thing' into the 'person' as 'not thing'" (pp. 9, 10).

6. "On the disappearance of the rhetorical aura," pp. 148–49. Farrell offers what is perhaps the most complete rendering of rhetorical coherence in contemporary rhetorical theory in *Norms of rhetorical culture*. While Farrell and I approach the notion of coherence from different perspectives we are both interested in finding a "middle way" in rhetorical theory and practice.

7. "In praise of Pirsig's *Zen and the art of motorcycle maintenance*, p. 169.

8. Quoted in Irene Ward's *Literacy, ideology, and dialogue*. Ward offers an extended analysis of dialogic pedagogy in composition, interrogating various perspectives and then offering her own "functional dialogism" for writing teachers. She contends that expressivists utilize dialogic approaches that vary from encouraging dialogue between students to emphasizing "internal" dialogue. "According to these compositionists, the role of the instructor is to provide an environment where the student can gain experience with writing, acting not as an instructor so much as an experienced coach or master craftsperson. In these classroom situations, students engage in dialogue with each other and with the instructor in order to provide one another with feedback about their writing processes and the work in progress. Each theorist's concept of the nature of the dialogue is different, leading to different goals and outcomes for the students, though the theoretical assumptions underlying the work of all the expressivists unifies them and their work" (p. 16).

9. Thomas O. Sloane, "Reinventing invention," p. 472.

10. Burke discusses consubstantiality in *A rhetoric of motives*. I would extend his usage to include relationships between individuals and texts to highlight its emphasis on the potential of symbolic action to transcend dualistic conceptions of reality.

11. David Payne draws on Burke's notions of identification and division in his discussion of the therapeutic uses of rhetoric. His analysis is particularly illuminating in light of the student's experience as described in her essay. "Human identity is defined as divided and capable of failure; the self internalizes 'fault' for flawed conditions and thus experiences them as proof of its divisions and failure. To repair this flawed identity the individual must seek out symbolic resolutions—those provided by therapeutic rhetorics found in religion, psychiatry, psychology, or, as I have sought to point out, the general rhetorical involvements available in social persuasion" (p. 35). I would extend Payne's analysis to include, as well, the internal dialogics of self-reflection.

12. *The rhetoric of Aristotle*, p. 6. The bracketed phrase "in a speech" is supplied by Cooper.

13. *Being and race: Black writing since 1970*, p. 47.

14. See Brian Wilkes's essay, "Kanji—the meaning of 'dojo,'" p. 40.

15. Mindell explains that "deep democracy" is found in all perennial spiritual traditions, especially the martial arts, Taoism, and Zen Buddhism: "It is our responsibility to follow the flow of nature, respect fate, energy, or in the Far East, Tao or Ki, and our role in cocreating history. Deep democracy is our sense that the world is here to help us become our entire selves, and that we are here to help the world become whole" (p. 5).

16. *Tao of jeet kun do*, p. 9. Lee invented his own style called Jeet Kune Do, and encouraged his students to "absorb what is useful" in the path toward mastery of the arts. His advice is also useful for students of rhetoric, who might do well to absorb these words: "Acceptance, denial and conviction prevent understanding. Let your mind move together with another's in understanding and sensitivity. Then, there is a possibility of real communication. To understand one another, there must be a state of choiceless awareness where this is no sense of comparison or condemnation, no waiting for a further development of discussion in order to agree or disagree. *Above all, don't start from a conclusion*" (p. 19).

REFERENCES

Adler, M. (1939). The crisis in contemporary education. *The Social Frontier*, 5, 141–44.

Anderson, T. (1988). Black encounter of racism and elitism in white academe: A critique of the system. *Journal of Black Studies*, 18 (3), 259–72.

Anderson, W. (1989). Scientific nomenclature and revolutionary rhetoric. *Rhetorica*, 7, 45–54.

Argüelles, J. (1975). *The transformative vision: Reflections on the nature and history of human expression.* Boulder, CO: Shambhala.

———. (1987). *The Mayan factor: Path beyond technology.* Santa Fe: Bear & Company.

Asante, M. (né Arthur Smith, 1972). Markings of an African concept of rhetoric. In A. Smith (ed.), *Language, communication, and rhetoric in Black America* (pp. 363–74). New York: Harper & Row.

———. (1974). Theoretical and research issues in black communication. In J. Daniel (ed.), *Black communication: Dimensions of research and instruction* (pp. 136–44). New York: Speech Communication Association.

Attenborough, R., ed. (1982). *The words of Gandhi.* New York: New Market Press.

Augros, R., and G. Stanciu (1986). *The new story of science.* New York: Bantam.

Awkward, M. (1988). Race, gender, and the politics of reading. *Black American Literary Forum*, 22, 5–27.

Bakhtin, M. (1990). *The dialogic imagination.* Trans. M. and C. Emerson. Austin, TX: University of Texas Press.

Baldwin, J. (1974). *If Beale street could talk.* New York: The Dial Press.

Baudrillard, J. (1988). On seduction. In M. Poster (ed.), *Jean Baudrillard: Selected writings*. Stanford: Stanford University Press.

Bartholomae, D. (1986). Inventing the university. *Journal of Basic Writing, 5* (1), 4–23.

Bazerman, C. (1988). *Shaping written knowledge: The genre and activity of the experimental article in science*. Madison, WI: University of Wisconsin Press.

Bell-Villada, G. (1991). Is the American mind getting dumber? *Monthly Review, 43,* 41–55.

Benz, E. (1976). Buddhist influences outside Asia. In H. Dumoulin and J. C. Maraldo (eds.), *Buddhism in the modern world* (pp. 305–22). New York and London: Macmillan.

Berstein, R. (1978). *The restructuring of social and political theory.* Philadelphia: University of Pennsylvania Press.

Besserman, P. and M. Steger (1991). *Crazy clouds: Zen radicals, rebels and reformers.* Boston and London: Shambhala.

Biesecker, B. (1993). Rhetoric, postmodernism, and desire. In R. McKerrow (ed.), *Argument and the postmodern challenge: Proceedings of the Eighth SCA/AFA Conference on Argumentation* (pp. 122–23). Annandale, VA: Speech Communication Association.

Blanshard, B. (1940). *The nature of thought.* New York: Macmillan.

Bloom, A. (1987). *The closing of the American mind: How democracy has impoverished the souls of today's students.* New York: Simon & Schuster.

Bobo, L. (1988). Group conflict, prejudice, and the paradox of contemporary racial attitudes. In P. Katz and D. Taylor (eds.), *Eliminating racism: Profiles in controversy* (pp. 85–114). New York: Plenum Press.

Bode, R. A. (1987). Mohandas Karamchand Gandhi's rhetorical theory: Implications for communication ethics. Unpublished doctoral dissertation, University of Oregon.

Bohm, D. (1983). *Wholeness and the implicate order.* New York: Routledge & Kegan Paul.

———. (1992). On dialogue. *Noetic Sciences Review, 23,* 16–18.

———. (1994). *Thought as system.* New York: Routledge.

Bohm, D., and F. D. Peat (1987). *Science, order and creativity.* New York: Bantam.

Bohr, N. (1963). *Essays, 1958–1962: On atomic physics and human knowledge.* New York: Interscience.

Bondurant, J. (1969). *The conquest of violence: The Gandhian philosophy of conflict.* Berkeley: University of California Press.

Booth, W. (1981). Mere rhetoric, rhetoric, and the search for common learning. In E. Boyer (ed.), *Common learning: Carnegie colloquim on general education* (pp. 23–55). Washington, DC: The Carnegie Foundation for the Advancement of Teaching.

———. (1986). Pluralism in the classroom. *Critical Inquiry, 12* (3), 468–79.

Bowser, B. P., and R. G. Hunt (1981). *Impacts of racism on white Americans.* Beverly Hills, CA: Sage Publications.

Boyer, E. L. (1987). *College: The undergraduate experience in America.* New York: Harper & Row.

Bradbury, R. (1990). *Zen in the art of writing.* Santa Barbara, CA: Capra Press.

Brandon, D. (1990). *Zen in the art of helping.* New York: Arkana.

Branham, R. (1991). *Debate and critical analysis: The harmony of conflict.* Hillsdale, NJ: Lawrence Erlbaum.

Brent, D. (1991). Young, Becker and Pike's Rogerian rhetoric: A twenty-year reassessment. *College English, 53,* 452–66.

Brinker, H. (1987). *Zen in the art of painting.* New York: Arkana.

Brock, B., and R. Scott (1982). *Methods of rhetorical criticism.* Detroit: Wayne State University Press.

Brockriede, W. (1972). Arguers as lovers. *Philosophy and Rhetoric, 5,* 1–11.

Brown, J. (1994). *Zen: The Eastern counterpart of cynicism.* Paper presented at the 1994 Speech Communication Association Convention, New Orleans.

Bruffee, K. (1986). Social construction, language, and the authority of knowledge: A bibliographical essay. *College English, 48,* 773–90.

Brummett, B. (1976). Some implications of "process" or "intersubjectivity": Postmodern rhetoric. *Philosophy & Rhetoric, 9,* 21–51.

————. (1990). A eulogy for epistemic rhetoric. *Quarterly Journal of Speech, 76,* 69–72.

Bump. J. (1983). Creativity, rationality, and metaphor in Robert Pirsig's *Zen and the art of motorcycle maintenance. The South Atlantic Quarterly, 82* (4), 370–80.

Burke, K. (1969). *A rhetoric of motives.* Berkeley, CA: University of California Press.

Campbell, J. A. (1989). The invisible rhetorician: Charles Darwin's "third party" strategy. *Rhetorica, 7* (1), 55–86.

Capra, F. (1984). *The tao of physics.* New York: Bantam.

Carlson, A. C. (1986). Gandhi and the comic frame: "Ad bellum purificandum." *Quarterly Journal of Speech, 72,* 446–55.

Carnoy, M. (1974). *Education as cultural imperialism.* New York: David McKay Company, Inc.

Carter, R. (1993). Thirty-five years later: New perspectives on Brown. In H. Hill and J. Jones (eds.), *Race in America: The struggle for equality* (pp. 83–96). Madison, WI: University of Wisconsin Press.

Chen, G. and J. Chung (1994). The impact of Confucianism on organizational communication. *Communication Quarterly, 42,* 93–105.

Cherwitz, R. A., and J. W. Hikins (1990). Burying the undertaker: A eulogy for the eulogists of rhetorical epistemology. *Quarterly Journal of Speech, 76,* 73–77.

Christian, B. (1987). The race for theory. *Cultural Critique, 6,* 51–63.

Chung, T. C. (1994). *Zen speaks: Shouts of nothingness.* Trans. B. Bruya. New York: Anchor Books.

Cleary, T., trans. (1993). *Zen antics: 100 stories of enlightenment.* Boston: Shambhala.

Coleman, T. (1990). Managing diversity at work: The new American dilemma. *Public Management, 72,* 2–3+.

Collison, M. (1987). More young blacks men choosing not to go to college. *The Chronicle of Higher Education, 34* (15), A1, A26.

Cooper, L., trans. (1960). *The rhetoric of Aristotle.* Englewood Cliffs, NJ: Prentice-Hall.

Copeland, L. (1987). Valuing workplace diversity. *Personnel Administrator, 33,* 38–40.

Crapanzano, V. (1985). *Waiting: The whites of South Africa.* New York: Random House.

Crowley, S. (1992). Reflections on the argument that won't go away: Or, a turn of the ideological screw. *The Quarterly Journal of Speech, 78,* 450–65.

Crusius, T. (1976). In praise of Pirsig's *Zen and the art of motorcycle maintenance. Western Speech Communication Journal, 40,* 168–77.

Cupach, W. R. and T. Imahori (1993). Managing social predicaments created by others: A comparison of Japanese and American face-work. *Western Journal of Communication, 57,* 431–44.

Degrood, D. (1970). *Philosophies of essence: An examination of the category of essence.* Gronigen, FRG: Wolters-Noordhoff.

de Man, P. (1983). The rhetoric of blindness. *Blindness and insight: Essays in the rhetoric of contemporary criticism.* Minneapolis: University of Minnesota Press.

Dennett, D. (1984). *Elbow room.* Cambridge, MA: MIT Press.

DeWine, S., A. M. Nicotera, A., M., and D. Parry (1981). Argumentativeness and aggressiveness: The flip side of gentle persuasion. *Management Communication Quarterly, 4,* 386–411.

Di Mare, L. (1990). Ma and Japan. *The Southern Communication Journal, 55,* 319–28.

Dobris, C., and C. White (1989). Rhetorical constructions of self and identity: Toward a genre view of feminist identity discourse. Paper presented at the Speech Communication Association Convention.

———. (1993). A chorus of discordant voices: Radical feminist confrontations with patriarchal religion. *The Southern Communication Journal, 58,* 239–46.

Donnellan, L. (1987). *Examining the ethos of science.* Paper presented to the 73rd Annual Meeting of the Speech Communication Association, Boston, MA.

Dumoulin, H., and J. C. Maraldo, eds. (1976). *Buddhism in the modern world.* New York and London: Macmillan.

Egami, S. (1976). *The heart of karate-do.* New York: Kodansha International Ltd.

Ehninger, D. (1984). Science, philosophy—and rhetoric: A look toward the future. In J. Golden, G. Berquist, and W. E. Coleman (eds.), *The rhetoric of Western thought* (pp. 454–64). Dubuque, IA: Kendall Hunt.

Entman, R. (1990). Modern racism and the images of blacks in local television news. *Critical Studies in Mass Communication, 7,* 332–45

Enzenberger, H. (1974). *The consciousness industry.* New York: Seabury.

Farber, J. (1969). *The student as nigger.* North Hollywood, CA: Contact Books.

———. (1990). Learning how to teach: A progress report. *College English,* 52, 135–41.

Farrell, T. (1990). From the parthenon to the bassinet: Along the epistemic trail. *Quarterly Journal of Speech, 76,* 78–84.

———. (1993). *Norms of rhetorical culture.* New Haven: Yale University Press.

———. (1993). On the dissappearance of the rhetorical aura. *Western Journal of Communication, 57,* 147–58.

Fine, M. (1991). New voices in the workplace: Research directions in multicultural communication. *The Journal of Business Communication, 28,* 259–75.

Fine, M., F. Johnson, and M. S. Ryan (1990). Cultural diversity in the workplace. *Public Personnel Management, 19,* 305–19.

Fiordo, R. (1993). Debate, pedagogy, and the Japanese RAM. In R. McKerrow (ed.), *Argument and the postmodern challenge: Proceedings of the Eighth SCA/AFA Conference on Argumentation* (pp. 72–75). Annandale, VA: Speech Communication Association.

Fitzgerald, T. (1992). Media, ethnicity and identity. In P. Scannel, P. Schlesinger, and C. Sparks (eds.),*Culture and power: A media, culture and society reader* (pp. 112–33). Beverly Hills, CA: Sage Publications

Foster, G. (1991). Cultural relativism and the theory of value: The educational implications. *The American Journal of Economics and Sociology, 50,* 257–67.

Frank, E. (1983). In search of peace: The rhetoric of nonviolent action. Unpublished Ph.D. dissertation, University of Oregon.

Freeman, K. (1977). *Ancilla to the pre-Socratic philosophers.* Cambridge, MA: Harvard University Press.

Freire, P. (1973). Education, liberation and the church. *Study Encounter,* 9 (1).

———. (1981). *Pedagogy of the oppressed.* New York: Continuum.

Gandal, A., and C. Hosterman (1982). Toward and examination of the rhetoric of ancient India. *The Southern Speech Communication Journal, 47,* 277–91.

Gard, R., ed. (1962) *Buddhism.* New York: George Braziller.

Garrett, M. (1989). Asian Challenge. In S. K. Foss, K. A. Foss, and R. Trapp (eds.), *Contemporary perspectives on rhetoric,* 2nd ed. (pp. 295–314). Prospect Heights, IL: Waveland Press.

———. (1993). *Pathos* reconsidered from the perspective of classical Chinese rhetorics. *Quarterly Journal of Speech, 79,* 19–39.

———. (1993). Wit, power, and oppositional groups: A case study of "pure talk." *Quarterly Journal of Speech, 79,* 303–18.

———. (1993). Classical Chinese conceptions of argumentation and persuasion. *Argumentation and Advocacy, 29,* 105–15

Gates, H. L., Jr., ed. (1984). Criticism in the jungle. In *Black literature and literary theory* (pp. 1–24). New York: Methuen.

Gearhart, S. M. (1979). The womanization of rhetoric. *Women's Studies International Quarterly, 2,* 195–201.

Geddes, D. (1994). *Using Zen principles in interpersonal communication.* Paper presented at the 1994 Speech Communication Association Convention, New Orleans.

Gregg, R. (1984). *Symbolic inducement and knowing: A study in the foundations of rhetoric.* Columbia, SC: University of South Carolina.

Gregory, B. (1988). *Inventing reality: Physics as language.* New York: John Wiley and Sons.

Gross, A. (1990). *The rhetoric of science.* Cambridge, MA: Harvard University Press.

———. (1990). Rhetoric of science *is* epistemic rhetoric. *Quarterly Journal of Speech, 76,* 304–6.

Guthrie, W. K. C. (1971). *The Sophists*. Cambridge: Cambridge University Press.

Habermas, J. (1970). Towards a theory of communicative competence. *Inquiry, 13*, 360–375.

———. (1971). *Knowledge and human interests*. Boston: Beacon Press.

———. (1973). *Theory and practice*. Boston: Beacon Press.

———. (1975). *Legitimation crisis*. Boston: Beacon Press.

———. (1979). *Communication and the evolution of society*. Boston: Beacon Press.

Hall, S. (1986). The problem of ideology: Marxism without guarantees. *Journal of Communication Inquiry, 10*, 28–43.

Hamera, J. (1990). Silence that reflects: Butoh, *Ma* and a crosscultural gaze. *Text and Performance Quarterly, 10*, 53–60.

Hamilton, E., and H. Cairns (1982). *Plato: Collected dialogues*. Princeton, NJ: Princeton University Press.

Hammitzsch, H. (1988). *Zen in the art of the tea ceremony*. New York: E. P. Dutton.

Harpham, G. (1988). Rhetoric and the madness of philosophy in Plato and Pirsig. *Contemporary Literature, 29* (1), 64–81.

Harriman, R. (1991). Critical rhetoric and postmodern theory. *The Quarterly Journal of Speech, 77* (1), 67–70.

Harris, R. A. (1991). Rhetoric of science. *College English, 53*, 282–307.

Hayles, N. K. (1984). *The cosmic web: scientific field models and literary strategies in the twentieth century*. Ithaca, NY: Cornell University Press.

———. (1990). *Chaos bound: Orderly disorder in contemporary literature and science*. Ithaca, NY: Cornell University Press.

Heisenberg, W. (1958). *Physics and philosophy*. New York: Harper & Row.

Heller, S. (1988). Bloom's best seller called "racist" and "elitist" by former SUNY chief. *The Chronicle of Higher Education, 34* (19), A1, A12.

Herrigel, E. (1971). *Zen in the art of archery*. New York: Vintage Books.

———. (1974). *The method of Zen*. New York: Random House.

Herrigel, G. (1987). *Zen in the art of flower arrangement*. New York: Arkana.

Hikins, J., and K. Zagacki (1988). Rhetoric, philosophy, and objectivism: An attenuation of the claims of the rhetoric of inquiry. *The Quarterly Journal of Speech, 74*, 201–28.

Hikins, J. (1990). Realism and its implications for rhetorical theory. In R. Cherwitz (ed.), *Rhetoric and philosophy* (pp. 21–78). Hillsdale, NJ: Lawrence Erlbaum.

Hill, H., and J. Jones, eds. (1993). *Race in America: The struggle for equality*. Madison, WI: University of Wisconsin Press.

Hillman, J. (1980). On the necessity of abnormal psychology: Ananke and Athena. In J. Hillman (ed.), *Facing the gods* (pp. 1–38). Irving: University of Dallas.

Hirschorn, M. W. (1987). Best-selling book makes the collegiate curriculum a burning public issue. *The Chronicle of Higher Education, 34* (17), 20–26.

Hook, S. (1989). *The closing of the American mind*: An intellectual best seller revisited. *The American Scholar 58*, 123–35.

hooks, b. (1984) *Feminist theory: From margin to center*. Boston: South End Press.

Horne, J. (1989). Rhetoric after Rorty. *Western Journal of Speech Communication, 53*, 247–59.

Hyams. J. (1979). *Zen in the martial arts*. New York: St. Martins.

Ijselling, S. (1976). *Rhetoric and philosophy in conflict: An historic survey*. The Hague: Martinus Nijhoff.

Ikeda, D. (1982). *Buddhism the first millennium*. Tokyo: Kodansha International.

Ishii, S. (1989). *Hyaku-nin Isshu* (Single poems by a hundred poets): A Japanese text-performance tradition. *Text and Performance Quarterly, 9*, 334–35.

Jaeger, W. (1979). *Paideia: The ideals of Greek culture*. New York: Oxford University Press.

Jarratt, S. (1991). *Rereading the Sophists: Classical rhetoric refigured*. Carbondale, IL: Southern Illinois University Press.

Jensen, J. V. (1987). Rhetorical emphases of Taoism. *Rhetorica, 5,* 219–30.

———. (1992). Values and practices in Asian argumentation. *Argumentation and Advocacy, 28,* 155–66.

Joachim, H. H. (1906). *The nature of truth.* New York: Oxford University Press.

Johannesen, R. (1971). The emerging concept of communication as dialogue. *The Quarterly Journal of Speech, 57,* 373–82.

———. (1983). *Ethics in human communication.* 2nd edition. Prospect Heights, IL: Waveland Press.

Johnson, C. (1988). *Being and race: Black writing since 1970.* Bloomington, IN: Indiana University Press.

Kehoe, B. (1992). *Zen and the art of the Internet.* Chester, PA: Brendan P. Kehoe.

Kerferd, G. B. (1981). *The sophistic movement.* Cambridge: Cambridge University Press.

King, M. L., Jr. (1964). *Why we can't wait.* New York: Mentor.

———. (1967). *The trumpet of conscience.* New York: Harper & Row.

King, W. L. (1993). *Zen and the way of the sword: Arming the samurai psyche.* Oxford University Press.

Kirk, G. S., and J. E. Raven (1966). *The presocratic philosophers.* Cambridge: Cambridge University Press.

Kirkwood, W. (1987). The turtle spoke, the donkey brayed: Fables about speech and silence in the *Panchatantra. Journal of Communication and Religion, 10,* 1–11.

———. (1989). Truthfulness as a standard for speech in ancient India. *Southern Communication Journal, 54,* 213–34.

———. (1990). Shiva's dance at sundown: Implications of Indian aesthetics for poetics and rhetoric. *Text and Performance Quarterly, 10,* 93–110.

Klopf, D. (1991). Japanese commnication practices: Recent comparative research. *Communication Quarterly, 39,* 130–43.

Kress, G., and R. Hodge (1979). *Language as ideology.* Boston: Routledge & Kegan Paul.

Krone, K. J., F. M. Jablin, and L. L. Putman (1987). Communication theory and organizational communication: Multiple perspectives. In F. Jablin, L. Putman, K. Roberts, and L. Porter (eds.), *Handbook of organizational communication* (pp. 18–40). Newbury Park, CA: Sage.

Kuhn, T. (1970). *The structure of scientific revolutions.* Chicago: University of Chicago Press.

Laclau, E. (1977). *Politics and ideology in Marxist theory.* London: New Left Books.

Laclau, E., and C. Mouffe (1989). *Hegemony and socialist strategy.* London: Verso.

Lanham, R. (1976). *The motives of eloquence.* New Haven: Yale University Press.

Lao Tzu (1985). *Tao te ching.* New York: Viking Penguin.

Lehrer, K. (1990). *Theory of knowledge.* Boulder, CO: Westview Press.

Lee, B. (1975). *Tao of jeet kune do.* Santa Clarita, CA: Ohara Publications.

Limaye, M., and D. Victor (1991). Cross-cultural business communication research: State of the art and hypotheses for the 1990s. *The Journal of Business Communication, 28,* 277–99.

Loden, M., and R. H. Loeser (1991). Working diversity: Managing the differences. *The Bureaucrat: The Journal for Public Managers, 20,* 21–25.

Lu, X., and D. Frank (1993). On the study of ancient Chinese Rhetoric/Bain. *Western Journal of Communication, 57,* 445–63.

Lyotard, J. F. (1988). *The differend: Phrases in dispute.* Minneapolis: University of Minnesota Press.

———. (1988). *The postmodern condition: A report on knowledge.* Minneapolis: University of Minnesota Press.

Lyotard, J. F., and J. Thébaud (1985). *Just gaming.* Minneapolis: University of Minnesota Press.

Machiorlatti, J. (1994). *Zen and the art of documentary: Resolving the attachment of self to subject.* Paper presented at the American Film and Video Association Annual Conference, Bozeman, MT.

Macke, F. (1993). The end of modernity and the ends of argumentation: A discourse on the notion of advocacy as rationality. In R.

McKerrow (ed.), *Argument and the postmodern challenge: Proceedings of the Eighth SCA/AFA Conference on Argumentation* (pp. 104–12). Annandale, VA: Speech Communication Association.

McCloskey, D. (1985). *The rhetoric of economics.* Madison, WI: University of Wisconsin Press.

McGee, M. (1993). Superficial confrontations. In R. McKerrow (ed.), *Argument and the postmodern challenge: Proceedings of the Eighth SCA/AFA Conference on Argumentation* (pp. 76–78.). Annandale, VA: Speech Communication Association.

McGuire, J. E., and T. Melia (1989). Some cautionary strictures on the writing of the rhetoric of science. *Rhetorica, 7,* 87–100.

McGuire, M. (1990). Materialism: Reductionist dogma or critical rhetoric? In R. Cherwitz (ed.), *Rhetoric and philosophy* (pp. 187–212). Hillsdale, NJ: Lawrence Erlbaum.

McKerrow, R. (1989). Critical rhetoric: Theory and praxis. *Communication Monographs, 56* (2), 91–111.

———. (1991). Critical rhetoric in a postmodern world. *The Quarterly Journal* of Speech, 77 (1), 75–78.

———. (1993). Overcoming fatalism: Rhetoric/argument in postmodernity. In R. McKerrow (ed.). *Argument and the postmodern challenge: Proceedings of the Eighth SCA/AFA Conference on Argumentation* (pp. 119–21). Annandale, VA: Speech Communication Association.

McPhail, M. (1993). *The rhetoric of racism.* Lanham, MD: University Press of America.

———. (1995). Coherence as representative anecdote in the rhetorics of Kenneth Burke and Ernesto Grassi. In B. Brock (ed.), *Kenneth Burke in contemporary Western thought: A rhetoric in transition* (pp. 76–118). Tuscaloosa, AL: University of Alabama Press.

———. (in press). Afrocentricity and complicity: An ethnophilosophical analysis. In J. Hamlet (ed.), *Afrocentric notions: Studies in culture and communication.* Dubuque, IA: Kendall Hunt

Meiland, J. (1981). *College thinking: How to get the best out of college.* New York: New American Library.

Memmi, A. (1967). *The colonizer and the colonized.* Boston: Beacon Press.

Mermin, N. D. (1990). *Boojums all the way through: Communicating science in a prosaic age.* Cambridge: Cambridge University Press.

Meyer, M. (1994). *Rhetoric, language* and *reason.* University Park, PA: Pennsylvania State University Press.

Miller, C. (1989). Some perspectives on rhetoric, science and history. *Rhetorica, 7,* 101–14.

Miller, S. (1991). *Textual carnivals: The politics of composition.* Carbondale, IL: Southern Illinois University Press.

Mindell, A. (1992). *The leader as martial artist: An introduction to deep democracy.* New York: HarperCollins.

Mitgang, L. (1987). Schools should stress thinking skills, report says. *The Ann Arbor News,* 12 March, C1.

Morrison, J. (1972). The absence of a rhetorical tradition in Japanese culture. *Western Speech, 36,* 89–102.

Moss, J. D. (1989). The interplay of science and rhetoric in seventeenth-century Italy. *Rhetorica, 7,* 23–44.

Murphy, H., and H. Hildebrandt (1991). *Effective business communication.* New York: McGraw-Hill.

Myers, G. (1986). Writing research and the sociology of scientific knowledge: A review of three new books. *College English, 48,* 595–610.

Nakagawa, G. (1990). "What are we doing here with all these Japanese?": Subject-constitution and strategies of discursive closure represented in stories of Japanese-American internment. *Communication Quarterly, 38,* 388–402.

Nelson, J., A. Megill, and D. McCloskey (1987). *The rhetoric of the human sciences: Language and argument in scholarship and public affairs.* Madison, WI: University of Wisconsin Press.

Nitobe, I. (1979). *Bushido: The warrior's code.* Burbank, CA: Ohara Publications.

Norris, C. (1984). *The deconstructive turn: Essays in the rhetoric of philosophy.* New York: Methuen.

Nussbaum, M. (1987). Undemocratic vistas. (Review of *The closing of the American mind* by Allan Bloom). *The New York Review of Books, 34* (7), 20–26.

Okabe, R. (1990). The impact of Western rhetoric on the East: The case of Japan. *Rhetorica, 8,* 371–88.

Oliver, R. (1971). *Communication and culture in ancient India and China*. Syracuse, NY: Syracuse University Press.

Paine, C. (1989). Relativism, radical pedagogy, and the ideology of paralysis. *College English, 51* (6), 557–70.

Parker, E. (1988). *The Zen of kenpo: Meaningful quotes from the teachings of Ed Parker*. Los Angeles: Delsby Publications.

Payne, D. (1989). *Coping with failure: The therapeutic uses of rhetoric*. Columbia, SC: University of South Carolina Press.

Parrinder, G., ed. (1971). *World religions: From ancient history to the present*. New York: Facts on File Publications.

Penrose, R. (1989). *The emperor's new mind: Concerning computers, minds, and the laws of physics*. Oxford: Oxford University Press.

Perelman, C., and L. Olbrechts-Tyteca (1982). *The new rhetoric: A treatise on argumentation*. Notre Dame, IN: University of Notre Dame Press.

Phillips, D. (1986). *Toward a just social order*. Princeton: Princeton University Press.

Pirsig, R. (1985). *Zen and the art of motorcycle maintenance*. New York: Bantam Books.

Pitturro, M., and S. Mahoney (1991). Managing diversity: The new multicultural workforce requires a simpatico style. *Executive Female*, May/June, 45–48.

Polanyi, M. (1986). *Personal knowledge: Towards a post critical philosophy*. Chicago: University of Chicago Press.

Poulakos, J. (1983). Toward a sophistic definition of rhetoric. *Philosophy and Rhetoric, 16*, 35–48.

———. (1984). Rhetoric, the sophists, and the possible. *Communication Monographs, 51*, 215–26.

———. (1987). Sophistical rhetoric as a critique of culture. In J. Wenzel (ed.), *Argument and critical practices: Proceedings of the Fifth SCA/AFA Conference on Argumentation* (pp. 97–101). Annandale, VA: Speech Communication Association.

———. (1990). Hegel's reception of the sophists. *Western Journal of Speech Communication, 54*, 160–71.

Poulet, G. (1981). Criticism and the experience of interiority. In J. Tompkins (ed.), *Reader-response criticism: From formalism to post-structuralism* (pp. 41–49). Baltimore: Johns Hopkins University Press.

Price, A. F., and M. Wong, trans. (1969). *The Diamond Sutra and the sutra of Hui Neng*. Boston: Shambhala.

Prigogine, I., and I. Stengers (1988). *Order out of chaos*. New York: Bantam.

Radhakrishnan, R. (1987). Ethnic identity and post-structuralist difference. *Cultural Critique, 6*, 199–220.

——— . (1988) Feminist historiography and post-structuralist thought: Intersections and departures. In E. Meese and A. Parker (eds.), *The difference within: Feminism and critical theory* (pp. 189–205). Philadelphia: John Benjamins Publishing Co.

Rahula, W. (1974). *What the Buddha taught*. New York: Grove Press.

Railsback, C. (1983). Beyond rhetorical relativism: A structural-material model of truth and objective reality. *Quarterly Journal of Speech, 69*, 351–63.

Rich, A. (1979). *On lies, secrets and silence: Selected prose, 1966–1978*. New York: W. W. Norton.

Rorty, R. (1979). *Philosophy and the mirror of nature*. Princeton, NJ: Princeton University Press.

Rossetti, L. (1988). The rhetoric of Zeno's paradoxes. *Philosophy and Rhetoric, 21*, 145–51.

Rowe, S. (1994). *Rediscovering the west: An inquiry into nothingness and relatedness*. Albany: SUNY Press.

Rushing, J. H. (1985). *E. T.* as rhetorical transcendence. *Quarterly Journal of Speech, 71*, 188–203.

Ryan, W. (1971). *Blaming the victim*. New York: Random House.

Sandmann, W. (1993). Gorgias and his postmodern cousins: Toward a skeptical view of argument. In R. McKerrow (ed.), *Argument and the postmodern challenge: Proceedings of the Eighth SCA/AFA Conference on Argumentation* (pp. 97–103). Annandale, VA: Speech Communication Association.

Schiappa, E. (1991). *Protagoras and logos: A study in Greek philosophy and rhetoric*. Columbia, SC: University of South Carolina Press.

————. (1992). Rhêtorikê: What's in a name? Toward a revised history of early Greek rhetorical theory. *Quarterly Journal of Speech, 78* (1), 1–15.

Schulke, F., and P. McPhee (1986). *King remembered.* New York: W. W. Norton.

Schwarze, S. (1987). Letter. *The Chronicle of Higher Education, 34* (7), B4.

Scott, R. (1967). On viewing rhetoric as epistemic. *Central States Speech Journal, 18,* 9–16.

————. (1990). Epistemic rhetoric and criticism: Where Barry Brummett goes wrong. *Quarterly Journal of Speech, 76,* 300–303.

————. (1993). Dialectical tensions of speaking and silence. *Quarterly Journal of Speech, 79,* 1–18.

————. (1993). Argument is; Therefore arguers are. In R. McKerrow (ed.), *Argument and the postmodern challenge: Proceedings of the Eighth SCA/AFA Conference on Argumentation* (pp. 91–96). Annandale, VA: Speech Communication Association.

Seager, R. H., ed. (1993). *The dawn of religious pluralism: Voices from the World's Parliament of Religions, 1893.* LaSalle, IL: Open Court.

Simons, H. W. (1989). *Rhetoric in the human sciences.* Newbury Park, CA: Sage.

Sloan, T. O. (1989). Reinventing invention. *College English, 51* (5), 461–73.

Smith, A. (1990). Mishima's *Seppuku* speech: A critical-cultural analysis. *Text and Performance Quarterly, 10,* 1–19.

————. (1990). Seeing through a mask's confession. *Text and Performance Quarterly, 9,* 132–52.

Smith, J. (1993). Allan Bloom, Mike Rose and Paul Goodman: In search of a lost pedagogical synthesis. *College English, 55,* 721–44.

Sosa, E. (1991). *Knowledge in perspective: Selected essays in epistemology.* Cambridge: Cambridge University Press.

St. Aubyn, G. (1985). *The art of argument.* New York: Taplinger Publishing Co., Inc.

Starosta, W., and A. Chaudhary (1993). "I can wait 40 or 400 years": Gandhian *Satyagraha* West and East. *International Philosophical Quarterly, 33,* 163–72.

Stewart, L., W. B. Gudykunst, S. Ting-Toomey, and T. Nishida (1986). The effects of decision-making on openness and satisfaction within Japanese organizations. *Communication Monographs, 53,* 236–51.

Stone, I. F. (1988). *The trial of Socrates.* Boston: Little, Brown and Company.

Styrk, L., and T. Ikemoto (1987). *Zen poems of China and Japan: The crane's bill.* New York: Grove Press.

Suzuki, D. T. (1964). *An introduction to Zen Buddhism.* New York: Grove Press.

———. (1973). *Zen and Japanese culture.* Princeton, NJ: Princeton University Press.

Suzuki, S. (1988). *Zen mind, beginner's mind.* New York: John Weatherhill Inc.

Talbot, M. (1988). *Beyond the quantum.* New York: Bantam.

Taylor, M. P. (1988). Review of *The closing of the American mind* by Allan Bloom. *Michigan Law Review, 86* (6), 1135–40.

Tompkins, J. P., ed. (1981). An introduction to reader response criticism. In *Reader-response criticism: From formalism to post-structuralism* (pp. ix–xxvi). Baltimore: Johns Hopkins University Press.

Trigg, R. (1980). *Reality at risk: A defense of realism in philosophy and the sciences.* Sussex, UK: The Harvester Press.

Trungpa, C. (1981). *Journey without goal: The tantric wisdom of the Buddha.* Boston: Shambala.

———. (1986). *Shambhala: The sacred path of the warrior.* New York: Bantam.

———. (1987). *Cutting through spiritual materialism.* Boston: Shambhala.

Tukey, D. (1990). Toward a research agenda for a spiritual rhetoric. *Journal of Communication and Religion, 13,* 66–76.

Tyler, S. (1987). *The unspeakable: Discourse, dialogue, and rhetoric in the postmodern world.* Madison: University of Wisconsin Press.

Unger, R. M. (1986). *The critical legal studies movement.* Cambridge, MA: Harvard University Press.

Valesio, P. (1980). *Novantiqua: Rhetorics as a contemporary theory.* Bloomington: Indiana University Press.

van Dijk, T. (1987). *Communicating racism.* Beverly Hills, CA: Sage Publications.

———. (1993). *Elite discourse and racism.* Beverly Hills, CA: Sage Publications.

Vernant, J. P. (1982). Greek tragedy: Problems of interpretation. In R. Macksey and E. Donato (eds.), *The structuralist controversy: The languages of criticism and the sciences of man* (pp. 273–89). Baltimore: John Hopkins University Press.

von Weizsacker, C. R. (1987). Parmenides and quantum theory. In J. H. Weaver (ed.), *The world of physics: A small library of the literature of physics from antiquity to the present* (pp. 101–9). New York: Simon & Schuster.

Wallace, B. A. (1989). *Choosing reality: A contemplative view of physics and the mind.* Boston: Shambhala.

Wallace, W. A. (1989). Aristotelian science and rhetoric in transition: The Middle Ages and the Renaissance. *Rhetorica, 7,* 7–22.

Ward, I. (1994). *Literacy, ideology, and dialogue: Towards a dialogic pedagogy.* Albany: SUNY Press.

Warren, R. P. (1980). *Being here: Poetry 1977–1980.* New York: Random House.

Watzlawick, P. (1977). *How real is real?* New York: Vintage Books.

Wellman, D. T. (1980). *Portraits of white racism.* Cambridge: Cambridge University Press.

West, C. (1993). *Prophetic reflections: Notes on race and power in America.* Monroe, ME: Common Courage Press.

Whitson, S. (1988). The *Phaedrus* complex. *PRE/TEXT: A Journal of Rhetorical Theory, 9,* 9–25.

Wilkes, B. (1994). Kanji—the meaning of "dojo". *Inside Karate, 15,* 36–45.

Wilkinson, D. (1991). The American university and the rhetoric of neo-conservatism. *Contemporary Sociology, 20,* 550–53.

Williams, D. (1993). Approaching the abyss: Argumentation theory and postmodernism. In R. McKerrow (ed.), *Argument and the post-modern challenge: Proceedings of the Eighth SCA/AFA Conference on Argumentation* (pp. 86–90). Annandale, VA: Speech Communication Association.

Wilson, W. S. (1982). *Ideals of the samurai: Writings of Japanese warriors.* Burbank: Ohara Publications, Inc.

Wolf, F. A. (1989). *Taking the quantum leap: The new physics for nonscientists.* New York: Harper & Row.

Wolf, F. A., and B. Toben (1975). *Space-time and beyond: Toward an explanation of the unexplainable.* New York: Dutton.

Woolf, V. (1978). *A room of one's own.* London: Hogarth Press.

Wright, D. S. (1992). Rethinking transcendence: The role of language in Zen experience. *Philosophy East & West, 42,* 113–38.

Young, R. E., A. L. Becker, and K. L. Pike (1970) *Rhetoric: Discovery and change.* New York: Harcourt, Brace & World.

Yum, J. O. (1988). The impact of Confucianism on interpersonal relationships and communication patterns in East Asia. *Communication Monographs, 55,* 374–88.

Zukav, G. (1979). *The dancing Wu Li masters: An overview of the new physics.* New York: William Morrow and Company.

Zulick, M. (1993). Standpoint, praxis, and postmodern argument: A feminist dilemma. In R. McKerrow (ed.), *Argument and the postmodern challenge: Proceedings of the Eighth SCA/AFA Conference on Argumentation* (pp. 124–27). Annandale, VA: Speech Communication Association.

INDEX

A

actively non-argumentative discourse, 14, 78, 90, 92, 114-115, 127-128, 153

Adler, Mortimer, 48, 177n

affirmation, 57, 76, 86, 91, 120, 125, 167, 188n, 193n; and coherence, 80, 112; "higher" in Zen Buddhism, 11, 15; of negative difference, 58;

affirmative action, 32, 53, 179n

Afrocentricity, 22; and coherence, 182n; and complicity, 60, 65-6, 182n

agonistic , 75, 101, 103, 110, 120

ancient Greece, 21-23, 62, 95, 99, 124, 131-2, 134; rhetoricians, 38; Sophists, 60, 67, 95, 104-106, 117, 128; and democracy, 120, 146

aretê, 117, 154, 190n, 192n; and techné 142, 161, 189n; and virtue, 131; as excellence 107, 147, 161

Argüelles, José, 93-94, 110-111, 144-145, 188n

Aristotle, 17, 34, 47, 125, 165, 182n, 191n; and Plato, 81, 105, 118; and rhetoric, 27, 61, 155, 185n; the *Rhetoric*, 174n, 176n, 194n

articulation, 69-71, 84-85, 182n

B

beginner's mind, 12-3, 17, 21, 41, 62, 115, 128; defined, 43

bivalence, 60, 108, 118, 140; *See also* law of the excluded middle

Blanshard, Brand, 83

Bloom, Alan, 12, 32, 35,41, 43-63, 131-2, 145, 177-181n; *See* chapter two

Bohm, David, 25, 101-3, 151-2, 174n, 183-4n, 187n; on dialogue, 78-79, 90

Booth, Wayne, 40, 60, 147

Brummett, Barry, 96, 109, 115, 116

Buddhism, 8, 63, 91, 152-3, 169n; Tibetan, 1; Zen, 3, 7, 155-6, 170n, 194n

Burke, Kenneth, 183n, 189n, 194n

C

Carnoy, Martin, 133, 145, 191n; *See also* colonized knowledge

Cherwitz, Richard, 96, 107

Chisholm, Roderick, 82-3, 183n

class, 24, 50, 67, 69, 71, 74, 136, 141; *See also* gender or race

classification, 50, 67, 71, 74, 141; essentialist, 46; systems of, 85, 90 coherence, viii, 2, 5, 56, 78, 119, 127, 139-140, 152, 154, 165-7, 182n; and dialogue, 25, 78-80, 86-90, 167; and rhetoric, 11, 15, 16, 17, 79, 80, 90, 111, 134, 153, 193n; epistemological, 13, 30, 54, 66, 69, 82-85, 107, 174n; 177n; rhetorical, 11, 41, 164, 172n; See chapter six.

colonized knowledge, 133, 145, 191n; See also Carnoy, Martin

compassion, 11, 12, 17, 18, and discipline, viii, ix, 10, 16, 17, 148, 154-5, 167, 192n; and beginner's mind, 43, 62; and Buddhism, 152; and Zen, 2

complicity, 26, 35, 57, 66-75, 84, 90, 119, 139, 173, 181; See chapter three

conventionalism, 61, 44-45, 57, 69-70, 75, 83, 85, 153, 177-8n; See also foundationism

Crapanzano, Vincent, 23, 45-6, 58, 67-8, 173n, 180n

D

democracy, 27, 44, 57, 86; and rhetoric, 6, 130, 145-6, 192n; deep, 166-7, 194n

Dewey, John, 56, 147, 180n

dialogue, 38, 56, 59, 148, 161, 183n, 193n; and coherence, 61-3, 164-7; and dialectic, 16, 17, 27, 29, 60, 157, 164; as non argumentative, 77-90, 101, 152; "of argumentation," 120; in Freire, 153, 175n

differend, 120-1, 190n

discipline, 8, 11, 165, 169n; and compassion, viii, ix, 10, 16, 17, 148, 154-5, 167, 192n; in Zen, 44

dissoi-logoi, 60, 62, 106-7, 117-8, 176n; compared to Zen, 4, 37

duality, 16, 91, 109, 110, 124, 126, 153, 156, 162, 163; and language, 13; and Zen, 3-5, 11-12, 62

E

emancipatory cognitive interest, 35, 38-9, 121-2

essentialism, 3, 12-14, 28, 35, 40, 44, 48-9, 55, 57, 75; and discourse, 35-6, 43, 55, 59-60, 80, 84, 141, and education, 26, 37, 133-135, 142-146; and epistemology, 41, 43, 47, 58, 67, 72, 75, 81, 119, 141, 145, 174n; and racism, 23, 45-6; and reality, 26, 45, 66, 67, 105, 132, 150, 152; and thought, 23, 25, 141

ethnocentricity, 22, 55, 173n

externalism, 14, 24, 98; in justification, 58, 66, 69, 81, 90-1, 137, 174n, 178n

F

Farber, Jerry, 28-9, 150-1, 175n

Farrell, Thomas, 96, 153, 164, 193n

feminism, 45, 47, 48, 55, 59 65, 66, 136, 139-40, 188n; and criticism, 70-74; and essentialism, 182n

forgiveness, 23, 35, 62

foundationism, 41, 55, 66-68, 90, 180n; and externalism, 14, 24, 62, 81, 91, 137, 174n; and conventionalism, 61, 44-45, 57, 69, 70, 75, 83, 85, 153, 177-8n;

fragmentation, vii, 14, 102, 151, 165-6, 184n, 186n; and postmodernism, 85, 128, 135; "exigence of," 110
Freire, Paulo, 20, 35, 40, 153, 175n

G

Gandhi, Mohandas K., 85-90, 171n, 193n
Gates, Henry Louis, 68, 82, 173n
gender, 24, 47, 58, 62, 66-84 , 91, 136, 182n; See also class or race
Golden Rule, 23, 88, 127; See also rule of justice
Gorgias, 81, 96, 105-6
Great Books, 48, 145, 177n, 178n
Gregory, Bruce, 103-4, 108-9

H

Habermas, Jürgen, 14, 35, 38, 119-125, 135, 176n, 191n
harmony, 14, 131, 139, 165, 183n
Hayles, N. Katherine, 95, 107, 155, 184n
hegemony, 5, 13, 85; and complicity, 69-72
Herrigel, Eugen, 2-3, 15-16, 37, 149
Herrigel, Gustie, 13, 43
Hikins, James, 96, 107, 186-7n

I

ideal speech situation, 38-9, 119, 121-3, 128, 150; See also Habermas, Jürgen
idealism, 23, 30, 49, 59, 65, 66, 75; 90, 102, 113, 114, 118, 123, 153, 174n, 175n, 177n, 183n;

and historicism, 44; and materialism, 65, 91, 93; personal, 87; See also realism
identification, 154, 164, 188n, 194n
identity, 45, 70, 85, 127, 129, 182n
interdependence, 76, 86, 88
interrelatedness, 78-80, 83, 86-87
intersubjectivity, 113, 115, 189n
Isocrates, 38

J

Joachim, H. H., 82-3
judgment, 23, 24, 35, 56, 58, 65, 78, 83, 87, 115, 119, 120, 123, 125, 126, 134, 135, 136, 139, 179n, 192n
justice, 46, 48, 120, 123-4, 146
justificatory strategies, 36, 63, 75, 81, 83, 86, 137, 140, 174n, 178n, 186n; coherentist, 66, 69; in closing of the American mind, 41, 45, 50, 55-58, 180n; essentialist, 67, 73, 74, 135; 185; See also conventionalism or foundationism

K

Kant, Immanuel, 122, 180n, 190n
King, Martin Luther, 85-88, 193n
King, Winston, 14, 19, 114, 188n
kinhin, 3-4
koan, 3-4, 14, 113-4, 128
Kuhn, Thomas, 94, 149, 151

L

Laclau, Ernesto, 69-70, 85, 182n
Lanham, Richard, 10, 16, 23, 29, 38, 49, 61-2, 68, 76, 82, 107,

Lanham, Richard *(continued)*
116, 126-7, 133, 140, 142,
169n, 176n, 183n; See also
rhetorical ideal of life
law of the excluded middle, 108-
9; See also bivalence
logocentricism, 22, 69, 173n
love, 8, 17, 65, 160, 167, 193; and
dialectic, 81, 150, 193n; and
dialogue, 153; and power, 151;
and Zen, 18
Lyotard, Jean François, 14, 106,
119, 123-6, 189n, 190n

M

martial arts, ix, 14, 148, 162, 164-
165, 172-3n, 194n; rhetoric as,
17, 154, 164
materialism, 2, 65, 91, 93, 134, 146
McKerrow, Raymie, 111-112,
116, 119, 188n, 189n
Merton, Thomas, 1, 12, 93, 170n
modernism, 58, 93, 122, 140; and
postmodernism, 14, 111, 115,
116, 118, 123, 125, 126,
127,189n, 190n
Mouffe, Chantal, 69-70, 85, 182n
multicultural communication,
139-141
mythos, 62, 128

N

negation, 6, 13, 68, 75, 81, 90,
102, 124, 126, 137, 138, 164,
188n
negative difference, 47, 49, 61-2,
128; and complicity, 66-91;
and judgment, 35, 60, 120, 138,
141-2; and racism, 23-25, 33
nomos, 61, 95, 185-6n; See also
physis
nonviolence, 17, 86-89, 127, 184

O

objectivity, 100, 104, 107-8, 113,
186-7n
opposition, 13, 59, 85, 178
oppositional criticism 63, 66, 69-
77, 84-6, 114, 181n; See chapter three
Other, 13, 24, 29, 59, 65-6, 76-7,
92, 150, 152

P

Parmenides, 15, 105-6
Peat, F. David, 78, 101, 151,
153
physics, 14, 25, 91-2, 94-111; See
chapter four
physis, 61, 95, 99, 185-6n; See
also nomos
physis-nomos antithesis, 44, 95,
106, 185-6n
Pirsig, Robert, viii, 10-12, 16-7,
21-2, 26-9, 31, 37, 62, 107, 128,
131, 152-164, 173n, 175n,
182n, 193n; See also Zen in
the art of motorcycle maintenance.
Plato, 21-22, 48, 46, 49, 68, 80,
81, 105, 123, 131, 167, 180n,
187n, 189n; and Socrates,
26-7, 30, 61; and Sophists;
117-8
Platonic dialogues, 105;
Cratylus, 48; *Gorgias*, 81, 105;
Phaedrus, 22, 68, 81-2;
Republic, 46, 143
postmodernism, 2, 5, 16, 84, 113;
and modernism, 14, 111, 115,
116, 118, 123, 125, 126,
127,189n, 190n; and rhetoric 5,
14, 96, 108, 109, 113-129; See
chapter five
Protagoras, 117-8, 176n

Q

quality, 9, 16, 154; in Pirsig, 10, 22, 155, 160-1
quantum physics, 91, 93-105, 108-110, 140, 186n

R

race, 12, 32, 39, 41, 65, 172n, 174n, 179n, 180n, 194n; and class/gender, 24, 62, 66-85, 134; and complicity, 66-85; and essentialism, 23, 43, 45; in *closing of the American mind*, 45-47, 50-62
Radhakrishnan, R., 70-1, 74
realism, 23, 30, 49, 59, 66, 75, 90, 102, 113, 114, 118, 153, 174n, 175n, 186-7n; See also idealism.
relativism, 36, 47-49, 56, 178n, 187n
rhetorical ideal of life, 16, 18, 23, 32, 37, 62, 107, 140, 154, 155, 176n; and postmodern rhetoric, 126-8
Rogerian rhetoric, 79-80, 183n
rule of justice, 35, 58, 62, 88, 146; defined, 24; in postmodern rhetoric, 124-127

S

Satyagrahis, 88, 171n, 184n
Scott, Robert, 96, 97, 171n, 173n
Socrates, 26-27, 37, 44, 48, 57, 61, 81-2, 150, 183n
Sophists 2, 11, 14, 15, 22, 25, 44, 67, 96, 109, 119, 126, 140, 146, 190n, 192n; and antilogic, 4-6, 37, 59-60, 62, 106-7, 116-8, 176n; in Lyotard, 120-1, 123-5; on success and truth, 128, 190n

special pleading, 33; and racism, 53-5, 174n; defined, 24
spirit, viii, 4, 11, 13, 78, 150, 165, 183n
spiritual, 2, 5, 9, 12, 83, 86, 172; rhetoric as, 147-155, 193n, 194n
Suzuki, Daisetz T., 3, 18, 107, 126, 170n
Suzuki, Shunryu, 18, 43, 62

T

Taoists, 3, 80, 171, 194n
Tao, 7, 105; *te Ching*, 172n, 192n; *of physics*, 102
techné, 138, 142, 161; *See also* areté
theory of the opposite party, 4, 80, 107; and complicity, 58-9, 67; and Sophistry, 117-8
Thrasymachus, 4, 59, 67, 80, 106, 117-8, 146
Trungpa, Chögyam, vii, 169n, 171n

U

uncertainty, 106-7
uncertainty principle, 100, 102, 108
unity, 11, 12, 76, 87, 93, 102, 111, 124, 127, 141; as multiplicity, 105; in plurality, 79
unspeakable, 114-5, 127

V

Vajrayana, 170n, 171n
Valesio, Paolo, 74, 116
validity claims, 189n, 191n
value laden hypothesis, 186n
valuing diversity, 136-141

Vernant, Jean-Pierre, 106, 176n
violence, 77, 149, 150
void, 16, 111

W

Wallace, B. Alan, 91, 102, 152-3
warfare of fixed opinions, 55, 60
warrior, vii, 20, 30, 35, 40-1, 153,
    192; of the word, 12, 167;
    rhetorical, 15, 20
wholeness, 102-104, 110-111
wisdom, vii, 29, 48, 63, 87; love
    of, 44, 148

Y

Yin and Yang, 80, 166-7

Z

Zagacki, Kenneth, 186n
Zen/chan, vii, 1-18, 19, 21, 43, 62,
    65, 131, 148, 149, 167, 169n,
    170n, 172n, 176n, 181n, 188n,
    190n, 194n; and antilogic, 4,
    37; and language, 5-7; and post-
    modernism; 5-7, 113-5, 125-8
Zen and the art of motorcycle
    maintenance, viii, 10, 21-2, 25,
    28, 107, 128, 154-164, 173n,
    175n, 182n, 193n; See also
    Pirsig, Robert
Zen masters, 2, 5, 6, 7, 15, 32, 40,
    41, 167, 171n
Zennists, 4, 114, 127
Zeno, 105-6, 187n